JUDGE FOR YOURSELF

Judge for Yourself

Peter Bristow

WILLIAM KIMBER · LONDON

First published in 1986 by
WILLIAM KIMBER & CO. LIMITED
100 Jermyn Street, London, SW1Y 6EE

© Sir Peter Bristow, 1986
ISBN 0-7183-0616-3

Photoset by Grove Graphics, Tring, Hertfordshire
and printed in Great Britain by
The Garden City Press Limited
Letchworth, Hertfordshire, SG6 1JS

To Elsa, who bore with and helped me
through the period of gestation

Acknowledgements

To Phil Davey and Diana Jones for typing and
William Kimber for encouragement, my thanks

Contents

8   *Contents*

List of Illustrations

Wind of Change

I was called to the Bar on November 1936 by the then Treasurer of the Middle Temple, Master Konstam, who was a judge of the Westminster County Court. There were twenty King's Bench judges. There were seven Lords Justices of Appeal. The Old Bailey was manned by the Recorder of London, the Common Serjeant, and an 'additional' judge, plus a periodic visiting King's Bench judge to deal with the capital cases and the other top level crime. Outside London, major crime was tried by jury with King's Bench judges going round the country on assize, on the pattern instituted by King Henry II. Run of the mill crime was tried by jury at Quarter Sessions, mostly with barristers acting part time as Recorders in boroughs, and as Chairmen or Deputy Chairmen in the counties, but still in part by lay magistrate Chairmen. Petty crime was tried by lay magistrates at Petty Sessions, and, exceptionally, in London and some other big cities, by full-time professionally qualified magistrates. Mr Pickwick and Mr Jorrocks would have recognized the scene. What went on in the field is beautifully illustrated and satirized by Theobald Matthews' *Forensic Fables*. A. P. Herbert's *Misleading Cases* satirize the law as it was in those days.

On 29th September 1985, I retired after fifteen years' service as a Queen's Bench judge, preceded by six years as Queen's Counsel. The remaining years, with a break for six years for Hitler's war and one year as a pupil in chambers, were spent in practice as a junior at the Common Law Bar. Then there were fifty Queen's Bench judges. Then there were twenty Lords Justices of Appeal. Then the Old Bailey was manned by the Recorder of London, the Common Serjeant, numerous 'additional judges' and enough Recorders to keep some nineteen courts in operation, plus a permanent presence of at least two visiting Queen's Bench judges. Assizes and Quarter

Sessions are no more. Outside London both major and run of the mill serious crime are tried by jury in the Crown Court. In the largest centres of population there is a continuous presence of visiting Queen's Bench judges, to deal with the most serious cases, and there are permanent full-time Circuit judges, reinforced by part-time Recorders or Assistant Recorders, drawn from both the Bar and from among solicitors. In all large centres there is a continuous second-level presence in the Crown Court of Circuit judges and there is a regular but periodical visiting Queen's Bench judge. The smaller centre Crown Courts are manned as required by Circuit judges and Recorders or Assistant Recorders. In the largest centres there are periodical visits by Family Division judges, who not only do Family Division work (in 1936 the province of the three judges of the Probate Divorce and Admiralty Division, none being done outside London) but help out the Queen's Bench visiting judges by trying civil actions and even crime. Only the set-up for trying petty crime remains unchanged. The magistrates do their same job in Petty Sessions.

The years 1830 to 1875 had been a period of revolutionary change. At the end of it you were still to be hung for murder, but not for forgery or the other multifarious offences which had carried the mandatory death penalty. The prisons were no longer simply holding establishments till your trial. 'Gateways,' as it has been wittily said, 'to the New World or the next.' Transportation had ceased and it had to be by prison in our Old World that you were to expiate your offence. Old civil courts went down like nine-pins, replaced by the Supreme Court of Judicature, High Court plus Court of Appeal. Ours is not the first age of revolutionary change. But it is the one which we have experienced at first hand. Here is my experience of it as a field worker, not a scholar or reformer, and here are some of my reflections as I look back.

PART ONE

In the Beginning

1. Qualification

As the son of a successful surgeon, brought up in Harley Street, in the Golden Age of private medicine, I flirted inevitably with the idea of following in my father's footsteps. I saw how happy he was and the good and useful life he led. But at school at the critical age of thirteen to fifteen I was off net with my science teachers and very much on net with my teachers of the humanities. Add that I am dysnumerate, and the pocket calculator was in the distant future, and it is not surprising that physics repelled me even more than biology attracted me and that after comprehensively failing the first MB exam, optimistically prepared for in four hours' work a week, I followed the line of least resistance and read Classics for my first two years at Cambridge.

I had tried, and failed, to get a scholarship to Trinity, but turned down the offer of an Exhibition at King's because it was to Trinity I wanted to go. To Trinity I went. Those were the days, but at least this arrogant decision kept me insulated from the Burgess-Maclean-Blunt ambience, then at King's at its most vigorous recruiting stage. You too can share in gaiety and treason! I had two years' unalloyed enjoyment of such by-ways of the classics as the *Characters of Theophrastus* whose 'disgusting man' initiated conversation by 'Yesterday I puked', and whose 'unfortunate man' on his way to the privy in the garden at night gets bitten by the dog; and Xenophon's treatise *Hunting and Cavalry Tactics*, the basic rule being, 'If you see a Spartan go the other way'. And I had time to spend majoring in sociology in the pubs; something which stood me in very good stead dealing with people in court later on.

Then my father said, as fathers do, 'What are you going to do for a living?' 'I don't know,' I said. 'What about the Bar?' he said. 'There are all those very nice KCs and judges we play golf with at Littlestone who appear to do all right and to enjoy themselves!' So that was decided upon. In year three at Cambridge I said goodbye to the Classics, which had been fun, and embarked full of enthusiasm on Part II of the Law Tripos. Part II of the Law Tripos came as a bit of a shock when you had been coasting along for two years in familiar waters, helping yourself without effort to a handsome second class plus a special commendation for the beauty of your Greek iambic verses.

The great Professor Harry Hollond, Dean of Trinity, was now my director of studies. Lecture 1 of his Course on Real Property was my first exposure to learning the law. It was entitled 'the Beatitude of Seisin' and I did not understand a single word! After that Harry was very kind and was content that I should work from the book and ask him when I got stuck. Percy Winfield on Torts was a consolation. In that field, academe was still reeling from the 1932 decision of the House of Lords in the snail-in-the-ginger-beer-bottle case, and Lord Atkins' great 'Who then is my neighbour?' The sting in the tail which cheered me up was that when the Scots Court, following the excursion to the Lords on the point of law, came to try the facts, it found that there never was a snail in the ginger beer bottle at all.

I had to grapple with the mysteries of 'jurisprudence', for me a non-subject if ever there was one. Legal history was more cheering, full of delicious Latin tags like the return to the Writ of Middlesex when it had not worked, '*Latitat et discurrit*', he lies hid and runs around; and of such nice concepts as the '*peine forte et dure*', when if you refused to plead to a charge of felony, you were sandwiched between two sheets of iron and weights were put on to you until you pleaded or were squashed to death. Provided you kept your mouth shut your estate was not forfeit to the Crown. Somehow or other, among all the Cambridge year three distractions, I struggled through to my honours degree with a modest third class.

In those days, if you wanted to pass your Bar exams without tears, you went to Gibson and Weldon's great establishment in Chancery Lane. Armed with their lecture notes, a degree of application, and the *Nutshell* series of helpful little textbooks, you could not fail. I started work with them in October. Roman Law, fresh territory to me, was splendidly potted in the appropriate *Nutshell* of some fifty pages. At beating the elementary nuts and bolts of subjects into you, the Gibson and Weldon lecturers were superb. Their quality is shown by the fact that after World War II, both John Widgery, later Lord

Chief Justice, and Ted Megarry, later Vice-Chancellor, spent some bread-and-butter time on the Gibson and Weldon lecturer strength.

I passed Part I at Christmas and the Final early the following May, painlessly. I spent half the day in the Part I time in the litigation department of my maternal grandfather's solicitor's firm, White and Leonard, under the wing of Eddie Keyse, managing clerk. I spent most Mondays in the Part II time fishing for salmon on the Test. But in between these distractions, I applied myself to the nuts and bolts. It was during my White and Leonard time that I finally concluded the whole operation might be worthwhile because of the impact of the legal concepts on real life.

It came about in this way. The firm had considerable London agency work for solicitors in Southampton. One of these solicitors had to take charge of a sad situation. A delicate little girl shop assistant from Ryde had fallen for, and married, a large tough farm labourer from the back of the Wight. She was too small and he was too large for them to be able to consummate their marriage, which could not survive the stress created by such a misfortune. So we were instructed by the Southampton solicitor to apply for a Poor Person's Certificate to enable her to take proceedings for annulment of the marriage on the grounds of non-consummation. If you got a certificate you had solicitors and counsel for nothing. Solicitors and counsel got nothing either. The legal aid cornucopia was still far away.

The Poor Persons' Department was situated in the bowels of the Divorce Courts. It was presided over by the brother of Canon Hassard-Short, for years the moving spirit of the AA. The brother was a very handsome and dignified old gentleman with lovely white hair and a classic profile. He wore what was even then becoming obsolete, a frock coat. Standing behind Eddie Keyse, I was deeply impressed by the solemnity of the ambience. Eddie deployed the sad facts before Mr Hassard-Short. Mr Hassard-Short sat for a while in thoughtful silence. Then he said to Eddie with sorrow in every syllable, 'You know, Mr Keyse what these two poor young people really need is not a Poor Persons' Certificate so as to take proceedings to get their marriage annulled. What they need is a spokeshave and a pair of glove stretchers.'

So I decided it was all worthwhile and stuck to Gibson and

Weldon and my *Nutshells*. After taking my finals, I made a precautionary sortie to Rhodesia, to see the Law of the Carriage and Goods by Sea in three dimensions on the ship on the way out, and to put six thousand miles between me and my father when the exam results were published in case I had failed. I passed.

2. Pupillage

Then, as now, it was extremely difficult to get good pupillage. The convention, for then it was no more, was that you should spend a year as a pupil, seeing how the law, which you had learned as an art or a science at the feet of the professors or from Gibson and Weldon and the *Nutshell* series, was actually used as a tool to resolve disputes which people could not resolve for themselves or to ensure the standard of behaviour which is necessary if society is to continue to exist. There was nothing to stop you from appearing for a client in court once you had passed the Bar exams and been called, except the good sense of solicitors in not briefing you and of the clerk in your pupil masters' chambers, whose interest it was that you should not let the side down. Then, as now, it helped if your father had friends. Then, as now, it helped if you had a solicitor somewhere in the family. You paid your pupil master a hundred guineas for the privilege of sitting at his feet for a year, or fifty for six months.

What with all the judges and KCs at Littlestone and my solicitor grandfather, I was privileged. Academic distinction was fortunately not regarded as something you cannot do without. The old boy net landed for me a first six months' pupillage with Valentine Holmes at the Common Law Bar, and a second six months with Wilfred Hunt in the Chancery scene. Each was generally regarded as the leading junior in his field. Only juniors could take pupils. Two more different people as pupil masters it would have been difficult to find. Their only common denominator was that both were much too busy to pretend to teach you anything.

When I went to see Val Holmes he made no bones about this, but said he would take me if I was prepared to come simply on the basis that I would be made free of all his work, and would teach myself. And what work it was. He was Common Law Treasury junior, handling all Common Law litigation involving the Government. Most counsel holding that position find time to do nothing else, and its importance is shown by the fact that, after a stint of five years or so, the convention is that you become a High Court judge without ever taking silk. Val added to the Treasury workload a very large commercial practice, big contract cases and cases on the carriage of goods by sea, and one of the two biggest practices in defamation.

To me, the defamation was the fun. When you saw a large number of libel cases and how the master handled them in the preliminary stages, in which most got settled, you soon became familiar with the law in that field, which when you are familiar with it and so are not scared or silly about it is not difficult and makes good sense. The human interest of the fact situations was absorbing. The villains on one side were gold-digging plaintiffs. The villains on the other side were spiteful individuals who could drag at their coat tails journalists who failed to get their facts right, and when shown they had got their facts wrong could not bear the loss of face involved in saying they were sorry.

Of course there were then, as now, gold-digging plaintiffs. Of course spiteful individuals can lead the newspapers and now the radio and television communicators up the garden path, so that, without meaning to, they do immense injury to honest and decent people. What was fascinating was to observe the master sifting the wheat from the chaff of the libel actions people wanted to bring or defend, saving them from making fools of themselves at great expense on the bad cases, but in those, and there were many, which as a matter of self-respect had to be bought or had to be defended, ensuring that his clients should be on ground at the trial which gave them the best position from which to fight. I have to confess that I found his cases which involved the small print on charter parties and bills of lading unexciting. I found the Treasury cases, bristling with legal concepts and important constitutional questions of bodies exceeding their statutory powers, positively dreary in comparison.

In those days, before World War II had, because of the shortage of newsprint, reduced the size of newspapers, sometimes three or four pages were filled with the reports of *causes célèbres*. The fashionable silks, the Pat Hastings and Norman Birketts, the Stafford Cripps and Roland Olivers, who performed in those cases, attracted public interest and adulation on the scale now accorded to pop stars. Then it was the fashionable silks who had the Rolls Royces, though if they were also Labour MPs they tended to leave their Rolls Royces in the Temple and finish their journey to the House in Austin Tens or by the District Line. Val was engaged in so many of the *causes célèbres* that, rather than waste his time, as he saw it, by sitting in court, where he could not smoke, listening to the performance of the prima donnas, he used to send his pupils to sit behind them instead, while he got on with his work in chambers. This was edifying, and occasionally daunting when, for example, Pat Hastings, having momentarily mislaid a document or his cue, turned upon you for assistance, and was not always pleased to find the back-up was you, not Val.

It was good sharpening-up stuff. Wilfred Hunt and the Chancery were a very different kettle of fish. Even in 1936 the doyen of the Chancery juniors and continuing in active practice into his eighties, he seemed to me, after my Common Law chambers baptism, wholly unworldly. For example, except when you are a specialist and know the law in your own field backwards, it is usually wise to check what you think the answer to the problem on your plate to be, by going to the books. Wilfred paid *Halsbury's Laws of England* the compliment of using it for this purpose. If you want to cite in the opinion which you write the cases which bear on your problem, not necessarily to blind your solicitor client with science but to give yourself a convenient reference point if the case comes back to you, most people simply cite the precedent without underlining that it has been culled from the footnotes in Halsbury. In that way you may convey an impression of total familiarity with the law. Not Wilfred!

He used to eschew such vanities, start by giving the Halsbury volume and paragraph number, and then the cases quoted in the footnote.

We, his pupils, were of course made free of all his work, but, like Val, he made no pretence of teaching us. Neither of them had us in to conferences, partly, I think, simply because they worked, in Goldsmith Buildings, Temple, and in New Court, Lincoln's Inn respectively, in such modest rooms that there would have been no space. We went to court with Wilfred, whose operations did not normally include *causes célèbres*, rare birds on the whole in Chancery work, but mostly involved multiple short appearances relating to the interpretation of wills and the winding up of companies, dull stuff to my taste.

On one unforgettable morning Wilfred was scheduled to make no less than five such appearances. Dyer, his clerk, was having an off day and had not only failed to arrange the five so that they were dovetailed but had failed to bring the briefs across to court. I found Wilfred standing in the court corridor, metaphorically wringing his hands, and saying, 'I have been a giddy goat, oh, I have been a giddy goat.'

Under Wilfred you not only learned that most wills achieved a result precisely opposite to what the testator intended. You learned the answer to the question, 'When is a drain not a drain?' which was, 'When it is a sewer.' The apogee of my Chancery pupillage experience was an action conducted by Wilfred on behalf of the Town Clerk of a Lancashire borough. The borough included a convent in a situation scheduled under the Town Planning scheme as a residential area. The Mother Superior had recently died, and the sisters had had her buried in the garden. So the court, via Wilfred, was called in to put an end to what I can only assume, because I failed to grasp the profound legal concepts involved, must have been a gross breach of planning and burial law. Wilfred proceeded forthwith to move for a mandatory injunction to dig her up, and up she came.

Far different was the stuff of Val's practice. I sat through the Talking Mongoose case, when Mr Lambert of the BBC sued Sir Cecil Levita who had said something nasty about him. It was a real nineteen-thirties blood-letting, with members of the Diamond

Syndicate as part of the full supporting programme in the witness box. But the most impressive moment I ever experienced in court came in the course of a libel action by a spiritualist medium who had been subjected to an attack by *John Bull*, which was campaigning against the exploitation of bereavement by fraudulent people describing themselves as mediums. The trial was before the Lord Chief Justice, Lord Hewart, and a jury. He was a formidable little man, apt to be sardonic on the Bench. Val was junior for *John Bull*, led by Gilbert Beyfus, a formidable big man, apt to be sardonic at the Bar. We in the audience expected a field day. The medium, represented by a team of much less weight than ours, was a tiny, dowdy little woman who might have been anything between forty and eighty. She gave her evidence-in-chief modestly enough, perched up in the witness box, which is on the Bench itself in the Lord Chief Justice's court. There was no aura of sympathy spreading along the Bench from Lord Hewart. You could not tell what the jury was making of it. Then Gilbert Beyfus rose to cross-examine. It started like this:

Q. 'Your name is Mrs X., is it not?'

A. 'Yes, Mr Beyfus.'

Q. 'And what is your address, Mrs X.?'

A. '225, Commercial Road, Boscombe, Mr Beyfus.'

Q. 'A very appropriate address is it not, Mrs X.?'

A. 'May God forgive you, Mr Beyfus.'

You could have heard a pin drop in that court. The steam had gone right out of *John Bull*'s case, and I myself left court shortly after, feeling exceedingly chastened and not wishing to listen to any more.

After this catholic pupillage experience, I was delighted to be offered a seat in Val's chambers, where my name went at the bottom of the list on the door in September 1937.

3. Real Life

So far, so good. You had wrestled with the law as an art or a science.
You had sat at the feet of the great and learnt how they applied the
law to the solution of disputes people could not resolve themselves,
to the righting of injustice, to the protection of the members of the
community from the villains who threaten them. But in spite of your
label 'barrister' you had still been *in statu pupillari*, carrying no
professional responsibility and earning no money from the exercise
of your profession. Now came the change. You were to get into the
front line yourself. The making of the opportunities depended
largely on the clerk of your chambers. What you made of them
depended on you.

The label 'barrister's clerk' is totally misleading. In reality the
'clerk' heads a small administrative team, in our case a junior-cum-
typist and a boy. The nearest parallel to his function is the
impresario managing a collection of prima donnas, and in effect
remunerated by a proportion of their earnings. With us the lion's
share of the goodwill, the work, and the remuneration, attached to
Val Holmes, our great man. The only difficulty for Frank, our
clerk, in managing Val was to try to ensure that he was not
committed in too many places at once, and, if he was, to make sure
that from among the rest of us an acceptable substitute or backer-up
could be provided. Because of Val's reputation, work which came
to chambers nominally for him, which he could not do because he
was too busy, or ought not to do because it was not sufficiently
important, was often available to be farmed out by Frank to more
junior members of chambers with the agreement of the solicitors,
who knew they could trust him. If you were in Val's chambers it was
naturally supposed by solicitors that you were not stupid, or you
would not be there.

So the crumbs fell from the rich man's table, and as they went
down the line some finally fell to me. The trouble with small units

like Val's chambers, which attracted primarily top quality work, was that there were not many crumbs small enough to be fit for the debutant. In our set-up you would have been pushed, in your first year or two, to keep going on your professional earnings alone. I was lucky in that the family kitty could and did contribute. Writing, teaching, and, for us, because of Val's libel practice and reputation, reading the newspapers for libel all helped the young to keep going.

Reading the papers for libel was an eye-opener. You went to the newspaper office and you were given one after the other the page proofs of each edition. You spotted something that was obviously defamatory and said so. Someone on the staff said, 'Can we print it?' You replied, 'Of course, if it's true. Is it?' There was never time to check. It was then an editorial decision whether or not to run the risk of printing, so you were left wondering what you were there for.

Until you began to get busy yourself, if you were wise you continued, as you had while a pupil, drafting for Val, and now also for other members of chambers. If they used your drafts, Frank would know about it, and begin to treat you as an actual asset rather than simply the potential asset who had been recruited. You might even get paid for the process, which was called devilling. If you were wise you went with other members of chambers to the courts you had never seen during pupillage, so far were they below the level of the greats. You went to the County Courts, then manned by some fierce old gentlemen who had settled for second best, though in their own eyes they were fit for higher things. They did not suffer incompetence gladly. You went to Magistrates' Courts and Coroner's Courts. After A. P. Herbert's Act in 1938 which turned on the divorce tap you went to the Divorce Courts. It was as well to have been with someone else before you were solo in the front line, if only to know the way to the robing room or the loo or to find out who was the person to ask.

The scene too sometimes took an unexpected turn. I was lucky enough to sit in Ewen Montagu's room. He was then a bright and omnivorous junior who had his nose into the big time but had not yet shed all his small work. He was kind, he was fun, and he had a fast car. Two educational sorties under his wing were unforgettable. The first was to Brighton County Court, then presided over by Judge Archer KC, ex-Chancery Division, who believed in getting to the heart of things by his own route. Ewen's case, about a breach of contract for the supply of ice-cream, was third in the list.

'We'll go in,' Ewen said, 'and listen to cases one and two so that you can get the County Court flavour.'

Counsel got up to open for the plaintiff in case one. I thought I knew the form. He would tell the story. He would call his client and examine him in chief. Then the other side would cross-examine. The judge might chip in a bit. Little did I know. In Brighton County Court there were two witness boxes, labelled 'Plaintiff' and 'Defendant' respectively. They were at either end of the Bench. Counsel had hardly opened his mouth before Judge Archer had both plaintiff and defendant in the same witness-box and was cross-examining both of them himself. After that it came as no surprise when our client's star witness, an Italian who had described himself as manager of the enterprise, when cornered in cross-examination about his lack of any knowledge about the contract, rolled his eyes to the ceiling, spread out his hands palms up, and said plaintively, 'I am only da working manager, I washa de dish.'

The other sortie, to Droitwich Magistrates' Court, was altogether higher class. Droitwich Spa has brine baths, useful in the treatment of rheumatism by reason of radioactivity in the brine. Adjacent to the baths was a large and very high class hotel, much patronised by old and wealthy rheumatism sufferers. On the outskirts of the town was a brash and forward-looking public house, the management of which had the bright idea of exploiting Droitwich's natural asset. So along the fence beside its swimming pool a large notice was put up: 'Come and swim in our genuine Droitwich brine.' Why the hotel management should have considered this a threat to their business is difficult to understand. In any case the salinity of Droitwich brine was such that unless enormously diluted, swimming in the pub pool would have been as tiresome as swimming in the Dead Sea. The hotel sought Val's advice. He pointed out that the danger they apprehended was perhaps chimerical, but, if they really wanted to take action, the only action available was a prosecution under the Merchandise Marks Act in the local Magistrates' Court. So that was decided upon, and since the conduct of such a far-fetched operation was beneath Val it was sub-contracted to Ewen.

The solicitors concerned were a distinguished firm in the City, whose litigation managing clerk, later to become a partner, was Charlie Connett. I thought I ought to see how a private prosecution was conducted, so I went along with Charlie and Ewen in Ewen's Lincoln Zephyr, an impressive twelve-cylinder monster. We travelled the evening before, and were accommodated in great comfort in the hotel. The manager was young and bright and French, and delighted to have any guest around who was not afflicted by rheumatism and was under seventy years old. We had an excellent dinner and a rather wild evening's snooker in the otherwise deserted billiard room. Next morning Charlie walked down the passage to the bathroom in his dressing gown singing, 'I'm a little prairie flower, growing wilder every hour', a song then all the rage. At 10am we were in a charming little courtroom. The pub's interests were in the hands of a local solicitor. When the three justices took their seats, the Chairman was in a suit of Bedford cord, with gaiters, and this set the tone. A key witness for our side was the Spa doctor, to explain that what was in the pub pool could not truthfully be described as genuine Droitwich brine, because of the enormous dilution, and that this would of course impair its radioactive properties.

'Doctor,' said the Chairman, 'would you be so good as to explain to the court what radium is?'

This was a fast one our witness had not expected, and to play safe, he said that there was some difficulty about its true nature.

'Thank you, Doctor,' said the Chairman. 'At any rate we know what it is used for. It's used for blowing up balloons.'

After a protracted retirement, the justices announced that by a majority they found in favour of the prosecution. When they had left the Bench, the defending solicitor asked their clerk to tell him, if it was not improper, which justice had been in his favour. The clerk, looking very knowing, said, 'I couldn't possibly tell you that, Mr Jones, but I can tell you this. They were two to one.' We had an excellent celebratory lunch at the hotel, and so back to London rejoicing.

Then came a six-year pause for Hitler's war.

4. The Modern Picture

I had just about achieved professional maturity by the path I have described, nearly three years after call to the Bar, and at the outbreak of Hitler's war. The present process by which you attain that state is very different. After Hitler's war there was an enormous influx of students from the Commonwealth countries, which for some time had no satisfactory system of legal education of their own. The ambitious young, with the careers of Mahatma Gandhi and Jawaharlal Nehru as examples, flocked to the Inns of Court. Members of the Inns of Court are now as a result at the helm in many of the new Commonwealth countries. Lee Kuan Yew can talk as a member of the Middle Temple to Margaret Thatcher as a member of Lincoln's Inn when they meet at Commonwealth conferences. But the modest facilities then provided for legal education by the Inns of Court were overwhelmed. Throughout the fifties and sixties, continuous efforts were made to improve matters, but the great change followed the report of the Ormerod Committee on Legal Education in 1970.

It is now recognised that the best place for you to learn the law as an art or science, whichever it is, is in the universities where it is so regarded. The university law faculties, partly funded by the state, exist for the study of the law in that way, and scholarships and local authority grants are available to help those, now the great majority, to whom help from the family kitty is not available as it was to me. But the Bar, and the judges who will, with few exceptions, be recruited from the Bar, are rarely concerned in the field with the law as an art or science. They have to use it as a tool for the resolution of disputes and the maintenance of order in the community. To learn how to do this simply in pupillage produces a dilemma. If your pupil master has an extensive and varied practice, the probability is that he will have neither the time nor the inclination to teach you at all. Skill in teaching is a rare bird. If he

27

has the time and the inclination to teach you, it may well be because
he has not a varied and extensive practice. In either case the work
which you will see either to teach yourself as a university graduate
should be able to do, or to be taught how to handle by your pupil
master, is inevitably only part of the whole spectrum.

The solution adopted, broadly speaking, has been this. To join an
Inn of Court you now have to have at least a second class honours
university law degree. You are then required to attend what is called
the 'Vocational Stage' of training at the Inns of Court School of Law
in London, a course which occupies one academic year and is
primarily intended to give preliminary practical training in the
professional skills you will have the opportunity to see used for real
in your pupillage. When you have passed the exams which crown
the course, you must spend a year as a pupil in chambers. In the
second six months of that year, you are free to take paid professional
work if it comes your way.

This should all lead to a higher degree of professional skill in the
newly fledged barrister than might have been expected of us at the
end of the year's pupillage which convention alone required us to
undergo. But, as usual, there are two sides to the half penny. The
present set-up is aimed at producing earlier professional maturity
than could be sensibly expected of us. The great increase of state-
remunerated work in the criminal courts has led the earlier
professional maturity aimed at by the present system of training
having to be taken for granted whether in your case it exists or not.
You may be set to run before you know how to walk very well, and
the result can be unhappy for justice.

No doubt judges complained in our day too that young counsel
were incompetent. No doubt the volume of complaints you hear now
reflects the increased turnover of work and the increased number of
young counsel. No doubt there will always be differences of
opinion about legal education. This was vividly illustrated by
the evidence given to the Ormerod Committee in the same week
by the Law Faculties of Oxford and of Cambridge. Oxford came
on Tuesday. Their attitude boiled down to this: 'We regard
law as a tight university discipline, of a quality equivalent to PPE.
We are not interested in whether what our students are exposed
to with us will be of any practical value to them if they adopt the

law as their profession. Ideally, we want them up for four years.'

Cambridge came on Thursday. Their attitude boiled down to this: 'We regard the law as a tight university discipline. We will be delighted to include in what we show our students any subject which the professions would wish. We see tax law, for example, as just as good educationally as real property. We do not want them to read law for more than two years. In two years they will learn enough to teach themselves any particular branch of the law they may need to know. In their first year, we like them to read something different; for example, economics. If they read law for three years, they will have too much of it. But they must stay up for three years, or they will be immature on graduation.'

For a different approach, note that at Harvard law is not a first but a second degree, and the teaching is by the 'case' method, quite unlike our teaching system. You then have to qualify in the law of the State in which you propose to practise. At least our young can get out of *status pupillaris* and to grips with real life by the time they are twenty-four.

PART TWO

At the Bar

1. The Post-War Scene

If we had to have Hitler's war, the timing could not have been happier for my convenience. I had done long enough before it broke out to know that the Bar was what I wanted to do, and not to be tempted by the offer of a permanent commission in the RAF. My practice was so modest in 1939 that I really had nothing to lose. Six years' flying and working in a Department of State, the Air Ministry, cured me forever of the illusion from which you can suffer in your youth and innocence that the law is all and that judges are almost as close to the Almighty as a Captain RN. All my pre-war contemporaries, except those handicapped by ill-health and except those who had not survived, were in the same boat as I was. The only real differences were that back-up means of support like the family kitty were getting thin on the ground, and what might need support as a briefless or under-briefed barrister was no longer a young bachelor but a married man plus child or children. The phenomenon of the working wife supporting the husband beginner which is now a commonplace had then hardly surfaced.

We got back from World War II to discover there were things called the Rent Acts, unheard of in the Bar Exam syllabus before the war, which were to be our bread and butter for the next few years. You dealt with these in the County Court, now manned by judges who were more human than the old lot, and apt to temper the wind to us, as our opponents were not. There was some good cut-throat advocacy, and dear Elizabeth Lane, later to be the first female High Court judge, was among the most formidable performers. There was undefended divorce work, which you could do with your eyes shut once you had learned the formula. There were motoring defences in the Magistrates' Courts, funded by the insurers who would be handling the compensation claims.

Giants still bestrode the scene. Lord Goddard and Lord Denning were in their full flowering. Gilbert Beyfus still maintained his

33

inimitable fortissimo. Geoffrey Lawrence and Leslie Scarman were hatching out from their administrative law chrysalis, Geoffrey to defend Dr Bodkin Adams and die too soon, Leslie to go to the High Court Bench, Divorce Division, like Tom Denning, and then, like Tom Denning, on to the Court of Appeal and House of Lords. When Leslie's appointment to the Divorce Division was announced he was heard in Middle Temple Lane to say: 'Now I must go and find out about "adultery".' Gerald Gardiner, ice-cold advocate, was on his way to the Woolsack. So was Quintin Hogg, his temperamental antithesis. Your close friends never look like giants to you, but Elwyn Jones, back from Nuremberg, was on the same road.

On the Northern Circuit there were two local giants whom I had the good fortune to see in operation. Edward Wool, still going strong in his high seventies, could cut any rash judge down to size. Once he was conducting at Assizes a hopeless criminal defence, as best he could, before a judge more familiar with civil actions than with criminal trials by jury. Puzzled, as well he might be, by drift of Edward Wool's cross-examination, the judge was unwise enough to ask in a tone of some exasperation: 'But what is your client's defence, Mr Wool?' Edward struck the desk with his fist and with his eyes flashing replied, in a voice of Lancastrian thunder, so that nothing might be lost on the jury; 'Not guilty, my Lord', an answer as technically accurate as it was devastating in forensic effect.

This retort was as characteristic as it was devastating. In 1919 Edward had served in the British Army of Occupation in the Rhineland. Between the wars he had reason to travel to Germany in circumstances which required him to fill in an application form for a visa. It went like this:

Q. Have you been to Germany before?   A. Yes.
Q. If yes, how many times?   A. Twice.
Q. In what capacity?   A. First time, student.
                                            Second time, con-
                                            queror.

The other was Noel Goldie, whose distinguished career in Parliament and at the Bar was crowned by a knighthood, and who in

his later years used often to sit as a commissioner to deal with
undefended divorces. He was given to the malapropos on a grand
scale, so that on the Northern Circuit there is a treasured corpus,
alas unpublished, of 'Goldiana'. I found myself conducting an
undefended divorce petition before him on behalf of a lady whose
husband had deserted her. In those days a petitioner who had
committed adultery had to disclose all to the court in what was called
a 'discretion statement'. As I led the lady through her uninteresting
evidence, Goldie was paying no attention, but reading the discretion
statement with obvious close attention. When I got to the end, and
asked him to exercise his discretion and grant a decree of divorce,
he looked up at the lady with a happy smile and said: 'Ah, Madam,
I see you have been committing adultery with a member of my old
school.'

You sometimes got some jam with your bread and butter. The
1945 General Election, and the early events in the House of
Commons which followed, resulted in a number of libel actions.
During the campaign Professor Harold Laski, then Chairman of the
Labour Party Executive, spoke in support of the Socialist
Parliamentary Candidate at Newark, and was reported to have said
in answer to heckling questions from a well-known journalist, James
Wentworth Day, that if the Socialists could not get the reforms
which they desired they would not hesitate to use violence, even if
it meant revolution. Publicity was given to this, as you would
expect, in the right-wing newspapers, as being splendid
Conservative election propaganda. Next day, Professor Laski issued
writs for libel against the *Express*, the *Standard*, the *Nottingham
Guardian*, and the *Newark Advertiser*, whose editor, Cyril Parlby, was
also joined in the writ against his newspaper.

Val Holmes, still a junior, was instructed to settle the statements
of claim, but before the actions came on for trial he took silk, and
so it was necessary to add another junior to the team. I was the lucky
one. Gerald Slade, soon to become a judge, was our No 1 leader.
The form in which the defences were cast, relying on extracts from
Professor Laski's numerous books, was intended to show that he had
always advocated the use of violence to achieve socialist aims if they
could not be achieved by peaceful means. This meant that someone
on our side had to check all the quoted passages and decide whether,

put in context, they bore out what the defence said about them, and to consider how each extract should be dealt with. It had to be me, and I spent much of the lovely summer of 1946 reading, mostly in the garden, every word that Laski had ever published, which was hard work. The only available copies of some of his works were those in the British Museum, so I also had the experience of following in the footsteps of Karl Marx and becoming a registered user of the British Museum reading room. This was fascinating, but I found the garden more agreeable.

As usual, there was another side to that halfpenny. One of those present at the Newark meeting had been Major Breene, acting British Consul in Trebizond. His evidence was wanted by the defence, but he could not come to London, and an order was made for him to be examined before the Consul-General in Istanbul. I was sent out on 12th November 1946 to cross-examine him. The Pera Palace Hotel, looking over the Bosphorus in the November sunshine after you had entered the city past the breach in its walls made by the Turks when they captured it in 1483, was a striking change from London's November gloom.

It was the *Newark Advertiser* action which came on for trial first, on 26th November. It lasted for five happy days before Lord Goddard and a jury. It was all a welcome change from Rent Act cases in Ilford County Court. The propaganda impact of the original publication had of course been totally overtaken by the Socialist landslide victory in the 1945 general election, but once you have issued a libel writ you may have to go through with it willy nilly, and the defence of justification, saying that Professor Laski was in truth someone who had advocated the use of violence if necessary to achieve the Socialist end, made a blood-letting inevitable. As a first line of defence it was said that anyway what was published was a fair and accurate report of what he had actually said at the Newark meeting.

The Lord Chief Justice, Lord Goddard, was in his prime. It was the first trial by jury of a civil action after the post-war reintroduction of juries in civil actions. The defence team was led by Patrick Hastings at his most formidable, so that you had the edifying spectacle of an ex-Labour Attorney General cross-examining the Chairman of the Labour Party Executive on a red-hot political issue. Gerald Slade, fresh from his magnificent treason defence of

Lord Haw-Haw, led for our side, with Val Holmes as his No 2. Gerald was a fine advocate. He was deeply interested in the law. His deep interest in the law had been a great strength in the Lord Haw-Haw defence, which involved consideration of the constitutional situation of an Irishman who, on the eve of the war, had chosen Germany but had done so armed with a British passport. Did he or did he not owe allegiance to the Crown so that to broadcast German propaganda was high treason?

Our Laski case was essentially a human problem, and turned on whether Professor Laski had, at Newark, said what he was said to have said and whether he had in truth in his writing preached that if you could not achieve the Socialist Utopia without the use of force then force would be used. It was not really concerned with the technicalities of the law of treason. Yet Gerald, during his opening speech to the jury, quoted to them the terms of the Treason Felony Act of 1848, couched in the archaic language you would expect, and the precedent given in the 31st Edition of the criminal practitioner's Bible, Archbold's *Criminal Pleading Evidence and Practice*, for an indictment for the offence of treason felony. This he followed, after observing that the jury would know what high treason was, by quoting a substantial passage from the same source defining and illustrating the offence of sedition. Archbold is not an exhilarating work. In the course of the trial Lord Goddard ruled as a matter of law that no question of treason or treason felony arose on the words of the report of which Professor Laski complained, and at most they amounted to a charge of sedition. So of course he directed the jury accordingly in his summing-up. You can see how little this would predispose the jury to think favourably of the rest of our case.

In the end they resolved the question, had Professor Laski said what the report said he had said, a question on which there was respectable evidence both ways, in favour of the defence. That made it unnecessary for them to decide whether what had been said would have warranted a charge of sedition against Professor Laski or not, and they did not do so. In his summing-up Lord Goddard had referred to the evidence of Major Breene as being what might be 'the parting of the ways'. Major Breene's evidence had in the end been undented by my cross-examination before the British-Consul General in Istanbul!

2. Advocacy

There are specialised fields at the Bar in which skill as an advocate in court is of less importance than the mastery of, for instance, the corpus of taxing statutes, or, for example, in the patent field, of scientific concepts. In fields of that nature a high proportion of the work is advisory, and if ever you get to a fight in the courts, the specialist junior will usually have the advantage of a non-specialist leader to translate the specialist problem into terms comprehensible to the non-specialist judge. But in general Common Law work, skill in advocacy is of paramount importance, and it is only in cases involving very large sums of money, or large scale 'face', that the junior is likely to have the advantage of a leader. Normally he has to deploy the advocacy skills himself, and he soon finds that the approach which rings the bell with one tribunal won't do for another or which switches on one judge will switch another right off. If you have not got the law which affects your problem at your fingertips you can always find it in the books. You cannot find the advocacy skills in the books. You have to learn them from your betters and think them through for yourself as you go along. You will often get very sharp lessons in court from your opponents. Not only do you have professional tribunals to persuade that your case ought to win. When you take criminal cases you must learn how to appeal to a jury, and how, if the judge is being unhelpful, to get the jury on your side in despite of the judge. This is primarily a challenge for the criminal practitioner, but some civil cases, principally cases of libel, are also tried by jury.

There are certain fundamental things which you discover sooner or later. About half the time your clients will be at the wrong end of the stick. It's no good expecting them all to be swans. Half will be geese, for whom you must do the best you can. When you open a case in court it will be, in all its detail, at your fingertips. But the jury, and indeed normally a judge, will know nothing about it at all.

So, unless you go what seems to you very slowly indeed, they will have no hope of keeping up. If you are dealing with a three-dimensional problem, you have to remember that photographs and drawings are not easy for everyone to follow, especially when movement is involved. So you get it into 3D if you can by persuading the judge to go and have a look, or at least give him a model to play with. I had a very difficult case at Exeter in the early days of refrigeration in the retail trade, to do with the breakdown of the cork insulation in a provision dealer's cold room. The opposition was full of fight, but we had brought to court a section of the wall of the room with its cork with a hole in it. Mr Justice Croom-Johnson, our present Lord Justice's father, not always the sunniest of tribunals to appear before, played with it happily on the Bench all morning, and after the lunch adjournment the other side threw its hand in.

Cross-examination is regarded as a great art. The truth is that whether you get anywhere depends on whether you have any material on which to attack the witness's story. If you have none, you had better not cross-examine at all. Of course if you have material it can be deployed with varying degrees of skill and effectiveness. Usually you will get more out of a witness by leading him delicately and kindly up the garden path, rather than by being tough with him, though you must be ready to be tough if needs must. When the gentle approach drops him in it and he suddenly realises what has happened, the effect can be dramatic. I saw one victim go down in a dead faint. When arguing a point to the judge or a jury you must go on till you are satisfied it has been hoisted in. If you go on for too long they will say to themselves that you must think they're stupid.

Getting problems into 3D involves a modicum of risk. Terry Read, one of our Hampshire Quarter Sessions regulars, found himself at Winchester Assizes defending a husband whose wife was seeking to divorce him on the grounds of cruelty. Divorce judges had only recently started to try cases on circuit instead of always in London, and Lord Merriman, then President of the Divorce Division, had gone to Winchester to see what it was like. The wife's complaint was that the husband threatened her with a revolver and put her in fear. His case was that while he did wave a revolver about it was only in fun, and his wife was not and could not have been put in fear by what he did. Terry rose to cross-examine the wife, and put to her her husband's case. She said she was terrified by what had been done. Terry then produced the revolver from under his desk and proceeded to wave it about as the husband would say he had done. He had failed to ensure that it was unloaded. It went off. Lord Merriman, like any wise World War I ex-serviceman, took cover behind his desk. Thereupon a voice from the back of the court said, in ringing tones, 'Christ, he's shot the old bugger!'

You need to study your tribunal's background and interests. In our chambers, we kept a drawer full of old school and club and regimental ties. Should you, for example, deploy service, club or old school tie? Before such tribunals as the Disciplinary Committee of the Kennel Club, before whom I had to appear twice for lady dog breeders charged with conduct unbecoming to lady dog breeders, it was good gamesmanship. When you had a thoroughly undeserving client, part of the art was to focus the attention of the tribunal on yourself and away from your client. In this way advocates blessed with charm can be a very great help to the undeserving.

A beautiful example of this happened lately when I was sitting on Criminal Appeals. A girl barrister was submitting that her client's sentence was too long for his modest part in the complex villainy for which he had been convicted. There was much to be said for that view, but she played the ace of trumps when she said that imprisonment was hitting her client particularly hard because his broad beans, on which he had lavished much love and hard work, were all ready to harvest and there was no one to harvest them. Two of the three members of the court, as she had no doubt discovered by a little research in *Who's Who*, were keen gardeners. That girl will go far.

3. Libel

Even after Val Holmes had retired from the Bar his reputation as a libel expert stood us, his successors, in good stead. A very high proportion of libel actions, however, are compromised, and never reach the public eye unless the compromise includes a statement in open court to vindicate the injured reputation of the plaintiff. As a libel junior the back room work of handling the tactics behind the scenes was your province. You handled things so as to make life as difficult as possible for the other side's team and to harry them so that they would come to hate the sight of the litigation, and compromise to your client's advantage. Since it is axiomatic that counsel must never disclose to anyone what passes between him and his client except in so far as it happens in open court for all the world to hear, it is only those cases which reached open court either by way of statement after compromise, or by way of fight, that we can look at.

Looking back from 1986 it seems odd that in 1948 actions for libel were deliberately excluded, along with actions for damages for breach of promise of marriage, from the provisions of the Legal Aid and Advice Act, which, subject to a means test, introduced for the first time support from the public purse for people involved in civil litigation. Libel was excluded for fear of encouraging the gold-digging plaintiff, but that is small comfort to the genuine plaintiff whose reputation has been massacred in the organs of mass communication, and who seeks the redress the law provides. It is as if sufferers from venereal disease had been excluded from the benefit of the National Health Service because venereal disease is often contracted in disreputable circumstances. If the law of libel is necessary to redress injury to reputation, as it clearly is, and your reputation is injured and you cannot afford to litigate on your own bottom, you need state help just as much as if you have been defrauded or caused physical injury. The situation that has obtained ever since 1948 is illogical and unjust. As to breach of promise of marriage, Parliament went the logical whole hog, and abolished the cause of action.

The first libel action in which I was involved after the war was the Laski action. Another political libel action following upon the 1945 election was brought by Mrs Bessie Braddock MP. She was a colourful and much liked and respected heavyweight, but in the heady weeks after the Labour Party's landslide victory she had allowed herself to display her high spirits by dancing across the floor of the House of Commons to sit in the seat normally occupied by Winston Churchill. This physical variant of Sir Hartley Shawcross's 'We are the masters now' attracted unfavourable comment in the press, upon which she brought a libel action. Like the Laski action, it was tried by Lord Goddard and a jury. It is memorable for his observation, when her counsel, during the opening speech to the jury, had the misfortune to upset his glass of water over his client sitting in front of him: 'Pouring cold water on your client's case, I see.'

Politics are a good source of the raw material of libel actions. The tradition of the English Bar is that you are, as it were, on the cab rank, available to whoever wants your services. Because of this tradition, before World War II Gerald Gardiner, later Socialist Lord Chancellor, found himself often in the position of appearing for Oswald Mosley and the British Union of Fascists. During the fifties I found myself in the position of appearing regularly for the League of Empire Loyalists, a body even more way out, though infinitely less dangerous, than our prewar Blackshirts. They were a litigious lot who properly attracted the disapprobation of Canon Collins of St Paul's in the attitudes they expressed towards the black inhabitants of the African sub-continent, then in the news because of Dr Banda's vigorous campaign for the independence of Nyasaland.

Canon Collins, generous supporter of the black African cause that he was, on one occasion went to town on the League of Empire Loyalists in the course of a sermon from the pulpit of St Paul's. But he had got his facts wrong, and to the action for slander which they promptly brought against him there was no available defence, although no doubt, because of what their reputation was, a jury would have awarded very modest damages. When you have got your facts wrong during an attack made from the best of motives on some body of which you profoundly and sincerely disapprove, it seems to be very difficult to bring yourself to say you are sorry. So the negotiations with the Canon's team, which had to save his face as far as possible, were long and, for them, trying.

At last the formula for the statement in open court which was to express the compromise was hammered out, and the case was to be heard on a Wednesday. On the preceding Saturday, Dr Banda in Nyasaland said or did something of which the League of Empire Loyalists disapproved, and when Canon Collins left home for St Paul's on Sunday morning, he found painted on his front door 'Dr Banda's London Headquarters'. By Monday morning the telephone lines in the Temple were nearly red-hot, but in the end tempers cooled and the compromise went through in open court as planned.

Though politics were well to the fore, there were many other sources of raw material, and so long as the human animal remains full of hatred, envy, malice and all uncharitableness, or is careless of what he allows his tongue to say, no doubt there always will be. The investigative journalist is particularly at risk, because it is so easy, if you are campaigning with generous enthusiasm against something you believe to be a bad thing, to accept as true information which supports the story you wish to tell but which is in fact not true. If you say something nasty about somebody in the course of a media campaign and get your facts wrong you have no defence. If you allow yourself the luxury of failing to apologise when your factual error is pointed out and try to brazen it out in court it will be very expensive. Juries like the communicators to say they are sorry if they have got it wrong. Of course, as a matter of law, libel does not have to be tried by jury, but ever since Fox's Libel Act of 1793 you have been entitled to have a jury if you want to, and bitter experience has shown me that the jury, the twelve-body random sample of public opinion, is the proper body to evaluate injury to reputation. It sometimes happens that by mishandling of the preliminaries or by what I would consider misjudgement by those concerned, you find a libel action tried by judge alone. It happened to me twice at the Bar, with disaster each time. On the Bench I once myself had to try a libel action without a jury, and very unsatisfactory I found it, although I am confident I gave the right answer, and am encouraged in that arrogant view by the fact that there was no appeal.

Both the disasters followed publications, one in *Men Only* and one in a BBC broadcast, of material intended to amuse. I will illustrate from the broadcast. Until recently the only road crossing of the river Ouse downstream from York was by the toll bridge at Selby. For much of the commercial traffic of the region, the inconvenience of using the toll bridge, dating as it did from the early nineteenth century, and the cost of paying the modest toll, was very well worth the great saving in distance which going through Selby produced. But for the inhabitants of Selby itself, who even on foot had to pay a few pence to cross the bridge to the other side of the river, the nuisance was no doubt irritating. This then was a cause which the BBC might espouse. Down went the team, and canvassed local opinion. The team also discovered that the private Act of Parliament of the reign of George III which empowered its promoters to build the bridge for what was then very much the public good provided that, as a reward for their enterprise, they and their successors should enjoy the tolls in perpetuity free of tax. What Parliament can do, it can undo, but it hadn't undone this, and what had looked perfectly reasonable in the fiscal climate of the reign of George III looked different in the mid-twentieth century, when the successors to the bridge builders were clearly on a very good thing.

So the team had the material on which to produce an amusing programme to highlight this fascinating anomaly in the interests of everyone except those who were in enjoyment of the very good thing. It set out all the facts with accuracy, but hyperbole had to break in, and the inhabitants of Selby were said in the broadcast to be anxious to blow up the toll bridge. The bridge proprietors brought an action for libel. The only thing the BBC could not prove to be true, chapter and verse, in what they had published, was that the inhabitants of Selby wanted to blow up the bridge. With a jury we would have laughed the action out of court. Because of a technical hitch in the preparation there was no jury. It chanced that the judge who tried it, a sound and reliable master of the law, was not himself given to hyperbole of any sort. Every word was taken deadly seriously. We could not call witnesses to prove that the inhabitants of Selby actually wished to perpetrate the disgraceful crime of blowing up the toll bridge? Then it did not matter that the real facts were true, and our defence failed. Moral: always have a jury, and humour can be dangerous!

4. Contract

To me the most interesting and entertaining aspect of practice at the Common Law Bar was the libel work. Most of the contract and personal injury work was mainly about money, but face might creep into that field as well, and for me it was the face rather than the money involved in litigation which was the fascination. Moreover, mastery of the back-room machinery could be as important in the other work as it was in libel. We hear much about the law's delays. In the civil scene my experience was that counsel who was master of the back-room machinery could accelerate or put the brakes on the litigation depending on which course suited his client's interest. I will cite the two extreme examples which I remember.

There were two picturesque young entrepreneurs who came to consult me one Monday morning in the middle 'fifties. Their problem was that they had bought US Army surplus trucks from Europe, which the Canadian buyer to whom they had sold them intended to use in the far north. If the trucks were not dispatched to the far north by the end of the week the winter freeze-up would prevent them from getting there during that season and the delivery date under the contract was geared to that vital consideration. The ship carrying the trucks had reached Montreal, but a third entrepreneur who maintained that my two owed him money had got his hands on the shipping documents with the result that my two could not get the trucks off the ship and to their buyer. What should they do? Was he in England? Yes. Did they owe him money? Well, yes. But I did not see by what right, even if they did, he had taken and was holding the shipping documents, so on Monday afternoon we issued a writ claiming an injunction to make him give them up. On Tuesday morning we were before the Judge in Chambers, who happened to be an experienced commercial lawyer. He gave us an injunction. On Thursday morning we were before the Court of Appeal, composed of one Lord Justice who was an experienced commercial lawyer, and two Lords Justices who were not. The experienced commercial lawyer was for rejecting the appeal, but the other two allowed it and discharged the injunction. At a score of two all, with the experts in the commercial field in our favour, I felt this was a moral victory even if it was a material defeat; but from start to finish the whole thing took exactly four days, and I doubt whether any legal system would get from writ to appeal judgement faster.

The other extreme went thus. In the 'fifties, a large corporation had a virtual monopoly in the United Kingdom of the manufacture of French letters, a monopoly which was very valuable in the days before the pill had achieved its present popularity. The corporation guarded its manufacturing process by secrecy. Two of its skilled employees, who knew the secret, left its employment and joined a small undertaking some hundred and fifty miles from London which till then had manufactured such articles as gumboots and rubber gloves. Naturally the large corporation suspected that its employees had been seduced in order that the monopoly should be broken by a treacherous disclosure of the secret, and a writ was issued claiming an injunction to stop the two from doing any such thing.

It is a difficult and interesting branch of the law where the competing concepts of good faith and of your right to exploit the skills you have acquired in your career come into conflict. The small undertaking consulted me. No, of course they had not seduced away the two so as to get them to betray their previous employers' secret processes for the manufacture of French letters. But yes, the manufacture of French letters was a field of commercial activity into which they had it in mind to diversify, and they had employed the

two because of the know-how they must obviously have in this
esoteric manufacturing field.

The injunction application was duly heard before the Judge in
Chambers. It was a close run thing. Instead of granting an
injunction he certified under the Rules of Court that the case was
fit for a speedy trial. There was no appeal from the refusal of the
injunction, but a flurry of interlocutory activity followed. What does
all that mean, they asked us. Not to worry, we said. More than two
years later the litigation came to an end when the small undertaking
was taken over by the large corporation lock, stock and barrel.

It is true that there are sometimes very gross delays in the civil
litigation scene due to the incompetence of the lawyers on one side
or the other. But the Rules of Court provide machinery by which
anyone who regards his client as prejudiced by delay can bring
matters to a head. It is often a very nice question whether you should
bring matters to a head or let sleeping dogs lie.

In the 'sixties there were heard two memorable contract actions
in which the money involved was no more than a side-effect. The
late Nubar Gulbenkian, son of 'Mr Five Percent' the oil multi-
millionaire, was a most attractive and picturesque feature of the
post-war scene. A man of originality and intelligence, in London he
used a decorative private taxi-cab instead of a car. He was a very
keen rider to hounds. When someone said to him that he was the
first man he had ever seen out hunting in the shires with an orchid
in his buttonhole, his riposte was, 'I expect I'm the first Armenian
you have ever seen out fox-hunting.'

He often disagreed with what was done by the trustees of the
Gulbenkian Foundation created by his father, and used to express
his disagreement loud and clear, in ways calculated to cause them
the maximum embarrassment. In the summer of 1961 the BBC was
in the process of producing a programme about the Foundation and
its work. Nubar was invited to take part. The letter of invitation,
observing that the fifty-guinea fee normally paid to participants in
such broadcasts would no doubt be of no interest to him, asked him
to say what recognition he would like instead, as a consideration for
his contribution. Nubar said he would simply want a copy of the
recording of the programme as broadcast. This was agreed. Nubar's
part took the form of answers to questions. The questions were in

a form which gave him the opportunity to express criticism of the way in which the trustees were managing the affairs of the Foundation, and he took the opportunity with characteristic vigour and panache.

The trustees of the Foundation, one of whom was the late Lord Radcliffe, Lord of Appeal in Ordinary, exercised characteristic good sense and discretion. They knew Nubar's form to an ounce, but critical comment by him broadcast to the world on the BBC was clearly calculated to be damaging to the Foundation. So the BBC received a solicitor's letter expressing the trustees' regret that the Corporation had given Nubar a platform from which to trumpet his unjustified criticisms to the world, and warning that any repetition would result in action against the BBC.

At much the same time, the Corporation received a letter from Nubar thanking the BBC for the programme and asking for his copy of the recording. If it was given to him and he gave it the publicity which was clearly the object of the exercise, the BBC would be responsible if, as they had been warned, it was libellous of the trustees. If it was not given to him, then they would be in breach of their contract with Nubar who was not the kind of person to take it lying down.

Faced with this dilemma the BBC refused to hand over a copy of the recording to him, and Nubar duly sued them for an injunction to make them hand it over. The action was a lawyer's paradise. The defence was: What you want it for is to republish what is a libel on the trustees. You are asking for an injunction which is an equitable remedy. It is a principle of equity that he who seeks equity must come with clean hands. Because of the use to which you are clearly going to put what you are asking for, your hands are not clean.

Because Nubar's action was founded on breach of contract it had been brought not in the Chancery but in the Queen's Bench Division, where more attention is apt to be paid to common sense than the finer niceties of equitable doctrine. Nubar disappointingly did not wear an orchid in the witness-box. In all other respects his evidence was as endearing as it was candid. We had the pleasure of Lord Radcliffe in the witness-box. I had the pleasure of being led by Tony Cripps for the BBC. The BBC was victorious, Nubar took defeat in excellent part, and you were left at the end feeling that

Sociology. The Pickerel, Cambridge, 1935.

Reading for Bar Finals, spring 1936.

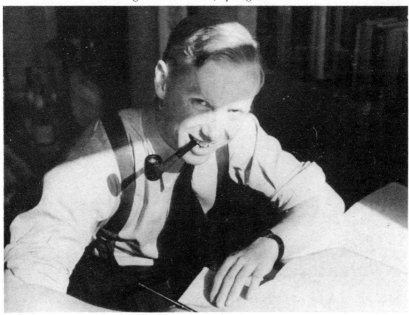

Pause for Hitler's War. Sergeant Pilot, ATS, Hullavington, December 1939.

everyone had had good fun and value for money, a situation in which you are very seldom left at the end of litigation.

Later in the sixties there was an unusual action in the Commercial Court over shares in a ship. Maria Callas, though perhaps past her peak as an opera star, had successfully shed the excess weight which had beset her earlier years as a singer, and was in her full bloom as a beautiful and attractive woman. She commanded the admiration and affection of an elderly Greek shipowner of tremendous respectability and he, by way of assisting her financially, provided her with an interest in a ship. Shortly afterwards Maria Callas attracted the admiration and affection of Aristotle Onassis, a more exciting figure than the other admirer, a man who, from nothing, had risen to millionaire status in the shipping world and become a friend of Winston Churchill in old age, taking him cruising in the Mediterranean on his magnificent yacht. The Onassis-Callas relationship soon became closer than Callas's relationship with the previous admirer, and Onassis set about clearing up the hitherto ambiguous nature of the Callas interest in the ship. The previous admirer took the view that he had not given Callas the interest outright, but only on terms that she should enjoy its fruit for the time being.

So an action was brought on Callas's behalf in the Commercial Court to establish that the interest in the ship was indeed hers. Those concerned except Callas were so wealthy and so well able to provide for her, irrespective of the interest in that ship, that the financial implications paled into insignificance before the human interest. In Greek shipping circles there was a saying, 'Ari gets what Ari wants.' There was no documentation to cast light on what the nature of the transaction had been. It had all been done by word of mouth, and it was inescapable that one side or the other was not telling the truth. Each side had a very obvious motive not to do so. Onassis had geographical connections with Ithaca, and if, like me, you had had a classical education you could not help thinking of 'Odysseus of many wiles' who had lived there. The Callas-Onassis team was led by Sir Milner Holland.

When I cross-examined Callas everyone was delighted to hear her from the witness-box apostrophise me as 'Sir Bristow', not being used to the niceties of the English title set-up. I was well teased over this premature promotion. The only document which threw any light on the problem pointed slightly in our favour, and I thought we ought to have won, but Mr Justice Roskill accepted the evidence which supported the Callas-Onassis case, and we lost. That it was another close-run thing is shown by the fact that the Court of Appeal decided in favour of the previous admirer, but the final dénouement of this needle match in the House of Lords was that Mr Justice Roskill had heard the witnesses and the Court of Appeal had not, and his judgement should be restored.

5. Off My Beaten Track

Unless you are a dyed-in-the-wool specialist, you will enjoy a wide variety of work at the Bar. As your experience increases, so your staple diet will alter as well. You get nearer the source of the crumbs which fall from the rich man's table, and you start shedding crumbs of your own. The first decisive upward step is when you say to your clerk, 'I do not want to go', or 'I will not go into the County Court any more'. The next is when you apply for silk, that is, to be a QC who wears a silk gown, and get it. In each case, you exclude yourself from much of what has hitherto been your bread and butter. In each case you widen your range, provided it does not involve professional suicide.

I duly graduated from rent restriction work in the County Court to libel and contract junior work. In our set-up we had very little of the personal injury work which is the staple diet of the majority of the Common Law Bar in London. I fell into the Church

Commissioners' landlord and tenant work, mostly concerning the Paddington Estate. This very rarely resulted in a trial in open court. Your real value was so to organise it all that there were no public blood-lettings.

Occasionally I found myself into crime. As a member of the Western Circuit, joined under Ewen Montagu's aegis before the war, I got, in my due turn, the occasional prosecuting brief from the Director of Public Prosecutions. What you got was normally the prosecuting brief in cases in which the plea was going to be guilty, and inexperience did not matter. The fights went to the experienced circuit practitioners like Hugh Park, Joe Molony, and Edgar Fay. So imagine my horror, on reading the brief kindly sent me by the Director to prosecute at Winchester Assizes in a father-grownup-daughter incest case in which both were charged, when I appreciated that this was going to be a fight. At that stage the criminal law, let alone the law of incest, was not my scene. There was a witness statement from younger sister maintaining that in the bedroom which the sisters shared she had seen father actually on the job. No jury will swallow that, I said to myself.

The fatal day came. The trial judge was Laurie Byrne, who had great experience of the criminal law and who later presided over the Lady Chatterley trial. In the Winchester Assize Court, which was then in the Great Hall of the Castle, the dock was at the back, and the witness-box was close to one end of the bench, high above where counsel sat. I opened the case to the jury with discretion, anticipating that our key witness, younger sister, would come unstuck.

I had to call mother first. She was so deaf that I had to leave my place at the Bar, stand directly below the witness-box, and shout the short and unattractive words up into her ear. This at least got us quickly over the embarrassment the short and unattractive words sometimes cause young counsel, though you get hardened in time. Then arrived the moment for younger sister to go into the box. She did so wearing the uniform of the Women's Land Army, fresh from the care of farm animals, and her evidence carried complete conviction. As a result of her occupation, there was clearly nothing she did not understand about sex among mammals.

When it came to the defence, daughter, who you might have

thought need not have been prosecuted anyway, did not go into the witness-box. Father raised a two-fold defence, which did not run easily in double harness. 'I never had intercourse with her. If I did, she was not my daughter.' Sister's evidence made the first limb difficult. After verdict, the shorthand writer, who could see them in the dock at which I had not had the sense to look, told me that they were so alike, sitting there side by side, that the second limb was equally unpromising. But it was accepted that, on the dates, the girl had been conceived before father's marriage, and he maintained that it was not by him.

My pedestrian cross-examination of him elicited a gem. If it was not he, I asked, who did he say it was? Anxious perhaps to ingratiate himself with a Winchester jury, he replied without hesitation: 'George, the butler at Eton College.' They were both convicted. Laurie, though not an Etonian, gave him three years, and put the girl on probation.

Another excursion into the criminal law took place after I had taken silk. Solicitor clients of our chambers who practised in the shipping world found themselves landed with the obligation to look after an employee of one of their shipping clients who had been on the strength as an apprentice ship's engineer and was charged with arson. He was to be tried at the Old Bailey. Our clerk, the inimitable Maureen, the first real Common Law lady clerk, who could twist anybody round her little finger and was as charming and skilful an impresario as she was attractive, landed me with the brief to defend him.

As I read the papers my heart sank. The boy was indicted on five counts of arson. Three related to fires which had happened while he was at college in the North-East studying marine engineering, and two to fires at sea in oil tankers on which he had been sailing as an apprentice engineer. He was a common factor in the circumstances of each fire. He had had the opportunity to initiate each fire. The prosecution case was to be, simply, 'Fire follows this boy'. If all five charges were dealt with together his chances of acquittal would be nil.

Apart from the opportunity to start each fire, there was no evidence that he had actually done it in any of the five cases. There was no connecting thread in the way in which the fires were started to point to the same hand having started them all. In each case there were other people who had as good an opportunity as he had had to start them. Though the fact was that he had had the opportunity to start each fire, there was no evidence against him other than opportunity, no evidence that he had been the one, out of the several in play and who had had the opportunity, who had started any of them. In each case evidence of opportunity alone was not enough of itself to prove guilt. Without a connecting link other than his opportunity, no evidence times five is still no evidence.

We spent the first two days of the Old Bailey trial contemplating this situation, in which, if my $0 \times 5 = 0$ proposition was right, it would have been absolutely wrong to try the indictment for five fires in one piece. 'Fire follows this boy' until you took it to pieces, looked damning. The judge was persuaded, and required the prosecution to go ahead on one fire only. They chose the best, the second oil tanker fire which it had taken the Royal Navy two days to put out and after which two CID officers had interrogated the boy on board all the way back from Gibraltar to Liverpool. In the course of the interrogations no evidence amounting to an admission that it was he, not someone else, who had started the fire, had been elicited. So at the end of the case, the boy was acquitted. The prosecution then very properly and inevitably offered no evidence on the other four charges, and the jury was required, on the direction of the judge, to bring in verdicts of not guilty on those charges as well. During that process their faces were a study in bewilderment.

Query, in that case was justice done? Justice according to law certainly was. Was the law an ass not to allow the prosecution case, 'fire follows this boy', to go forward? If you think that, how do you get round $0 \times 5 = 0$? Does the fact that he was in play when each fire was started make it more likely that it was he rather than one of the others in play who started it, or is the reality of the situation like the roulette systems? After red has turned up fifteen times the odds on black turning up on the sixteenth spin are the same as on the first.

As you mature at the Bar, you may find yourself involved in unorthodox operations. I found myself engaged in two out of the three Tribunals of Inquiry set up since the war under the Tribunals of Inquiry (Evidence) Act 1921. The first, in which I was not involved, concerned a junior minister in the Attlee Government who had used an insufficiently long spoon when supping with a colourful entrepreneur called Sidney Stanley. Stanley later migrated to Israel and became Schlomo ben Haim. This afforded the opportunity for a display of forensic virtuosity by Hartley Shawcross as Attorney-General. The way he conducted the case demonstrated that in the exercise of his office, the Attorney-General lays aside totally any political partisanship. He conducts the investigation, and presents the case in public before the tribunal, as a minister of Justice helping the tribunal, irrespective of party politics, to reach the right answer to the problem of serious public concern which it has been set up to unravel. The Sidney Stanley experience showed that tribunals under the 1921 Act come very expensive. They are therefore not popular, and are only set up when a scandal, or supposed scandal, of obvious public importance which must give rise to real public concern is in the wind.

The next after the Sidney Stanley affair was the tribunal set up to investigate a supposed budget leak in the nineteen-fifties. Christopher Chataway's sister worked in the Conservative Central office, and used to commute between London and Woking by train. Shortly before Budget Day she was in company on the train with a civil servant whom she thought needed teasing, and whom she teased by saying, quite untruly, that she knew about the contents of the budget soon to be revealed to the House of Commons.

The civil servant did not realise he was being teased. He concluded that budget secrets had been leaked to the Conservative Central Office and had become known to this very young girl who in a junior capacity worked there. If true, that would have been a very serious matter, and, having swallowed the tease hook line and sinker, he saw it as his duty to report it to a Labour Member of Parliament. That member, as was his duty, brought it to the attention of his front benchers, including Harold Wilson, and so the fat was in the fire. A Tribunal of Inquiry under the 1921 Act was set up so that this apparent grave scandal could be fully and publicly investigated. The Attorney-General, Reginald Manningham-Buller, Lord Chancellor-to-be, swept into action, backed by Roger Winn, Common Law Treasury junior counsel and judge-to-be, and full supporting programme. Other matters of suspicion about leaks were disclosed during their investigations, including an article by the City Editor of a daily newspaper, now defunct, for whom I was instructed. Where could he have got what appeared in his article from, if not from a leak?

When the case was presented before the tribunal, it occupied several days. Each suspicion was pursued to its bitter end. One mare's nest turned out to be Miss Chataway's unhappy tease. Another turned out to be that our City Editor really had written his article off the top of his head. All the suspicions on investigation turned out to be mare's nests. Clearly this was a good thing, but forensic fireworks from the prima donnas cost money, and somebody has to pay. The judges who man the tribunal are removed from their ordinary work, so that arrears accumulate. The advantage of the 1921 Act Tribunal is that it avoids the party political problems which arise when things are investigated by parliamentary committee. The tribunal, though its procedure is inquisitorial, is a judicial body. The Attorney-General and his team of inquisitors operate as servants of a judicial master appointed by Parliament, not as agents of Parliament itself. Anyone whose good name is at risk in the proceedings can apply to be represented, and to test, by cross-examination, the story that comes out.

The third tribunal set up under the Act was, to date, the last. It was the most spectacular, and may be thought to have had the most far-reaching results. It all took place in 1962 in the shadow of the Burgess-Maclean-you-too-can-be-a-gay-traitor syndrome. A low-ranking civil servant called Vassal, who worked in an Admiralty Supply branch, was caught and convicted of spying. The junior minister who had the responsibility for that branch was Tam Galbraith, Conservative member for one of the Glasgow constituencies, a married man of total respectability and blameless reputation. In the line of duty he had had personal contact with Vassal. When out of England he had occasion to communicate with Vassal, and had done so in the terms in which you would expect an English, or Scottish, gentleman to communicate with a trusted, if unimportant, subordinate.

Upon this innocuous basis there was erected a press campaign which culminated in the plain accusation that he had had a homosexual relationship with Vassal, and was about to defect with him but had been prevented because of Vassal's arrest. Difficult to imagine a more serious accusation? It was certainly a public accusation which called for top-level public investigation.

A tribunal was set up under the 1921 Act. The Attorney-General John Hobson, swept into action backed by John Donaldson, Master-of-the-Rolls-to-be, and full supporting programme. I was among those instructed to look after the interests of Tam Galbraith who was not unnaturally surprised by what had been going on in the press. Accusations like that do not help your future even if they are totally and publicly refuted, and even when the law of libel means that there will be financial compensation from those who make them.

Tam Galbraith's conduct in the matter was put under the microscope. The journalists responsible for what had been published were gone over with a fine tooth comb. What had been the 'source' of the river of assertion of treason-cum-homosexuality became more and more elusive the further upstream investigations took you. It had become crystal clear early on during the tribunal hearing that whatever its source the assertion was totally untrue. Ultimately the investigation reached two individual journalists. Unless they would reveal where they had got what they passed on, you could get no further. Both were called to give evidence before the tribunal. Each maintained that he had a source for what he had written. Each said that whatever the law might say, or however much the tribunal might urge that the public interest required that his source should be revealed, his professional ethos prevented him from revealing it even if proceedings for contempt of the tribunal might follow against him, with the risk that he would go to prison.

To some, it might seem quixotic that your professional ethos should forbid you to disclose who it was who told you the wicked lie that led you to accuse a blameless Government minister falsely of buggery and treason. Both journalists maintained their refusal to reveal their source. Proceedings for contempt followed against both, and both went to prison. Since then there has been a coolness, to say the least, in the relations between the Bar and the press which did not exist before.

Once you were a QC you were at risk of being asked to conduct various para-legal operations in which someone independent, with no obvious axe to grind, would be likely to promote some degree of confidence in the outcome. At least, that is what those who appointed you hoped. The strangest with which I found myself involved was in the autumn of 1969. It was the time at which containers were beginning to be extensively used for the carriage of goods by sea. To use the correct technical terminology, the container could be 'stuffed' or 'stripped' anywhere. All that was needed at the dockside was the crane which transferred it between road or rail vehicle and the ship, and the wires securing ship to shore. This was a good thing for cargo owners because apart from crane operator and wire handlers no dock labour was involved.

By the sixties the industrial dice, which in the bad old days of casual dock labour had been very heavily loaded against dockers, were very heavily loaded against the port employers, now legally required to pay every registered docker whether there was work for him or not. The dockers' unions had achieved a virtual monopoly of cargo handling in spite of my efforts as counsel at a recent dock labour public enquiry. I had appeared on behalf of the port employers of Mostyn, a mud hole on the Welsh side of the Dee Estuary, with a dock labour force then in the order of ten men, and Watchet in Somerset, a port from which the glory had so long departed that there were only two dockers left. These two were able to spend more and more pleasant time cultivating their gardens than handling cargo, something which although it occurred frequently at Mostyn was very rare at Watchet.

The use of containers introduced a new situation. The problem came to a head first in the Port of London, when the owners of Hay's Wharf effectively closed down their riverside operation and started up a container handling operation just across the street. The dockers' unions were outraged, and a national dock strike was threatened at a time when it would have been even more damaging than usual to the national economy.

Someone had the bright idea that a compromise which might avert disaster would be to extend the port boundaries within which the dock labour monopoly in cargo handling applied, so that you couldn't avoid the monopoly by just crossing the street from Hay's Wharf. A committee was set up with dockers' union representatives deployed down the left-hand side of a rectangular table in the

Ministry of Employment's St James's Square offices, and the port employers down the right-hand side. It was to try to redraw the port boundaries. I was laid on as chairman who knew nothing about the industry anyway but who was for that very reason manifestly independent, and as a QC capable, it was hoped, of wrestling with the jungle of statutory instruments by then surrounding the dock labour scheme. London, where we sat, gave rise to the immediate crisis, so it seemed sensible to tackle the boundaries of the Port of London first.

When you have fought your way through the delegated legislation, the enclosed docks presented no problem. Otherwise the boundary of the port seemed to be as far from the centre of the river as where you would get your feet wet at high water springs if the wharves were not there, all the way from Tilbury to Teddington on both banks. How to extend this to defuse the dockers' sense of outrage at the Hay's Wharf affair? It was not really difficult to feel a way towards agreement between the unions concerned and the port employers, though the negotiators on either side of the table made few bones about the extent to which they were inhibited by their own wild men. It was the port employers' customers, and other riverside undertakings who did their own cargo handling at their own riverside premises without ever having had to employ registered dockers, who would be adversely affected by any boundary alteration. None of them was represented on our committee.

Some of the opening gambits with us were fairly wild, including a proposal that the boundary line should be drawn far enough on either side of the river to include, measuring from the Teddington end, London Airport. In the end, agreement was reached between those present, and I wrote a solemn report which included the caveat that our conclusion did not take into account the views of others who might be affected, as if the Ministry did not know.

We then addressed ourselves to Stage 2, the other ports. These, it had seemed to me, should cause less difficulty than London, at least those with a high proportion of enclosed docks like Liverpool. After meeting No 2 on Stage 2, I came to the conclusion that no one was trying any more and we were wasting our time. So I said that I intended to report in those terms, and wind up the committee, a proposal that met with immediate enthusiastic and universal assent. But there was no dock strike.

In 1967, an Argonaut four-engined airliner of British Midland Airways returning from Spain on a charter flight with a full complement of passengers crash-landed in the middle of Stockport and was destroyed by fire with heavy casualties including 69 dead. It was an old aircraft, like so many charter aircraft in service at that time, and the accident caused grave public disquiet about the maintenance arrangements for aircraft of that age in general. In addition, there was the obvious need to find out how and why the Stockport accident had happened.

When you apply for silk, to become a QC, you are required to send the Lord Chancellor a personal history of yourself so that he can decide whether to make you a QC or not. That history is from then on enshrined in the Lord Chancellor's Department files, and those who are given silk form a pool from which the department picks people to man such things as inquiries into this and that, and ultimately to become part-time Assistant Recorders and Recorders, or full-time judges at Circuit judge or High Court level. My personal history in the Lord Chancellor's Department file included the fact that I had spent Hitler's war as a pilot in the RAF, so it was assumed that I knew something about aircraft. I was invited to preside over the public inquiry into the Stockport accident, with the help of a commercial pilot, Captain Brentnall, and an aeronautical engineer, Bill Sturrock, as assessors.

Almost the first thing that happened after the arrival on my desk of the great volume of statements which were to form the basis of the presentation of the problem to the inquiry by the Attorney General, Elwyn Jones, Lord Chancellor-to-be, was an application by the BBC to be allowed to film the proceedings. The BBC was producing a feature on air accident investigation, so this was a natural for them.

Since 1926 you have not been allowed to make drawings or take photographs in court. An Act of Parliament says so. Though an inquiry would not be a court it would have most of the characteristics of a court. If filming would be undesirable in court, by distracting or inhibiting the performers in court or leading to them playing to the gallery, the same considerations would apply to the inquiry. Though the Act did not apply to us, reference to the Lord Chancellor naturally elicited an immediate 'No'.

As a compromise, the BBC was allowed, before the proceedings had actually started on Day 1, to film me, as Commissioner, solemnly walking in with my assessors and sitting down. After that we walked out again, unfilmed, before coming in once more to take our seats for real. In 1926 the speed of film, the nature of flash equipment, and the size and noise made by movie cameras may well have been such that the Parliamentary inhibition on photography was wise, to prevent distraction in court. A discreetly placed camera using modern fast film could hardly act as a distraction. Why should it, you might ask, inhibit the performers in court or lead them to play to the gallery any more than the presence of the press in the form of reporters? Of course reports of what goes on in court can, indeed must, be edited. But that applies to the reporter's note, or if he were to use tape, the reporter's tape, just as much as to television film. It is the media of communication which lend reality to our basic principle that justice should be done in public, especially since no one may now sit in the public galleries of the Law Courts in the Strand for reasons of security. The cameras are in the House of Lords. Why not in the courts?

As the inquiry proceeded it soon emerged that anxiety about the maintenance of old aircraft, and this old aircraft in particular, was unjustified. The real problem was why, shortly before he was in a position to make his final approach to Manchester Airport, the pilot had suddenly lost both engines on one side. His decision then to turn away and try to restore power was criticised by no one, although in the end it turned out to be unfortunate. Had he gone straight in, he had enough height to give him a chance to make a safe landing. As it was, he was unable either to restore power or to maintain sufficient height to reach the airport. Height ran out in the centre of Stockport but he was able to put the aircraft down in an open site just short of the Town Hall, without injury to anyone on the ground.

The Argonaut, a variant of the DC4, which had for years been in quantity service worldwide, had a complicated fuel system of main tanks and auxiliary tanks in the wing feeding each engine. The system included arrangements for cross-feed so that in case the fuel in the tanks designed to feed a particular engine ran low, that engine could be fed through the cross-feed from tanks designed to serve a different engine. The selector levers enabling the pilots of the aircraft sitting in the cockpit seats to select which tank should feed which engine were awkwardly placed. To make your selection you moved the lever to a position where it reached a detent, which was not always easy to feel. If you did not move the lever fully into the desired detent, fuel might not feed the engine you intended it to feed but might feed a different engine altogether, an engine not at risk of impending fuel starvation. Things had happened during the operation of other DC4s, and of Argonauts operated by the same company, which pointed towards random maldistribution of fuel by reason of failure to get selector levers properly into detents. There had been one very close call where an Argonaut lost both engines on one side at the end of its landing run, but no accident from this cause had happened, and the danger caused by failure to get the selector fully into the detent had not been appreciated and reported.

Both the Accident Investigation Branch of the Ministry, and the Air Registration Board, which is the UK body primarily concerned wth aircraft safety, were represented before us. When the first engine failed, the pilot took action to restore fuel through the cross-feed system to the failed engine. The action he took was immediately followed by failure of the second engine. There was a head-on collision between the AIB experts and the ARB experts on whether what he did could have caused the second engine to stop, or whether it too must have stopped simply through random maldistribution of fuel already caused by failure to get a selector lever fully into the desired detent.

How to decide between them? Another of the company's Argonauts was already at the RAF Experimental Establishment at Boscombe Down for tests on its handling characteristics with both engines stopped on one side. Well then, we said, we will adjourn the inquiry while you see which body of experts had got it right. Try it out in the air. So they tried it out in the air and on the ground as well, and we got the definitive answer. As a result of the inquiry, the detent hazard was published to all users of the aircraft worldwide. As far as I know, there has been no DC4 accident caused by random maldistribution of fuel since, though the aircraft remained in operation as a work-horse for many years. It is one of the attractions of life at the Bar that with luck you will experience in your work infinite variety, and you will from time to time participate in the achievement of something widely useful.

6. Part-time Judging

There was another thing which might happen to you when you got on a bit as a silk, or even as a junior, in the era before Beeching. You might be asked to do part-time judge work at Quarter Sessions. You might become the Recorder of a borough, or the Chairman or Deputy Chairman of County Quarter Sessions. As a Recorder, an office I never held, you not only presided over jury trials at your Borough Quarter Sessions, but being appointed by the borough, you were very much part of the borough brass, with your place in the hierarchy on borough official occasions. You sat in robes, without justices. At County Quarter Sessions you sat with justices and in ordinary clothes. The court was administered by the Clerk of the Peace for the county, and sat in the traditional County Quarter Session centres, primarily the county towns. Recorders and Chairman or Deputy Chairman of County Quarter Sessions were expected to have a close territorial connection with their borough or county. When you became, as I did, a Deputy Chairman of Hants Quarter Sessions, the convention was to make you also a Justice of the Peace for the local bench of magistrates nearest to where you lived. My residential connection with Hampshire was my cruising yawl based at Lymington, so I became also a JP for Lymington.

All this gave you strong local ties, and you got to know the local form of your fellow-magistrates, who sat with you at Quarter Sessions and participated with you as equals in the sentencing process; of the administrators in the office of the Clerk of the Peace for the county; and of the villains in the county catchment area. You also got to know the local Bar, and they got to know you.

In Hampshire the catchment area and the villains it threw up were thoroughly mixed. In the north-east were Aldershot and, Farnborough where soldiers and airmen used to get into trouble. Apart from some more soldiers at Bordon and RAF at Odiham, which was usually law-abiding, the centre was firmly agricultural. In the north, along the escarpment of the Hampshire Downs, there was a strong gipsy element in the population. Both to them and to the gipsies of the New Forest telephone wires and their copper content seemed to be a grave temptation. The law-abiding New Foresters themselves created temptation because banks were relatively inaccessible, so that money accumulated accessibly in teapots and under mattresses.

To the south lay the industrial hinterland of Southampton and Portsmouth. Outside Portsmouth was a monocultural housing estate, built to accommodate the bombed-out inhabitants of Portsea Island, which was a foretaste of the law and order problems now so common in connection with much of the post-war planners' rehousing achievements. The coastal villains had a flavour all their own, but of course their opportunities, for example to steal outboard motors, were different. Sitting part-time at County Quarter Sessions gave you a wide exposure to human frailty, but you had the support of the local magistrates to help you to a sensible answer in dealing with it.

Our Chairman of Quarter Sessions in 1964 when I was recruited to help with the workload was Eustace Roskill, Law-Lord-to-be, then recently promoted from the commercial Bar to the High Court Bench. Eustace had become Deputy Chairman of Quarter Sessions in 1951 as a corrective to the study of the small print on Charter parties and bills of lading which forms the staple diet of the commercial Bar. By reason of his Quarter Sessions stint, he was already an experienced criminal judge when he went up to the Queen's Bench Division. He continued to sit as Chairman of

Quarter Sessions during vacation after his appointment to the High
Court Bench.

In those days the Chairman sat in the Great Hall of Winchester
Castle under the fourteenth century replica of King Arthur's Round
Table. To hear Eustace putting an eighteen-year-old malefactor on
probation in this splendid environment was a memorable
experience. But incongruity could creep in. The Alresford
magistrates were much troubled by a local poacher of pheasants who
was brought before them with such regularity that they ran out of
ideas about what to do with him. Finally the local prosecuting
authority charged him with an offence under the Night Poaching
Act 1828. The offence, although no longer punishable by
Transportation to Botany Bay for seven years, was not triable at
Petty Sessions, and it duly came before Eustace in the Great Hall
at Winchester.

Having seen from the papers that the problem was pheasant
poaching, Eustace asked why it was brought before him at
Winchester rather than being dealt with by the Alresford Bench.
'Not triable at Petty Sessions,' said prosecuting counsel. Eustace
turned to defence counsel. 'Are you going to call a psychiatrist, Mr
X, to say that this man is in need of treatment and should be put
on probation?' In fact defence counsel was going to do just that. The
unhappy defendant genuinely suffered from the delusion that unless
he ate pheasant every day he would lose his sexual potency. So a
probation order with a condition of treatment as an in-patient was
duly made, and you wonder what the catering staff of the mental
hospital that got him was able to make of it.

The light relief came of course mostly from the rural areas. Two
case examples, one rural and the other urban, may help to give the
Quarter Sessions flavour. In the second case, the justice sitting with
me was Mrs Prue Balfour. The first was a very sad story of how an
unforeseen accident can mar the best-laid criminal plan. A greedy
Hampshire farmer had under his control two point-to-point horses
which looked very similar. One was fast and a good jumper, the
other was not. So what was decided was that the faster horse should
assume the identity of the other with the help of a little dye to
obliterate marks by which it might have been identified. In order not
to arouse suspicion when a horse, supposedly so slow, won the race

(*Left*) Maureen, our impresario, 1964.

(*Below*) Guernsey Court of Appeal, 1970. From left to right, Alun Talfan Davies QC, Peter Stanley Price QC, P.B. QC.

Leaving St Petroc's after the court service, Bodmin. Marshal, Judge, Clerk, High Sheriff, Chaplin, Under Sheriff, Chief Executive North Cornwall D.C., Mayor of Bodmin, Mace bearers, Beadle.

Assize farewell dinner, Leicester, November 1971.

on which the betting coup was to be brought off, the ringer was entered for a race at a previous point-to-point in very low-class company, which it could have won on its head. But it was to be discreetly pulled so that it came in second, and this, while not seriously affecting the odds in the subsequent betting coup race, would disarm suspicion when it won that one.

All went well till the last fence of the first race. The ringer, pulled hard, was lying a poor second, with the rest of the field trailing. At the last fence the leading horse fell, and it was then not possible to prevent the ringer from coming in first. When the news reached Wetherbys that the supposed tortoise among point-to-pointers had won a race, suspicion was immediately aroused, the ringer was disqualified from running in the race in which the coup was to have been staged, and the police were brought in. The farmer was prosecuted and deployed a vigorous defence, but after three happy days which included an inspection by the jury of the ringer in the castle yard, he was convicted.

The urban example concerned that very common public-house offence called, for short, glassing. The defendant was cross-examined about why he should have made an attack on his victim, who had red hair. Prue and I were together on the bench without a second magistrate. She had, and has, a notable head of red hair. In those days there was more red and less white in mine, of course not concealed by a wig. When the defendant was driven into a corner he finally said he'd attacked the victim because he couldn't stand people with red hair. He then looked away from cross-examining counsel, looked up at the Bench, and with a gasp of horror covered his face with his hands.

Quarter Sessions were abolished on 31st December 1971. Quarter Sessions judicial work is now done in the Crown Court. There are Crown Courts in the centres where Quarter Sessions used to be held. Instead of being administered by the counties or the boroughs, the Crown Court is administered by the Lord Chancellor's Department, Central Government, through the Court Service. In each of the six circuits into which England and Wales divided for the purpose of administering justice there is a Circuit Administrator, who belongs to the Lord Chancellor's Department. Each circuit is subdivided into areas which normally cover several Crown

Court Centres, with each area administered by a Courts Administrator, answering to the Circuit Administrator. Big Brother, with
the best will in the world, cannot maintain the intimate local cohesion
between part-time judges, county and borough Clerks of the Peace,
and local Bar, which so strongly promoted the quality of justice at
Quarter Sessions.

The full-time Circuit judges are the Crown Court work horses.
Mainly they are deployed in the areas in which they practised at the
Bar, but once appointed they are no longer part and parcel of the
Bar. The administration, with the help and advice of the Presiding
Judges for the time being of the circuit, do their best to deploy both
the part-time Recorders and full-time Circuit judges in their areas
so as to promote local cohesion, but I wonder if under the Crown
Court set-up you could match this?

Sitting as Deputy Chairman of Quarter Sessions at Winchester
with two justices we had to try a man on a charge of drunken
driving. It was shortly before the 'blow in the bag' legislation was
passed. Bob Alexander, then still a promising Quarter Sessions
junior, now a distinguished QC and Chairman of the Bar Council,
was prosecuting. The man refused legal aid and defended himself.
When it came to the summing-up, I thought the prosecution case
was a bit thin, so, in order to correct the advocacy imbalance caused
by the defendant defending himself, I thought it right to stress the
inadequacies of the prosecution case rather than its strengths. The
jury very sensibly convicted without hesitation.

When we had passed sentence, the justices and I left court and
went to our retiring room to put on our coats. There was a knock
at the door. In breezed Bob with a big smile on his face.

'Peter,' he said to me, 'that summing-up defence speech was well
worth 50 guineas of anybody's money.'

If you were very lucky, you might get the most pleasant part-time
assignment of all. The Channel Islands consists of two quite
independent Bailiwicks; Jersey, with its off-lying reefs, the
Minquiers and the Ecrehos, and Guernsey, which includes
Alderney and Sark and the other small islands. Each Bailiwick has
its Royal Court, presided over by the Bailiff of Jersey and of
Guernsey respectively. Not only does the law of England not apply
in the islands but the law of Jersey, and its legal system, differs

from that of Guernsey. Jersey, for example, uses a jury of 24 to try serious crime. Guernsey has no jury in the modern sense. The jury function there is performed by the Jurats, distinguished local inhabitants who are permanent members of the Royal Court and participate also in the sentencing process. The law in each Bailiwick, in so far as it is not contained in Statutory Instruments issued by the Privy Council in England at the request of the Island Legislatures, called the States, is its own variant of the *Ancien Coutûme de Normandie*, before King John lost the Duchy to the French: for the Queen is Queen of Jersey and Guernsey in her right as Duke of Normandy, and the link between the islands and the Crown is not Parliament or any English government ministry, but the Privy Council.

Before the nineteen-sixties the only appeal from the island Royal Courts was direct to the Privy Council. The procedure was expensive and inconvenient. After World War II the Bailiff of Jersey, Alex Contanche, who had steered his island through the horrors and privations of the German occupation, decided that something ought to be done about it. The plan he devised was that there should be a Channel Island Court of Appeal, to consist of both Bailiffs, and a panel of English Queen's Counsel, so that the appeal from, for example, the Guernsey Royal Court would come before the Bailiff of Jersey and two English silks. English silks were needed because the island local Bars were too small to provide appellate judges. In 1949 all the necessary Statutory Instruments were prepared by the Privy Council. All that remained before they would take effect was the formal approval of the States in each island. But their mutual jealousy and mistrust was such that neither would approve. If there was one thing a Jerseyman distrusted more than an Englishman, it was a Guernseyman.

The whole project remained on ice for ten years. Then the problem was resolved by means of which the Irish would have been proud. A separate Court of Appeal was set up for each Bailiwick, to be manned by the same judges. This was a better solution than Alex's original plan, because each Court of Appeal could be serviced by the Royal Court administration in its own Bailiwick, and no new secretariat had to be created with all the inter-island jealousies and Parkinson's Law implications that would have been involved.

In 1965 I became one of the English QC panel of appeal judges. If you were lucky you were called on to go to one island or the other about twice a year. Small is beautiful. Bill Arnold and Bob LeMesurier, the Bailiffs, became your good friends, and you soon got the flavour of justice in a small community where sentencing is tougher because the crime is so much closer to everybody. A Manchester murder has little real impact in London. A St Sampson murder has considerable immediacy in St Peter Port. Proceedings in court started with prayers in Norman French. You sat in your silk gowns, but without wigs. In Guernsey, Bill Arnold, more of a traditionalist than Bob LeMesurier, organised for us to come in and go out wearing the toque as worn by him, the Jurats, and the Advocates, in the French fashion. These are made only in Paris, and there was considerable confusion before you could convert size seven and three-eighths into the circumference of your head in centimetres.

Most of the work was criminal appeals, simply how the particular Statutory Instrument applied to the facts found by the Royal Courts, and so no problem to the English silks who had not studied the *Ancien Coutûme de Normandie* at Caen University where all the experts are. But we had one splendid case in Guernsey. It was a dispute over title to a house in Sark. Round 1 was in the Court of the Seneschal in Sark. Round 2 was an appeal to the Guernsey Royal Court. Round 3 was before us, with Bob LeMesurier in the chair, and Godfrey LeQuesue, himself a Jerseyman, and Bristow, a mere Londoner as the English QC wing-men. Round 4 was the appeal from us to the Privy Council who said, in their innocence, that we had got it wrong, and sent it back for Round 5 to Square 1, the Court of the Seneschal in Sark. The Seneschal, with all the learning deployed in Rounds 2, 3 and 4 under his nose, came to a decision which restored our Round 3 result. It had all been a real lawyers' benefit. We started our examination of the law with Justinian and really finished with King John plus some Channel Island nineteenth-century commentators. Pothier, the French Blackstone, was thrown to the winds as modern stuff with which we had no concern. You hoped it was all worth while. It was said to be a very nice house.

Footnotes to the Channel Island experience

1. The prisons in both islands are George III vintage, and so grim

that anyone who got more than twelve months served it, by arrangement with the Home Office, in England. This created a cogent motive for appeals however hopeless, because as an appellant you came over from Wandsworth and saw your family even if it meant 48 hours in George III conditions.

2. Guernsey in the sixties retained corporal punishment. One of our regular Hants Quarter Sessions nuisance criminals, who, from us, got imprisonment, fine, probation, you name it, he got it, and came back for more, shipped one day as a foredeck hand on an oil tanker sailing from Fawley to St Sampson. There he went on shore on Friday evening, which he spent as he would have spent it in Southampton. He was before the Royal Court at St Peter Port at 10.00 on Saturday morning. At 12.30, when his ship took the tide out of St Sampson, he was back on board after the execution of a sentence of X strokes of the birch had been carried out on him. As far as I know he never troubled Hampshire Quarter Sessions again. *Post hoc*? *Propter hoc*?

PART THREE

Queen's Bench Judge

1. Transformation

The moment comes when you are asked to go to see the Lord Chancellor. The invitation was, in my case, conveyed in July 1970 by Dennis Dobson, a fellow Middle Temple Bencher, the Lord Chancellor's No 1 civil servant, the head of his department, as we were washing our hands together before lunch. So I went, and the Lord Chancellor, an old friend and opponent, said that he intended to make me a Queen's Bench judge. I knew he knew my form, because during his times in Opposition he had always gone back to practise at the Bar, and we had been against each other occasionally both as juniors and in silk. Our libel actions we usually managed to compromise, but we had had one contract battle *à l'outrance* over spotty mirrors. Rather like Hitler's war, the timing of transformation fell happily for me because I had lost my much-loved first wife, Joey, after a long illness, six months before, my children were out of the nest, and so my pattern of life was in flux anyway. Part-time judging, at Quarter Sessions and in the Channel Islands, broke you in to the judicial function. But you till now remained firmly based on the Bar, in what the sociologists would call the structured environment of your chambers, still for most of your time the advocate prima donna managed by your impresario clerk and with the problem of how to pay next year's tax bill a very real fact of life.

On translation to the High Court Bench the change in your situation was total. You passed from one structured environment into another, totally different. Instead of a professional income which might fluctuate wildly and on which income tax was payable one year and surtax in those days two years after you had earned the money, you now received a monthly salary credit from which tax had been deducted before ever it reached you, and although your salary was likely to be lower, for some people much lower, than your professional earnings had been, year by year you would clock up an increasing pension which after fifteen years' service would be 50% of your salary at retirement date. Once you had shaken out the complications involved in winding up the tax on your outstanding Bar earnings, and your financial obligations to your clerk and your chambers, you could fairly be said to be relieved of financial worry, with your bottom firmly based on the Consolidated Fund. To those who all their working lives had to pay their taxes in arrear, PAYE came as an enormous blessing.

Next, in secret until your appointment was officially announced at a date most convenient to the Treasury, with no one to know except your impresario and your nearest and dearest, you had to acquire your very expensive and elaborate outfit of judge's robes, and your judge's clerk, a most important factor in your future well-being. In the old days of small chambers units the newly appointed judge very often took his Bar clerk with him. This cannot have been very convenient for the rest of the chambers whom he left behind. By 1970 no active Bar clerk could afford to demote himself from his situation as high earning impresario to become a civil servant earning the judge's clerk's modest salary.

In the old days, by reason of an anomaly in the tax law which was not intended to be for his benefit, the newly appointed judge's Bar fees not yet paid at the date of his appointment did not attract tax. By 1970 a government which appeared to regard a tax-free bonus to cushion the end of a career at the Bar, however hard it had been earned, as sinful, had legislated to remove the tax anomaly. It had then found it was necessary to provide the newly appointed judge with a generous allowance towards the purchase of his robes, including all that ermine. As a QC you already had your full-bottomed wig, the cost of which indicates the labour-intensive nature of its manufacture. I took advantage of Harry Fisher's early retirement from the Bench that summer to acquire his outfit. Some of it he too had acquired second-hand and I soon had to replace it, but his working wig I have ever since regarded as my honorary fellowship of All Souls, and my friends have observed a marked improvement in my intellectual power when I have it on my head.

You also select your clerk. In my case three prospective judges attended an office in the nuts and bolts section of the Lord Chancellor's Department in Page Street, Westminster, to be confronted with three prospective judges' clerks and their curricula vitae. To my lot fell John Sowter, to my great good fortune. Son of a Loughborough engineer, he got tired of an apprenticeship which meant filing pieces of metal to the same shape for months on end. He joined first the Royal Marines, too young, and then the Royal Navy. He was selected for a pilot's flying course, and got all the way to Pensacola before they registered that he was colour-blind and was not allowed to fly. After what must have been a very frustrating time earthbound in the Fleet Air Arm, at the end of the war he was demobilised and at once joined the British South Africa Police, in whose service he spent the next twenty-five years in Southern Rhodesia, finishing with the equivalent rank of lieutenant-colonel, and commanding the Native Constables Training College.

When he retired, Cynthia, his South African wife, decided that England was where they should be. They returned to Lough-borough. After some weeks working with his hands in a timber undertaking, John saw a Civil Service advertisement for judges' clerks, answered it, and that is how I acquired an excellent clerk and a very real friend. Of course he was much too good for the job, but it was for family reasons that he ultimately left me to don a wig and gown as a court clerk at Nottingham Crown Court, where he has been a tower of strength ever since. Phil Davey took over and nursed me after John.

John had an endearing lack of inhibition about the English court scene. In September 1971 as a very junior judge I found myself landed with the long vacation stint at the Central Criminal Court. The other Queen's Bench vacation stints then were August or September as vacation judge at the Law Courts. The peace of the long vacation in the old days, when the judges and the Bar, like the members of the House of Commons and nearly everyone else, had to go home to get their harvests in and there was no railway to make London accessible, was still largely unbroken.

The Old Bailey is full of tradition. The visiting Red Judge does not sit in the imposing chair in the middle of the Bench in No 1 Court. To remind you that the Queen's justice is administered in the City of London by courtesy of the City, the centre chair is reserved for the Lord Mayor, and on 8th September, for the opening of the session, you went in behind a procession of the City Marshal, the

Sword Bearer, the Duty Alderman, the Lord Mayor, the Recorder of London, and I don't remember who else, and the day's work started with the whole party on the Bench, the Lord Mayor in his chair in the middle. You then had to engineer a discreet natural break, so that they could all file out again in a flurry of ceremonial bowing.

Before you come in, the Bench is, in accordance with tradition, strewn with dried herbs and you are presented with a posy. This had been to preserve you from infection by, and the aroma of, the prisoners at the Bar from Newgate prison. The tradition was unfamiliar to John. When he took my papers and notebook in to deploy them on the bench before the ceremonial arrival he saw what appeared to him to be a lot of mess that the cleaners had missed, and to the consternation of the court usher invited him to clear it up smartly.

John's sense of fun is both marked and Rabelaisian. After he had left me and gone as a court clerk to Nottingham Crown Court he was entrusted with the task of training a lady aspirant to that office whom he thought to be rather strait-laced. They found themselves dealing with a slightly eccentric father and daughter incest trial. Part of the court clerk's duty is to ensure that exhibits are duly recorded and preserved, and correctly labelled.

The father's defence was that the incest charge against him was a frame-up on the part of his daughter, with whom he had fallen out. The cross-examination of the daughter elicited that before the intercourse with which father was charged she had been able to look closely at his penis. Was there anything extraordinary about it? No. When father went into the witness-box he said triumphantly that this proved daughter was lying, because he had a very extraordinary penis. It bore a very striking tattoo.

After father's evidence had been given, John whispered to his trainee that father's penis would probably be made an exhibit and if so it would be her duty to tie the appropriately numbered label to it. It took her a little time to appreciate that she was being teased.

Having acquired your outfit and your clerk, and an admiring country having been told of your appointment, you next put on the full ceremonial gear and were driven from the Law Courts to the House of Lords, with your Bar clerk and your nearest loved ones in company, to be sworn in. For me the legal service on the first Sunday in October to mark the start of the legal year, with everyone on parade and the Lord Chancellor reading the lesson, followed almost immediately, and I was forthwith deployed to Winchester Assizes, together with John. So there I was, transformation complete.

2. The Judicial Function

When you are sworn in, you swear to do justice according to law.

What's the law then? someone may ask. The answer is this. One element is what Parliament has said it is to be in statutes which are passed, or in statutory instruments made under powers delegated by Parliament by statute, to constitutional organs like government departments or local authorities. Statutes are usually aimed at particular targets, for example industrial relations, town planning, taxation, Army and Air Force discipline, the use of water resources, or specific crimes. They do not necessarily have much relation to common sense, or in the case of taxing statutes, any relation to justice. They are ad hoc rules imposed on the community by Parliament, sometimes with all-party consent, more often at the instigation of the Government of the day.

The other element is the Common Law. For me it was most happily defined by Lord Reid in the speech he made after being entertained to dinner by the profession to celebrate the completion of his twenty-fifth year as a member of the Judicial Committee of the House of Lords. He said that he had always regarded the law, and he must have meant the Common Law, as systematised common sense. This struck home into many legal bosoms because in those twenty-five years it had very often been Scott Reid's down-to-earth question in the course of argument which had pricked the bubble of counsel's elaborate and learned argument. He also added that while importance was an occupational hazard for judges it helped to guard against it if you had to do your own washing-up.

If that's the law, someone may ask, how do you set about doing justice according to it then? The answer has to be twofold, because your function is quite different depending on whether you are working with a jury, or by yourself. In nearly all civil, as opposed to criminal, trials you sit without a jury.

What's a civil case, then? A civil case is where X sues Y to enforce a private right or get compensation from Y for injury he has suffered by reason of Y infringing a private right which he has. Example: X has a right to the integrity of his person. Y negligently runs him over. X's case against Y for compensation is a civil case. But if Y deliberately drives his car at X intending to hurt him, that will result in Y being prosecuted by the Crown, that is, the community at large, for an offence against the criminal, public, law.

Where, exceptionally in civil cases, as in libel actions, there is a jury, your function is to see fair play through the trial, sort out any legal problems which arise during the trial, tell the jury what the law is that they have to apply, and put the whole problem fairly on the setting board for them to sort out. By and large, they have to do the rest. They are the ultimate decision makers, you are not.

Sitting without a jury it is you who have to make the decision. What you are faced with is a dispute which the parties have been unable to sort out for themselves, so they come to court for it to be sorted out. It is in only a small proportion of cases that the problem is or includes a question of what the law is that you have to apply. Usually you are faced with a straight question of disputed fact. Then what you have to do is sit back and listen to the evidence. Sometimes you can see that a witness is lying. Usually you have to come to your conclusion on your own judgement about which version of what happened makes sense. In commercial problems the answer is usually there on the documents if you look close enough. In cases to do with machinery, or accidents of any kind involving personal injury, going to have a look is a great help.

I had to try a case at Exeter where a tractor driver had lost his eye as a result of a stone thrown up by a flail-type clover-cutting machine. An expert witness was called who had proved conclusively to his own satisfaction that the geometry was such that the machine could not have thrown up a stone which might hit the tractor driver in the eye. But he'd lost his eye, and there did not appear to be any alternative explanation.

'We'll go and have a look,' I said.

Tractor and machine were set up for me in a muddy farmyard near Cullompton. I had my own gumboots with me, always good one-upmanship in a judge, and I borrowed a storekeeper's coat. As I sat on the tractor seat and contemplated the driving wheel tyres, the light dawned at once. The expert had drawn his lines and measure his angles, as he had to, from the starting point of the tractor and its wheels at rest. You had only to look at the tread on the driving wheel tyres and think of them in motion to see that a stone thrown up by the flails which hit a tyre could ricochet in any direction depending where it struck the tread, and could certainly hit the driver in the eye.

So what you have to do is listen to the evidence, apply your common sense to it, see what help you can get from counsel by involving them in dialogue, and then, for better or for worse, make up your own mind. The French have a nice expression for it. They say: *'Faut trancher la question.'* Having made up your mind you are then to say in your judgement what you have decided and why, so that the parties can understand. You should also say what you have to say in such a way that, if one of the parties thinks you got it wrong and goes to the Court of Appeal, that court does not have to do all the work all over again but can pick up the problem where you left off and simply see whether or not it thinks you gave the right answer.

When you are faced with having to decide a disputed question of law you may first have to decide the facts, or there may be no dispute about the facts. Then you listen to what counsel on each side has to say about the law. Judges in England enjoy the enormous advantage that no one in his senses expects you to 'know the law'. The spectrum is after all rather wide, and while you will have been involved in part of the law in depth during your time at the Bar, much of it you will not have been exposed to at all. Our set-up is based on the proposition that the judge can expect to have these conflicting propositions of law competently deployed for him on either side, supported by the citation of whatever previous decisions there may be which might throw light upon what is the right answer. He is entitled to assume that counsel, who will after all have gone into it before bringing their clients onto the battlefield, will have done their homework properly and will present the proposition on their side honestly, warts and all.

All the judge should have to do is listen, make sure, if necessary by involving counsel in dialogue, that he understands the proposition on each side, and then make up his mind which to him makes the better sense. He can be confident that if he really is in the presence of a disputed question of law where the frontiers have to be enlarged, the problem will most likely be taken to the Court of Appeal whatever he decides, and quite possibly, whatever that court decides, to the House of Lords. It is satisfactory, when you have decided that the right answer is Black but the Court of Appeal said it was White, if 'the voices of ultimate infallibility', as Lord Justice Scrutton described the Law Lords, decide that it was Black after all.

It is because the judge can trust counsel to present cases so that all he has to do is listen and make up his mind, that in England we have had so few judges per head of population, and that they do their ordinary civil work sitting alone. In France, certainly in the criminal courts, judges sit three strong, afternoons only. They have to do their own homework, and need the morning to do it. In the United States Federal Court the judge has his law clerk, a recently qualified university graduate, to help him in his research and in drafting his judgements, which tend to be reserved more often than judgements are reserved in England. Neither in France nor in the United States is there a Bar in our sense, which is a separate profession, on which the judges can rely in the way the English judge can and does rely on the English Bar, and from the ranks of which the English High Court judges are all drawn.

This was brought home to me vividly shortly after the war. A solicitor's clerk, also an ex-airman, who was a good friend as well as a good client, had a father who owned a London hotel. He telephoned one day to say that over some beer in father's hotel the

CHURCH and STATE
June 1973.

(*Right*) Red Judge with Lord John
Manners, High Sheriff, Leicester.

(*Below*) Red Judge with the
Provost, Southwell Minster.

John with Carlisle Lodgings' staff and pinkfoot goose, January 1971.

Judge's Clerk and Marshal fishing the Lune. Short day at Lancaster, March 1971.

previous evening he discovered that father's hotel guest with whom he was enjoying his drink was a Federal judge from Indiana who was over on holiday and very anxious to have a look at the English courts. Could I make time to show him around? He himself was already committed.

Of course I could. He was a nice friendly Federal judge and I had what I thought was the great good fortune to be able to show him Mr Justice Stable trying a money-lender's action. Counsel on one side was the present Lord Chancellor, on the other Harry Phillimore, later a Lord Justice. With that team it had to be superb entertainment value with the money-lender in the witness-box, and it was.

After ten minutes I thought my Federal judge ought to be brought back to earth, so I got him out into the court corridor and before taking him to a Divorce Court asked him how he had enjoyed it. His reaction astonished me. It was: 'How did the judge come to allow counsel such latitude?' So I explained that there were only some two thousand counsel in England and Wales, as was then the fact; that because of the small numbers and the collegiate system of the Inns of Court most of the more senior were known personally or by reputation to the judges; that if any counsel was untrustworthy the word went around like a flash; and that since the two very distinguished counsel dealing with the money-lender's case were both known to Mr Justice Stable personally, all he had to do was sit back and listen and enjoy the performance and then make up his mind.

'Well,' said my Federal judge, 'in my jurisdiction in Indiana there are about twenty-five thousand counsellors who have the right of audience before me. I seldom see any of them more than once. Because they do so little advocacy, since there is no separate Bar, they are nearly all incompetent as advocates and I have to do most of the work myself, which takes a long time. But because of the way they are paid, by a percentage of the damages they get for their client and no win, no pay, I cannot trust any of them to play the game straight.'

Your work in the criminal field is different. The trial process, and your function to see fair play throughout and sort out any legal problems which arise as you go along, is much the same as in a civil case with a jury. So is the business of telling the jury what the law is that they must apply, and of putting the case on both sides fairly on the setting board for their consideration. It is not easy when there is a multiplicity of defendants on a multiplicity of charges, with many available permutations and combinations of verdict. In all cases where you have a jury it is of enormous importance that they should trust you, and you should be their friend. For judge and jury to be at cross-purposes, so that counsel can play one off against the other for his client's benefit, is a recipe for disaster to justice. By making it clear that you are interested in their comfort and convenience you should be able to get off to a good start. When the rapport is established it is very recognisable, and is a great help in ensuring that ingenious advocacy does not get them into a muddle. They will very seldom come to what you think to be a wrong verdict either of conviction or acquittal, and it is of very great importance that they should get it right. Sometimes they reach a verdict you had not thought of yourself, but when they have, you can see how right they are. The real difference from your function in civil comes after a plea or verdict of guilty, except in the case of murder, where the mandatory sentence of life imprisonment has replaced the mandatory sentence of death. The judge has to decide on the proper disposal of the guilty defendant. The plea or verdict 'guilty of murder' relieves you of having to say more to the defendant than the law requires you to pass 'sentence of life imprisonment'. If you have a vestige of humanity you will explain to the defendant, unless it was a very wicked killing, that the sentence does not mean he will be kept in prison for life but that progress in prison will be monitored and he will be released when those in charge of him think that it is right in the public interest to release him.

The other thing is that you should write to the Home Secretary giving him your opinion on the wickedness or otherwise of the killing, and, if you have any views on it, how long it should be before release. There is a great difference between a deliberate killing for money and a killing in heat in the course of a domestic dispute which goes too far but which fits the law's definition of murder. Yet the law requires the killer in each case to be sentenced to imprisonment for life.

3. Sentencing

This I suppose most judges would say is the most difficult of all their various functions. You get played in by sitting as a part-time judge, in my time at Quarter Sessions, now as Deputy Recorder or Recorder. Now before you sit in that capacity you are required to sit under instruction on the bench at the Crown Court for a period with a Circuit judge, so that you may see how he deals with the sort of problems with which you will be faced. In my time you were thrown in off the deep end with only your experience as counsel in criminal trials to help you, and an admirable little Home Office booklet, then in 1964 just published for the first time, to tell you what disposals were available and what they were intended to achieve. You also had the criminal practitioner's bible, *Archbold*. Now, at all levels, you will from time to time be required to attend residential seminars, and the Presiding Judges of the circuits have day-long sentencing conferences once a year for all the Circuit judges, Recorders, and Assistant Recorders on the circuit for which they are responsible.

The seminar and conference machinery consists in the consideration, by syndicates of those attending, of case problems, selected to illustrate particular aspects which give difficulty, and founded on actual cases recently dealt with in the Court of Appeal Criminal Division. Each syndicate decides on its own answer, and all the answers are deployed at the end of the day, sometimes accompanied by an ex-cathedra pronouncement from the presiding genius which, provided it happens after the announcement of the syndicate answers, can be helpful.

A case problem set at an early High Court level sentencing conference involved a rape by a Cambridge undergraduate in the spring of the year in which he was expected to get a brilliant first class Honours degree. The lesson to be incalculated was that for an offence so serious the fact that a prison sentence would have a disastrous effect on a university student's career must not deter the court from passing a prison sentence. The syndicate leaders duly announced their syndicates' answer, two years, three years, and so on. Leader of the last syndicate was Mr Justice Melford Stevenson, PC. 'Our syndicate has been astonished,' he said, 'at the sentences we have heard proposed. We were thinking of giving the boy a Blue.' A good reminder that the exercise in which we were then engaged was academic!

The weakness of the whole exercise process is that it is inevitably two-dimensional, and tends to be focused on the offence rather than the person committing it. You do not have the full social inquiry report which is a most important factor in the great majority of real cases. The books also cannot escape the same weakness, and all tend to fuel what to me is the ultimate sentencing heresy, the 'tariff' concept. Of course as a beginner it is helpful to have been exposed to the exercise and the books. Yet for the beginner, and for the public at large, the 'tariff' concept can lead to the belief that what you are doing is dealing with a criminal offence. What else do such expressions as 'tariff for armed robbery ten to fifteen years' immediately convey to someone unfamiliar with the scene? Of course fully spelt out it means that the order of sentence appropriate to most villains guilty of armed robbery in which there are neither aggravating nor extenuating circumstances attaching to the offence itself or to the offender will be from ten to fifteen years in prison.

The truth is, of course, that you are not dealing with a criminal offence. That has taken place, and cannot be undone. You are dealing with a person who has offended. Not only do armed robberies vary enormously, from the experienced and professional gang doing a street hold up of a bullion truck at gun-point to the Walter Mitty teenager with his toy pistol trying to scare the village post mistress into opening the till. The members of the gang itself will be very various people with various criminal records and family backgrounds. For some of them more than fifteen years is clearly necessary, and for some, less than ten would be clearly appropriate. So beware the tariff concept.

For twenty-two years at one level or another I have been involved in the sentencing process. I started with the advantage of having done very little criminal work at the Bar. Percy Russell, our much-loved top Hampshire probation officer, once said that the reason sentences in England tended to be higher than in Europe was that most of our Circuit judges and Recorders have had wide criminal experience at the Bar and so are conditioned in their thinking on sentencing by the sentences which the previous generation of judges passed upon their clients. European judges are not recruited from European advocates. The European lawyer at once becomes, and throughout remains, either advocate or judge. If he becomes a judge he will start as a very small judge, and then go up the judicial ladder. He will never have been an advocate at all, and so will not be conditioned in his approach to sentencing by his own experience as a fieldworker in court. When I started sentencing as a Deputy Chairman of Quarter Sessions I had no experience at the Bar of what sentences were passed at Quarter Sessions, and had to work it out from the little Home Office booklet and *Archbold* for myself, with what help I could get from the magistrates who sat with me at County Quarter Sessions and were full participants in the sentencing process. The magistrates themselves at Quarter Sessions were out of their usual scene, in which the maximum sentence they had jurisdiction to pass was very modest and the crime they had to deal with much less serious.

Your choice of alternatives to a prison sentence is now much wider than it was in 1964. In addition to fine, probation, conditional or absolute discharge, and bind-over, which were then available, you can now suspend a prison sentence of two years or less either completely or in part. You can make a community service order. You can use probation hostels, if they will take the person in. There are of course medical disposals available, but they are limited by what the doctors and the relevant statutes have to say. So how are you to choose between this wealth of possibilities, and what machinery, if any, is there in this computerised age to help you to know afterwards if you got it right?

In practice you are faced with three main situations. There is the villain who on form is never likely to get back on the rails and is a real danger or a real intolerable nuisance to the rest of the community. In such a case there is nothing constructive you can do. All you can do is to pass a sentence of imprisonment which will contain him for the length of time you think necessary and which must not be inappropriate to the offence for which you are sentencing him. Five years would be over the odds even for a hardened and incurable petty shoplifter. In picking the length of sentence, you bear in mind that one third will be remitted for good behaviour, and that after serving one third your villain will be eligible for parole, though if the Parole Board takes the same view of him as you do he won't get it.

The second situation is where the nature of the offence which your defendant has committed is such as to arouse proper indignation in his local community or in the community as a whole. Here even though the offence may have been committed in circumstances which are never likely to recur, and your defendant is never likely to do such a thing again, it is essential to recognise in the sentence you pass the proper public indignation which the crime has aroused. If you do not perform this 'lightning conductor' function there is a danger that you will destroy respect for the law and that people will be tempted to take the law into their own hands.

I had a sad example of the 'lightning conductor' situation while sitting at Newcastle. Two teenage boys took two younger teenage girls out for the afternoon without the knowledge of their parents and without any sinister intention. One thing led to another, as it so often does, and the afternoon finished with the girls dead and the boys in hiding. They were of course quickly found and arrested, and the public outcry in the area was such that the boys' families had to leave home and move away.

The prosecution very properly accepted the boys' pleas of guilty to manslaughter, but so great and so well justified was the feeling of horror and indignation in the local community that I decided that a sentence of detention for life was necessary, though the boys realised the enormity of what they had done, were overwhelmed with remorse, and were clearly never going to get into the same sort of situation again. A life sentence anyway has the advantage that when an appropriate period for expiation has elapsed they could be released to start life again somewhere else. Nothing anyone could do could bring the poor girls back to life.

The child-battering cases are a very sad illustration of the lightning conductor situation. More often than not you are faced with totally inadequate parents. Mother is not competent to look after the baby properly, and too stupid to get help. So the baby can't stop crying, and father can't cope either and hits him, so he cries some more. No one meant to hurt him, but you finish up with the baby seriously hurt or even dead, and father has to go to prison, the social services are under fire, and the family is totally destroyed.

Sometimes of course you are in the presence not of incompetence, but of real wickedness, usually in a step-father. I had one terrible case at Chester were step-father crowned a long course of maltreatment of his seven-year-old step-daughter by literally crucifying her against the kitchen door. This was too much even for the terrified mother who finally raised the alarm, and the child was rescued and survived.

Naturally this caused an immense public outcry, and it seemed to me to call for a sentence of fifteen years' imprisonment. It was heartening that afterwards I had several letters from members of the public enclosing money to buy toys for the girl and her small brother who had had his fair share of step-father's attentions as well. When you spend a protracted period trying serious criminal cases, as often you do on circuit, it is a comfort when something happens to persuade you that not everyone is as nasty as that.

Another situation in which the lightning conductor function is at present becoming paramount is rape. In dealing recently with sixteen appeals against rape and attempted rape sentences, Lord Lane said that while the number of rape cases had not increased over the years their nastiness had. This had given rise to disquiet, expressed both in Parliament and in the country. Sentencing for rape had been criticised as too lenient. Home Office statistics for 1984 showed that 95 per cent of those convicted got custodial sentences. 2 per cent had been sentenced to imprisonment for life, and a further 6 per cent for more than five years. Lord Lane commented that this suggested an approach by the judges resulting in sentences being too low, and set out starting points for judges to follow in the future in sentencing for various classes of rape, ranging from life imprisonment for those who would be a permanent danger to women, fifteen years for those conducting campaigns of rape, like 'the Fox' in Bedfordshire, eight years for gang rapists, burglar rapists, abductors, and those who had responsibilities towards their victims, down to five years for adults found guilty after not guilty pleas in cases where there were no aggravating or mitigating circumstances.

The press greeted what he said with such headlines as 'Longer Jail Sentences for Rapists, New Guidelines to End Leniency'. Query, what trend will the 1986 Home Office statistics show? When you are in the field it is easy enough to see into which category the case in which you have to pass sentence falls. The life sentence category is really self-evident, for the public safety he must be out of circulation for good. The 'campaign' rapist you might think is likely to be just as dangerous, and if he gets fifteen years and so is released, with remission, after ten, is the unscrupulous sexual drive which led to the 'campaign' likely to have vanished?

With the other categories it is the aggravating and mitigating circumstances which cause the difficulty and which inevitably result in what looks like inconsistency in sentencing. Where the circumstances of the rapist, his victim, and what he has done and how he has done it are different in every case, as they are, apparent consistency in sentencing is crying for the moon. Unless you have sat through or read full reports of two cases the sentences in which are different though the category of offence looked the same, you are in no position to assess whether those sentences are consistent or not.

Like homicide, rape is rarely a premeditated cold-blooded crime. Usually it happens because the man is disinhibited by alcohol and allows his sex imperative to take charge. Is it realistic to think of him saying to himself, I will stop this because I will get five years if I'm caught? Could the cry 'Longer Sentences for Rapists' make him think twice when the trouble is that he's not thinking with his head anyway?

The third situation is mercifully the usual one with which you are faced, and is one in which you can and should be constructive. Your villain, however near or far down the criminal road, does not have to be treated as 'irretrievable, for containment only': what has been done is not so horrific as to make the lightning conductor factor paramount. Here is someone who is off the rails, and whom it is in the best interests of the community to get back on the rails. The criminal law is all about the good of the community in general, and the sentencing options are about how it is be achieved. Crime and punishment in its simplistic sense is something that we have painfully grown out of through our history, just as the New

Testament overtook the Old Testament's eye for an eye and tooth for a tooth syndrome. Iran ought to discourage us from going back to the Middle Ages for our crime and punishment concepts.

Depending on what you make of your villain, so you will decide which of the available options is the most promising for getting him back on the rails. For some, a sharp sentence may well be the only sensible answer. I can remember several instances while I was on the Parole Board of men serving sentences of three years or more who were assessed by the prison officers who had to report on them, officers not in an occupation which leads you to become starry-eyed, as having reached the stage where the game was no longer worth the candle. With all the conveniences of the modern prison, if you are lucky enough to be in a modern prison, it still by and large means no beer, no smoking, and no wife to keep you warm at night.

You may conclude that a taste of prison, 'the clang of the prison gates', plus the certainty of more if you don't behave, is likely to be the right answer. So, a part suspended sentence with only a short time inside if you can keep your nose clean afterwards. Or it may be a case which cries out for the sort of help the probation service can give. In the case of the irresponsible young, particularly if unemployed, the community service order, provided your villain is acceptable to the management, is a first-rate constructive answer. All these options have teeth in them. If he does not play ball he will be brought back and worse will befall him. Making the choice is often easy, sometimes not, and you will make mistakes. It is the mistakes, not the unsung successes, that hit the headlines.

How then are you to know when you get it right, and when you do not? The best place for the unfavourable fan mail which you get, or I at any rate have got from time to time, is the waste-paper basket. The favourable fan mail which you also get from time to time, while more encouraging, is not worth any more. Both are the products of opinion, usually based on reporting in the newspapers or on the telly. The reporting itself, certainly in long cases, may through no fault of the reporter be very misleading. He will report prosecuting counsel's opening, based on prosecuting counsel's instructions on paper, and putting the prosecution case hot and strong. There follow days, sometimes weeks, spent in testing the evidence and fitting together the jigsaw. This process, quite

unreportable and wholly indigestible even if you get it word for word
in transcript of the shorthand note, often results in a picture
significantly different from the picture presented in the opening.
The summing up, apart from the occasional purple passage which
by and large the judge hopes to avoid, is unreportable because it is
a selective and allusive appreciation of the jury's problem. The next
thing to hit the headlines is the sentence. This you hope will be right
for the picture as it stands at the end of the trial, but it may look very
wrong set against counsel's opening. Even if the Court of Appeal
has to consider your sentence, whether it thinks it was right or
wrong is still its opinion.

What you want, in order to know whether you got it right, is fact.
What happened to the man in prison, on community service, on
probation? Did he survive his probationary period? After it was all
over, whatever it was, has he offended again? I find it extraordinary
that in this computer age there is really no machinery yet set up
through which you can discover any of these things. The best you
can do is to ask for reports on progress from the Probation Service.
Percy Russell always saw to it that we had quarterly reports on all
our Hants Quarter Sessions probationers, and I have always insisted
on this for myself up and down England and Wales, and even at the
Old Bailey, ever since. The probation officers appear delighted that
you are still taking an interest, and sometimes ask your opinion on
what they intend to do now with their problem that you originally
landed them with. You can see how each case worked out.

You can get the same follow-up on suspended sentence
supervision orders and community service orders. Of course you
can't remember them all, but many you do, especially the ones
where you were taking a long shot. It helps when the next borderline
probation prospect comes up. But you never know if after the order
is successfully completed the subject goes straight. You never know
what happens during or after a prison sentence unless by chance a
familiar name comes up when you are working on the Parole Board.
Only one came up with me. Why can you not get an annual
computer print-out on the progress of all your convicted villains
which would show you whether in fact, and not as a matter of
opinion, you were getting your sentences about right? Writing the
programmes for the computer might be a very useful exercise for the

University criminologists. Once the programmes are written, as I understand it, the machine does the rest with no trouble at all. Imagine, if you would, a Judges' meeting at the beginning of the legal year when everybody's factual results are displayed as a league table, with a sabbatical year studying other countries' sentencing form as the first prize.

4. Life on Circuit before Beeching

(Beeching-the-Courts; not Beeching-the-Trains)

My first assignment as a High Court judge was to Winchester Assizes. There was a very long case to be tried, and long cases did not fit conveniently into the pattern, unchanged in its essentials since the time of Henry II, upon which criminal justice was dealt with outside London. I arrived at the judges' lodgings, a charming Queen Anne house in the Cathedral Close just across from the Deanery with the Cathedral brooding over us, to find I was judge number 4. Before I set out, Hubert Parker, the Lord Chief Justice, had told me I was to deal with the marathon case and stay put in Winchester till the end of term dealing with any other Red Judge work which was wished my way.

Red Judge work is shorthand for criminal work, which the High Court judge tries in his scarlet robes. That the robes are scarlet is accidental, not significant. It used to be the convention that the sovereign on his accession made gifts of cloth to his senior officials, among them the judges, so that they could have new outfits for the new reign. They didn't hold with that sort of thing during the

Commonwealth. At the Restoration, Charles II, in a confused situation for which no one was prepared but being anxious to do as his predecessors on the throne had done, had to do the best he could with what cloth was to hand. This happened to be scarlet. When Charles died, James II was too busy with Monmouth's Rebellion to do anything about new outfits for his judges. After the Glorious Revolution, during which the actors had other preoccupations, the judges were no longer the sovereign's officials, removable at his pleasure. They were expressly made into an estate of the realm, irremovable except on a vote of both Houses of Parliament. They were independent of the sovereign. One of their chief functions ever since has been to stand between the sovereign, and now the executive, and the ordinary citizen. So the robes have stayed in Charles II's scarlet ever since.

On the day after I arrived, we all set out in procession in two limousines to court, attended by the High Sheriff and two Under Sheriffs, and a judge's marshal or so. The senior judge sat in the Great Hall, where the Commission of Assize, which made us all operational, was read. I was dropped off at the Council Chamber, the only place usable as a court commodious enough to accommodate the nine Spitalfields heroes whom I had to try. In principle the thing was that some of them had come to the conclusion that their profit margins would be improved if they did not have to pay for the raw materials which they subsequently sold in Spitalfields market. From this initial breakthrough it was a short step to a realisation that it was a pity to have to pay for your transport, so they started to steal the articulated lorries on which the raw materials were carried, as well as their loads. The crowning touch was to steal the tarpaulins with which to cover the loads.

It was a large-scale operation stretching into Scotland as well as over the Home Counties and the Midlands. Happily the first police capture took place in Portsmouth and as a result it was the Hampshire police and prosecuting authority which brought the whole thing to court at Winchester. The surprise and indignation of some of the villains, who had been briefed that if there was trouble they should get in touch with the Gaffer at such and such a police station in the Metropolitan Police Area and did so only to find he would not help them because it was the rotten Hampshire police who were running the case, was both obvious, comic and disturbing. Things have changed since 1970.

We settled down to seven interesting weeks' sorting out a complex evidence jigsaw which in the end required the jury to find some 57 verdicts. Meanwhile after the first fortnight my three brother judges, having for the time being disposed of the available Hants Assize work, set off with their clerks and marshals and cook and butlers, one professional, the other a Law Courts' usher thinly disguised, for points west, following the path beaten by judges going the Western Circuit since the Middle Ages; Dorchester, Exeter, Bodmin, Bristol, Taunton or Wells, Devizes or Salisbury, and finally back to Winchester for the last fortnight before Christmas. So there I was, the sole object of attention for the lodgings staff, in solitary state in that lovely house but for my clerk, John, good company and a tower of strength.

John Pelly, the High Sheriff, and Hazel his wife took me under their wing. John took me twice after court to shoot an evening flight in his little flight pond on the high chalk above the Meon valley. He lent me a gun, since I had not then the foresight to take my own, and I much surprised myself, and I suspect John and the Preshaw keeper, by killing the first two duck to come in as a right and left.

During week seven I summed up for two and a half days, and the jury returned all its 57 verdicts within the day, acquitting only Ginger Tom. He was out of the council chamber like a flash before the families of the convicted defendants could lynch him.

It was altogether a fun trial for my initial first XI appearance. The real high spot for me was this. It was a very hot October, so we sat with the council chamber windows wide open. One day I was asked, would I arrange my lunchtime movements so as not to clash with a ceremonial march down past the castle by the Army Pay Corps, led by the Green Jackets band, on their way to receive the freedom of the City. 'Of course,' I said. By 12.30 it was very hot in court, and the windows were wide open. One of the defence teams, provenance Old Bailey, had just concluded a particularly dreary submission of law about the admissibilty of evidence or some equally exhilarating question. I had launched into what I intended to be a witty and luminous ruling on the submission when I was silenced by the Green Jackets band marching past our open window. What they were playing was 'Colonel Bogey'. By the time any of us could make ourselves heard again, I thought it better that I should be the one to grasp the nettle. I observed to counsel that we ought to take the music as a coincidence rather than as a comment on my ruling on the submission.

There followed a prosecution for the illegal importation of Pakistanis from Cherbourg, in a converted lifeboat in midwinter, to Langston Harbour, where the police, alerted in the Franco-British customs grapevine, were waiting to welcome what was left of them after a miserable crossing. It was an open-and-shut case, with a charming but, by Hampshire standards, inexperienced counsel of Pakistani origin appearing for some of the defendants. I suspect I got over-enthusiastic about the maritime aspects of the problem. I have made many small boat passages between Cherbourg and the Solent in bad weather, and felt desperately sorry for the unhappy imports. Anyway, disaster! The jury disagreed. The retrial later, by a non-marine judge, reached the appropriate conclusion.

My last memory of a memorable twelve-week virgin exposure to the Assize scene is this. After my brothers' return from points west, as judge 4 I was roosting once again in the lodgings attic, and sitting in the Guildhall in what was normally the City Recorder's Court where he performed his Quarter Sessions duties. It is a long way from the castle, so the junior judge went off in a separate limousine with his clerk and a very tall Under Sheriff.

The Guildhall is a fine example of Victorian Gothic, fit to have been celebrated by John Betjeman. It stands towards the bottom of the High Street, by King Alfred's statue. The Recorder's Court and retiring room are on what you should I suppose call the entresol, reached by an imposing double stairway from the pavement which meets at the top on an open platform from which you go in through the door. On the platform was sited the municipal Christmas tree. Behold, in our last week the Christmas tree is adorned with fairy lights. I arrive, in scarlet and ermine, topped off with a wig, at the foot of the stairway, emerging from the limo preceded by the tall Under Sheriff with his magic wand. He in turn is preceded by a very large city policeman carrying a pike. We process up the stairway. I am followed by John, also very large, top hat in hand. Another enormous policeman, plus pike, brings up the rear. On the pavement is a young mother with her little boy. She has brought him to see the Christmas tree. Faced with our procession he is, not unnaturally, about to burst into tears. With a piece of superb quick thinking she saves the day. 'Look, Willie, Father Christmas.'

The Courts Act, the fruit of the Beeching reforms, came into operation on 1st January 1972. Before Beeching, when you were out of London on circuit, it was for the whole law term. My next assignment was to be on the Northern Circuit, terra incognita to me. The schedule was: 11th January 1971 to 29th January 1971 Carlisle – solo; 1st February 1971 to 12 March 1971 Manchester – with others; 15th March 1971 to 8th April 1971 Liverpool – with others.

This made a good sample of the old assize scene, with Carlisle as a typical small assize town and Manchester and Liverpool as typical large ones. Lancaster, the original Lancashire assize town before Liverpool and Manchester had experienced the Industrial Revolution and were still not much more than villages, was manned for a stretch by another of the Red Judges out on the Northern Circuit, who also had to take his turn at Manchester or Liverpool.

I went north on the night sleeper, this time remembering to take my gun. The Under Sheriff, Lionel Lightfoot, very much Mr Cumberland, met me at the station at the appallingly early hour when the train deposited me on the platform. He gave me my instructions for the assize service at ten o'clock, before the day's work was to start. He told me that the county justices would all be on parade at the sitting of the court. I was driven to the lodgings for a bath and breakfast. Then it was change into ceremonial gear, full-bottomed wig and hood but no knee breeches. The lodgings staff was enchanting, all being retainers of Lionel's. Janet, the butler, was aged 82. Her 86-year-old sister was the cook. Their niece, a chick in her sixties, was the housekeeper, and the team took over the house from its owner for such time, not more than nine weeks in the year, as a Red Judge was in Carlisle for the assizes.

Before Beeching, it was the county which had to provide the nuts and bolts so that the Queen's assize level justice could be done. The county had to provide, maintain, and staff the courts and the judges' lodgings, and produce the juries so that the gaols could be cleared of prisoners awaiting trial. The ultimate responsibility rested on the High Sheriff as the Queen's officer for the administration of justice in the county, with his Under Sheriff to do the work and the necessary County Council committees to provide the means. At Petty and Quarter Sessions level as opposed to the assizes the judges, as judges, had nothing to do with it, though they might, like Eustace in Hampshire, be involved as Chairman of Quarter Sessions.

It was the justices, below assize level, who kept the Queen's peace, hence the label JPs. So the administration of justice was very much an integral part of the county scene, and the periodic visits of Her Majesty's judges was a minor state occasion. In theory the judge on assize was the sovereign and strict ceremonial and protocol were observed, particularly if Lionel Lightfoot was the Under Sheriff. In old-fashioned cities like Exeter, with narrow streets, in 1971 old gentlemen on the pavements still doffed their caps as the Red Judge was driven past. In Carlisle, where you had enthusiastic police motor-cyclist outriders enjoying the break from their normal duties, the whole circus swept past too fast for anything like that.

After church, when you were greeted by a fanfare of trumpets, you proceeded, and I mean proceeded, to court. Still in your full-bottomed wig, you stood on the Bench while the Clerk of Assize read the commission. When he got to your name you picked your black tricorn hat off the desk, put it on top of your wig, took it off again, and then sat down. Bows all round, of course. When he finished reading the commission, you retired to your room and cleared for action. Off hoods, off full-bottomed wigs and on with the Honorary Fellowship of All Souls. Then to work.

On that occasion all the villains in the Carlisle calendar pleaded guilty. Compared to my Spitalfields villains at Winchester, all their offences were kids' stuff, and I sentenced them on the same basis on which I had been dealing with my Hants Quarter Sessions customers for the last six years. This made a big impression on the Northern Circuit, which was reflected in a speech made by Godfrey Heilpern, the leader, when the circuit entertained the assizes' judges to dinner at Manchester while I was there that summer. The custom is for the Bar to tease the judges a bit in order to save them from the occupational hazard of importance.

'Last,' said Godfrey, 'I come to Mr Justice Bristow. He has not heard of any sentence other than "absolute discharge".'

Years later Ben Hytner, another distinguished Northern Circuit

(*Top left*) Bill Potter, butler, Exeter Lodgings 1973.

(*Top right*) Helen Potter, housekeeper and cook, with Malcolm Fortune, Marshal, Exeter 1973.

(*Bottom right*) George Hill, doyen of itinerant butlers, Plymouth, 1973.

Judges' lodgings, Ludlow Castle. (So sited to protect the Red Judge from the natives).

John and Mike Mitchell (NZ Marshal) Mam Tor. Short day from Manchester.

silk, reminded me of this and said that my approach had since become the circuit norm.

Having got through all the crime so happily on Day 1 I was left with a certain amount of civil work plus even some divorce. Civil work often involves the production of plans. The plaintiff's expert's plan is usually drawn the other way up from the defendant's expert's plan, and this, unless each has included a north point so that you can see where you are, involves confusion and delay. I expressed myself about this during the first civil case in which there were plans with no north point. Thereafter, in every case, whether a plan was necessary or not, a plan was ostentatiously produced complete with north point. This delicate tease by the Northern Circuit Bar of the judge who was a stranger in those parts was much appreciated, and illustrates the English bench and Bar relationship at its happiest.

The divorce work I was landed with revealed that in the Cumberland mining communities it is an occupational hazard for wives to get a belting on pay day, but if you got one on a Sunday night as well, that is regarded as grounds for divorce. When I was working in Nottinghamshire I was told a story which suggests that Cumberland is not unique in this respect. A distinguished solicitor practising in the north of the county spent most of his professional time looking after the affairs of large landowners in the Dukeries. But he also let the Worksop magistrates and the local police know that he was ready to help people in magistrate's court trouble for nothing in case of need.

One Saturday night the Worksop station sergeant very apologetically telephoned to say that he had Mrs X in the cells, in serious need of help. He explained that she had been arrested on the previous Saturday night for hitting her husband on the head with a hatchet, fortunately without causing serious injury. The magistrates had bailed her on Monday, but she had just had to be arrested again because she had hit her husband on the head with a hammer and done him no good at all.

So the solicitor went along to Worksop police station and was shown into a cell where he saw a very small lady who might have been aged anything from forty to eighty, sitting on the edge of the bunk. She was so small that her feet did not reach the ground. The solicitor explained who he was, and that he had come to see her because the sergeant thought she needed help. 'Oh yes,' she said, and the conversation went like this:

'The sergeant tells me that last Saturday you hit your old man on the head with a hatchet. Is that right?'

'Oh yes.'

'Why did you do that?'

'Well, sir, you know what these pitmen are like. I'd had a belting from him nearly every Saturday night for the last 25 years and last Saturday I'd had enough, so I took the hatchet and hit him with it.'

'I quite understand, but, Mrs X, the sergeant says that's not all. He tells me that tonight you hit your old man on the head with a hammer. Is that right?'

'Oh yes.'

'Why did you do that to him?'

'Well, the police had taken away the hatchet.'

The collapse of the Carlisle criminal work gave me considerable free time, and the weather was beautiful. John and I went along the Solway shore past Port Carlisle towards Silloth to look at the wild geese. One afternoon, with the sun low in the west, the whole pack of Pinkfeet, I suppose two or three thousand, took off together from where they had been feeding on someone's winter crops, concealed from where we stood on the salt marsh by the sea wall. As the whole pack turned together their undersides were lit a rosy red by the low sun before they flew out to roost on the sandbanks in the estuary. There were Roman remains to be seen everywhere. I had a day's salmon fishing, unfruitful, on the Eden.

Also I fulfilled a lifelong ambition. I was invited to a morning flight for geese on Rockliffe marshes. The rendezvous was at 0730 at the shed on the edge of the marsh between the mouth of the Eden and the Border Esk from which in the old days if you were bold enough you could take horse at low water and ride across the estuary to Scotland. It seems it was a bad insurance risk, because the sands shift and are very soft in parts.

By great good luck I was deployed at the end of the line of guns to which, as it happened, the geese came in. John had come with me to see, as a judge's clerk should, that I did not get into trouble. We took post in a wet ditch with a bank on the seaward side and waited.

As the dawn broke so the chatter of geese talking out on the sand banks rose in a crescendo, and finally they all took off to come inland to feed, positively shouting to one another in flight, so that you realised the full meaning of Peter Scott's book title *Wild Chorus*. In they came. I missed the first that passed within shot, but killed the second clean. After that I left my gun unloaded, and watched. Three of these splendid creatures landed within fifteen yards of us and started grazing. One stood on watch while the other two had their heads down on the grass, and they took it in turn to be sentry. Finally as the light increased they spotted us and moved away. We were lucky to have been at our end of the line. None of the other guns had any shooting, and the mass of the geese were well outside us.

At nine o'clock the spectre of sitting in court at Carlisle at ten-thirty began to rear its ugly head. We collected the dead goose, said good-bye and thank you for what was an unforgettable experience, and went back to the lodgings for breakfast.

Of course all this was too good to last. That very day there came a phone call from London. Have you really finished the work at Carlisle? they asked. We had to say yes. Well then, they said, go down to Liverpool and help out for the rest of the week there. So we did, and of course that messed up the Liverpool listing. The newly arrived judge 3 felt he was wasting his time, and might better have stayed in solitary glory among the delights of Carlisle.

When I moved to Manchester I was again judge 3, with Elizabeth Lane as senior judge in command, and Stephen Chapman, on his native heath, as judge 2. We had a very happy time. It snowed, and Elizabeth disapproved of me wearing my snowboots to court. Not wishing to risk having to sit all morning with wet feet, I asserted my male chauvinist independence by persisting. We had the nicest possible High Sheriff of Lancashire in John Darlington, who had to service three judges sitting in Manchester, two in Liverpool, and one on his doorstep in Lancaster, so he had his work cut out. I was trying mainly crime, which was squalid and unmemorable. As the days lengthened and the weather improved, John and I sometimes got out for the afternoon to the Peak District. We reconnoitred the Snake Pass and Edale, because John wanted to walk the Pennine

Way next summer with his teenage boy. The project did not look very appealing in March.

Then back to Liverpool, where I was judge 2 to James Stirling as senior judge. He did the divorce work and the civil. I did the crime, even more squalid than in Manchester. Kidnapping plus rape seemed to be the speciality. There was a club in Liverpool, not listed in the telephone book, called the Drizzler. It was a popular spot for assignations for sexual gratification. One such assignation was such a success as far as the coloured gentleman participant was concerned that when the uncoloured lady participant, having as she thought performed her contract, wished to return to the Drizzler to pick up someone else, he would not allow it but kept her in his house for the next forty-eight hours. The prosecution case was that not only was she unwilling to stay with him, but that she was an unwilling participant in the further sexual gratification exercises on which he insisted. Finally he made the error of going out for some cigarettes without locking the door behind him, whereupon she fled, uncharacteristically, into the arms of the Liverpool police.

In this unmemorable scene John Darlington, the High Sheriff, was a great help. He had me to stay for the weekend at his home just outside Lancaster, and introduced me to Lunedale and the River Lune. He organised for me a lovely Saturday salmon fishing, again unsuccessful, at Rigmaden under the wing of Eric Wilson, one-time High Sheriff of Westmorland when the assizes were held at Appleby. It made a nice change from Liverpool. The judges' lodgings at Liverpool are in a magnificent Regency palace, on the edge of a public park which used to be the demesne of the brewer who built it. You sweep off to work with your two police motor-cyclist outriders through a desolation of ancient and modern slum housing and the outriders get you through the one-way maelstrom of traffic that whirls round St George's Hall where the courts are housed. There you are welcomed by the largest policemen I have ever seen.

One night in the lodgings my pyjama jacket split right down the back due to old age and long service. John had been told that our case for next morning would probably collapse. It did, so he arranged that we would park my car at St George's Hall and walk just down the street to Marks and Spencer. We went back to the lodgings in the official limo, plus outriders, changed out of scarlet and ermine, and set off in my car. We reached the circumference of the maelstrom, with no police outriders to hold up the traffic and get us across to the car park. There was nothing to do but take a deep breath, stop shivering on the brink, and launch away. Before you could say Jack Robinson we found ourselves in the Mersey Tunnel, and finished up by buying the new pyjamas in Marks and Spencer's in Birkenhead.

On 8th April 1971 the Easter term finally expired. It seemed a long time since Lionel Lightfoot had met me on Carlisle station platform in the small hours of 12th January, but I felt I now knew something about north-western England and the Northern Circuit. There followed a spell in London till Whitsun, and after the Whitsun vacation, I set off to Manchester again on 8th June, and then on 5th July to Lancaster, where I spent from 5th to 29th July.

Lancaster, now no more a Red Judge centre, had all that Manchester had not. The judges' lodgings were a family-sized Stuart house halfway up the hill to the castle. The castle housed, as it always had, both the prison and the Assize Court. It was quicker and easier to walk up to the court than to be driven in the county's ancient Rolls Royce hired for the purpose. Below the dock, to encourage those about to be tried, were a couple of Norman remand cells, with electric light as the only visible alteration since Henry II's time. The back of the dock was still furnished with fetters to hold the hand of the convicted felon while 'F' was branded on his palm by the branding iron, still kept handy. It was in that very Assize Courtroom that James I personally tried the Pendle Hill witches, who were subsequently burned to death in the castle courtyard. After a summer day trying crime in that formidable environment it was nice to get out, and there were wonderful places within easy reach. You could drive down across the marshes to Sunderland Point where the Lune flows into the sea. You could walk up Clougha Scarr, behind the town, to be scolded by the cock grouse in the heather. One very clear evening up there I could see Snowdon some eighty-five miles away to the south-west, and Snaefell on the Isle of Man some seventy miles to the west.

You could fish for, and catch, brown trout on the Lune near Tunstall under Tommy Catlow's wing, though the water that

month was very low. As far as I was concerned the salmon and sea
trout remained imaginary. No doubt you could have gone
shrimping in Morecambe Bay, also on your doorstep. Mrs Heath,
the Lodgings cook and housekeeper, used to buy shrimps in
Lancaster market and pot them herself. You had the Lake District
in reach to the north and the Pennines to the east for week-end
sorties. All in all it was a good place to spend July trying crime.

To call what followed 'the long vacation' was a mockery because
it included my stint at the Old Bailey. The on 4th October Her
Majesty's Queen Bench judges set out on the last Assize of some
eight hundred years, with the Beeching axe at its roots. My itinerary
was Lincoln, 14th to 19th October, Northampton 20th October to
1st November, Leicester 2nd November to 15th November, and
Nottingham 16th November to 17th December. This was a typical
Midland circuit pattern for the judges who escaped Birmingham.
What was unusual was that because someone else was ill I found
myself as senior judge for the first three whistle stops with Raymond
Philips, just appointed, as my No 2. I reverted to my usual judge
3 status at Nottingham while Ray went to Birmingham. At each
assize town there was a tremendous 'Farewell to the Assizes' party,
After all, to demolish what has been part of English and Welsh
provincial life for some eight hundred years, and put something
brand spanking new in its place, is not something that happens
every day.

5. Beeching

What had been cost effective and good time and motion in Henry II's time, before MacAdam or the railways and when getting in the harvest was for all a first priority, was not necessarily cost effective or good time and motion in the nineteen-sixties. It was wasteful in bricks and mortar resources and in spite of palliative reforms applied from time to time the Assize and Quarter Session pattern of administering justice seemed to be a major reason for unacceptable delays in bringing those accused of serious crime to trial.

When Gerald Gardiner became Lord Chancellor in 1964 he decided that a root and branch attack on the problem was called for. A commission was set up under the chairmanship of Dr Beeching, a distinguished accountant who had not long before been turned loose on the intractable problem of rationalising the railway system. Put broadly, the solution reached for the courts was to abolish Assize and Quarter Sessions and the artificial division of classes of crime which could be tried in one and not the other, and to substitute a new animal, the Crown Court. The High Court judges on circuit sitting in the Crown Court centres would function as they always had. Below them there would be full-time Circuit judges, permanently attached to their own areas, plus a backup of part-timers called Recorders, nothing to do with the old Recorders of Borough Quarter Session, now extinct.

The administration of the Crown Court was to be nothing to do with the counties. A new Courts Service, an organ of Central Government, was to run the whole affair. The circuits were in the main left untouched but for the amalgamation of the Midland and the Oxford circuits, who used to share Birmingham anyway, and the transfer of Gloucester to the Western Circuit. Each circuit was to have a Circuit Administrator at the head of the appropriate civil service administrative hierarchy, with Courts Administrators answering to him for their own areas. Central Government was taking over lock stock and barrel the responsibilities hitherto discharged locally on a county basis.

Question: What about the judges, either the Circuit Judges and Recorders, or the Red Judges when out in the field? Can the Circuit Administrator push them around, if he is that sort of person?

Nothing was written into the Courts Act about this, but the independence of the judiciary from interference by the executive in the form of Court Service officials creates, as you would expect, no problem. On each circuit there are two Presiding Judges, three on the South-Eastern because it includes London, so that one at least is out on the circuit at any one time. The Presiding Judge is responsible, not to anybody but responsible, for the welfare, and so the efficiency, of all the judges and Recorders working in his circuit. It is to him that they are to turn if they want help. It is to him that the administrators are to turn if they think things are going wrong on the judges' front and could be better. It is he who has to initiate action if something goes wrong at the sharp end in the courts or in judges' lodgings.

The smooth running of the circuits depends to a large degree on good relations between the Presiding Judges and the Circuit Administrators. In the early days after 1st January 1972, good relations were sometimes noticeable by their absence. Some Circuit Administrators were less wise than others, and were not going to have judges treading on what they regarded as their preserves. Some judges were less wise than others and saw in every activity of the administrators a potential trespass on the sacred independence of the judiciary. But after a few years have passed it is easier to remember that judges and administrators are complementary. Both are there to see that justice can be, and is, done.

How, to a field worker, does it look as if it has all worked out? From the time and motion angle the Crown Court should be, and usually is, more efficient and elastic than the old set-up. If, for example, Reading, South-Eastern Circuit, is over-loaded and Winchester, Western, is running light, you can readily switch Reading work to Winchester. Of course whether you are overloaded or not depends not only on the current incidence of villainy in your catchment area, but on the efficiency of your court listing officials. Listing for trials is a difficult art. The listing officer has to sense how long cases are going to last, and this is affected by many imponderables. Will there be a compromise plea of guilty? Are counsel terse or long-winded? Have you got a quick or a slow judge? One of the Crown Court snags is that the Courts Service regards the listing job as just another step in a civil servant's career. You can get someone in what is the key position in the court machinery who does not even realise that he or she is faced, not with a job, but with an art. By the time they've learned the hard way what it is all about and how you handle difficult counsel's clerks and fractious judges, they are posted away and someone else has to learn it all over again.

But at any rate no longer do judges' lodgings at centres on the scale of Winchester or Nottingham or Cardiff accommodate a clutch of judges for a few weeks in the year, and lie fallow for the rest. No longer should you get court buildings under-used because it is not assize time and the part-timers, who are the Quarter Sessions judges, are not available because they are inextricably tied up with their Bar practices when there is a courtroom void to fill. But no longer are your top-level courts run in principle by a tiny team on each circuit, going circuit with the Bar and living in the Bar mess on intimate terms. The Clerk of Assize on the circuit was, and needed to be, everybody's friend, and if he did not play ball with the Bar or the Bar did not play ball with him over listing, it was sorted out after dinner in mess. No longer are second-level courts run by a tiny team in the department of the Clerk of the Peace for the county. At above Petty Sessions level the administration of justice is out of the counties' hands. Instead the Crown Courts in the provinces, and the Law Courts in London and the London area Crown Courts including the Old Bailey, are all serviced by Central Government.

When the Courts Service was set up Parkinson's Law reigned so supreme that constant efforts have been made since to reduce the cost in money and manpower. When I was Presiding Judge of the Western Circuit and the committee then on the economy hunt told me that they were considering putting the same Circuit Administrator in charge of both the Western and the Wales and Chester Circuits. To be fair, they did say they realised that his office would need to be in the middle of the Severn Bridge.

I expect they had heard what happened when it had been

proposed to the Beeching Commission that those two circuits should be amalgamated and administered from Bristol. Tasker Watkins VC., now Lord Justice, then the leader of the circuit, formed up to them and is reported to have said: 'There are some thousands of solicitors in Cardiff. Not one of them speaks Welsh. But if you do this, they will all be on the barricades and I will be at their head.' Responsible officers at Court Administrator level themselves say the set-up is gravely over-administered, and that they have to spend a disproportionate amount of their time on returns which will ultimately bear statistical fruit which is not worth the effort. Putting Parkinson's Law into reverse is not easy.

The buildings which house the administration of justice, including judges' lodgings, are now the responsibility of the Property Services Agency. From experience, here are two homely examples of how PSA works:

One: The retiring rooms for the Circuit judges and Recorders who sit in the brand new courts at Portsmouth are furnished with showers as well as loos. Even in Portsmouth a trial does not involve for the judge the sort of stress which demands a shower afterwards.

Two: In mid-February 1971, on arriving at Bristol lodgings as Presiding Judge of the circuit, I found the lodgings' refrigerator to be unserviceable. Steps were being taken to get a replacement. There was some delay while minds were made up what type the replacement was to be. That sorted out, the replacement was ordered through the PSA central purchasing arrangements, designed no doubt to save money. Time passed. No fridge. Being on the spot, a quarter of a mile from the circuit office, I wanted to know the reason why. It had to come from Southampton, it was all ready, but could not be dispatched till there was a full load for the lorry. Time passed. After six weeks with no replacement refrigerator I left Bristol for the Easter vacation. The replacement refrigerator beat the judge replacement by a short head, arriving the day before he did for the following term. Before Beeching, the housekeeper or I would have got on to the High Sheriff who would have got on to the Council Judges' Lodgings Committee, and a replacement would have been produced at the drop of a hat.

Big is not beautiful! But it is also right to say that after a few initial hiccoughs the quality of judges' lodgings regular staff has much improved. When I started going circuit I found it a necessary precaution to take a set of Carrier cookery cards with me, and to spend time in most of the judges' lodgings kitchens myself.

There is a more considerable criticism to be made of centralising the administration. It has been one of the axioms of doing justice in England and Wales that a man should be 'tried by his peers'. In our now mixed society there are problems in achieving this which did not exist before. Should you impanel a jury of Pakistani ethnic origin to try in Leeds a Pakistani ethnic origin accused, or is it right that he should be tried by a random sample of the population of West Yorks, predominantly white? What about second generation children of West Indian immigrants in South London? What does being 'tried by your peers' really mean? The one thing it has never meant is that if you are a Glaswegian who gets into trouble while doing a summer job at Blackpool you will be tried by a jury of Glaswegians. You will be tried by a Lancashire jury, who may have grave difficulty in understanding the language which you speak.

'Trial by your peers' has really meant trial by a twelve- person random sample of the inhabitants of the area where you are brought to trial. Before Beeching, this was at assizes or Quarter Sessions in the county, a relatively small area in which some of the jury at least would be likely to be familiar with local conditions, knowledge of which may be important to get the case in perspective. In 1981 I found myself trying a young man on a rape charge. His defence was: she wanted it. The trial was at Winchester, before a Hampshire jury. The sexual congress on the nature of which they had to decide had taken place in Weymouth on a wet Sunday evening in February. The girl had been picked up by the young man in the bar of the hotel where she worked. No Hampshire juror could begin to appreciate what Weymouth is like on a wet Sunday evening in February, and the temptation this would put in a girl's way to take comfort in a little consensual sex, of which she might afterwards think better.

Had it not been for the fact that in March 1941 when my squadron was at Warmwell for some air firing on the West Bay ranges I had experience as a humble pilot officer of what a wet Sunday evening in Weymouth was like, and was able to get the flavour across to the Hampshire jury, injustice might have been done. A Dorset jury would not have needed any help from me.

The reason the young man was being tried at Winchester was this. Although Dorchester is nominally a Crown Court Centre where you have a Red Judge from time to time, the cost of maintaining judges' lodgings is considered to be disproportionate to the volume of Red Judge work to be expected there. When, as an administrator, you look at the map, you say to yourself, you can get to Winchester from Dorchester and those parts easily by rail or road, so it is reasonable time and motion, and good economy, to try your Dorset Red Judge crime at Winchester, where there are judges' lodgings in permanent commission overflowing with Red Judges. We will do that and save the cost of Dorchester judges' lodgings. So you take the accused and all the witnesses to Winchester and try him in front of a Hampshire jury who speak with a quite different accent, instead of taking one Red Judge and his clerk to lodgings in Dorchester and trying him by his peers. The judge could not try a case at Dorchester from the Winchester lodgings. He would not have time to do the homework which a serious trial involves. The distance is too great.

I live just over the border from Dorset in East Devon. While I was Presiding Judge I was able to sit at Dorchester when there was Red Judge crime to be tried there, based at home. In one week one year I had the following Red Judge work to deal with. Two homicides. A rape. A young man who planted home-made but effective bombs all over Yeovil in aid of a Walter Mitty bank robbery. A Bonnie and Clyde armed robbery operation involving a police chase round the Isle of Purbeck culminating in a shoot-out on the army tank ranges at Lulworth. It would have been expensive to move all the people concerned in those trials to and from Winchester every day or to pay them their overnight expenses in Winchester, and you do ask yourself whether, even on a time and motion and cost effectiveness approach, to scrub the judges' lodgings at Dorchester has been worth while.

6. Life on Circuit after Beeching

The immediate impact of the establishment of the Crown Court in place of assizes and Quarter Sessions was to turn into full-time Circuit judges a large number of members of the Bar who had been part-time Chairmen and Deputy Chairmen of Quarter Sessions and Recorders. It did not greatly affect the situation of the Red Judge on circuit to begin with. Some of the smaller assize centres, for example Salisbury, Hereford and Warwick, became Crown Court centres planned for no Red Judge presence. Plymouth, which had never had assizes, became Crown Court centre planned for a Red Judge presence. The general effect was that on each circuit you found yourself in fewer places, but for a longer time in each.

Later, as the administrators really got stuck in, some Crown Court centres planned for a Red Judge presence in effect lost it by being deprived for reasons of economy of their judges' lodgings. On the Western Circuit this happened to Dorchester and Gloucester, though it is possible for a Red Judge housed in the Bristol lodgings to try cases at Gloucester. In the back of a big car you can do homework during forty minutes out and forty minutes home on the M5. In addition to the 'trial by your peers' consideration, the blow to local amour propre of being deprived of periodic Red Judge visits which you have enjoyed for centuries is very real. It is no consolation to the High Sheriff of Gloucestershire or to the mayor and the locals when you explain that though when the Courts Act was passed Gloucester was set up as a Crown Court Centre with a Red Judge presence, Central Government will not provide the money for judges' lodgings which alone make any real Red Judge presence possible. The Presiding Judges can do something in the way of showing the flag, but unless you can house your Red Judge on the spot it is showing the flag, no more.

On circuit the principal change you find is in the nature of the criminal work that you do. Before Beeching, the Quarter Sessions

109

jurisdiction was strictly limited, and the assize judge had to deal with the rest. You tried all sorts of fairly modest stuff in the way of public-house fights, charged as 'doing grievous bodily harm with intent', motor manslaughter, run of the mill robbery, and so on. Now the Circuit judges have jurisdiction to try nearly everything, though it is one of the Presiding Judge's important functions to decide which of the Circuit judges in each centre on the circuit should be entrusted with trial of the most difficult cases. As a result, by far the greater part of your criminal work as Red Judge on circuit is homicide and rape. You will also of course find yourself trying other cases which have locally or nationally sensitive implications, and which for that reason are better dealt with at top level by a judge who is not part of the local furniture, however easy or difficult they may be.

Apart from the nature of the work, the change is still not marked. In the small centres, like Lewes or Plymouth or Caernarvon, where there is a periodic Red Judge presence on very much the same scale as there was in the days of the assizes, you will find you start your visit with a welcome from the High Sheriff, if not from the mayor and entourage. You will normally have a church service before you start your first working day. Your arrival is still a matter of note locally. You may even feature in the local television news. The ceremonial fanfare outside church or as you arrive at court afterwards means something, like the Union Jack flying outside judges' lodgings while you are there. In Cardiff there are two flag staffs, one with the Union Jack and the other with the Welsh dragon. Both flags were impartially stolen on the first night I arrived.

In the large centres, like Birmingham, Manchester, Liverpool, there had been a more or less continuous assize judge presence anyway, with a church service only at the beginning of term. Now the major services are organised by circuits. In the North-East, for example, there is a service at York in the autumn and Durham in the spring. On the Western Circuit there are services at Winchester and Bristol in the autumn, at Exeter in the spring. The ceremonial trumpet fanfare for the arrival of the judges at court is sometimes handicapped by the design of the modern courts. In the old courts you were apt to go in through the main entrance, with everyone falling back on either side to make way. In the new courts at Leeds the judges' entrance is in the subterranean car park.

Sheffield when I was last there, perhaps characteristically, managed the worst of both worlds in its old building. You went in through the main entrance, but instead of finding yourself in an open space with everyone falling back on either side to make way, you found that the open space had been turned into a cafeteria of which British Rail would not have been proud. You made your way through past the empty saucers.

The other major difference in circuit life for the Red Judge since Beeching is in fact nothing to do with Beeching. Now you do not go on circuit for the whole term. You spend half the term on circuit, and half in London. So if you have children still at school or university and a wife who is still tied to base, the separation will only be six or seven weeks, and not twelve or thirteen, and life must be very much easier. It is of course a side-effect of the new arrangements that if a very long case has to be tried on circuit and cannot be tried by a suitable Circuit judge because its nature calls for top-level treatment, special arrangements for what the administrators call additional 'judge power' have to be laid on. The normal allocation of Red Judges to the circuits spreads them very thin. On the Western Circuit, for instance, covering the area Aldershot to the Scillies east–west, and Gloucester to the English Channel north–south, there are at any one period only three Red Judges, plus a Family Division judge for half the time. If you are landed with a long case on top of the normal Red Judge workload you need extra help to cope.

So, in the small centres, little change. In Bodmin you would notice no difference. If you are a gardener, camellia time is the time to go. Go in July for the night fishing for sea trout, which does not bite into your working time, though you may be sleepy after lunch. The Mayor will welcome you, will go to St Petroc's church for the service with mace bearers and councillors complete, and be in court for the reading of the proclamation which has replaced the Commission of Assize even though you would be operational without it. In the big centres, little change. Cross-pollination with the city brass absent. It is now Central Government, not the Liverpool ratepayers, which pays for driving you to and from court.

The loss which I regret is that of the historic assize towns, swamped by the attraction for the administrators of their Industrial

Revolution conurbation neighbours. To lose Warwick to Birmingham, Lancaster to Preston, York to Leeds, is a slap in the face for English history. York touches me most closely, for it was there that I reached my circuit social apogee. There the convention was that at 1700 hours on the evening of the Red Judge's arrival the Lord Mayor attended the lodgings, an exquisite Queen Anne house just up the road from the Mansion House, to welcome him to the city. I was briefed that it was also the convention that the Lord Mayor and party would be delighted if the Red Judge gave them a drink.

So I drove hot foot from London to York, arriving just in time for a cup of tea and a short breather before the witching hour. The lodgings' staff, familiar with the score, had laid out the drinks on the side. The Lord Mayor arrived, ushered in by the Sword Bearer and attended by his chaplain. The Chief Constable came too, and the City Sheriff attended, as I remember, by his chaplain. The Chief Executive also arrived. All were in full robes or uniform, the Chief Executive complete with wig. What would the Lord Mayor care to drink? Whisky and soda, please. And his chaplain? Gin and tonic. And so on till we came to the Chief Executive. 'And what would you like, Mr X?' 'Do I see a bottle of Kümmel on the sideboard?' 'You do.' 'I would very much like a Kümmel.' We had a jolly relaxed half hour before Lord Mayor and party, preceded by Sword Bearer, departed to perform the next Lord Mayoral obligation of the evening.

It happened that I was at York once more the very next year. The same protocol was observed, though there was of course a new Lord Mayor and a new chaplain, but my friend the Chief Executive was still of the party. What would the new Lord Mayor care to drink? 'Whisky and soda, please', and so on till I came to Mr X. 'I know what you'd like, Mr X,' I said. 'You'd like a nice Kümmel.' 'Oh, I would, how did you guess?' Leeds may be all very well, but that could not happen at Leeds.

To do work, however engrossing, which keeps you away from home for even six weeks at a time three times a year, the normal Red Judge pattern, is not without its disadvantages. If you go home most week-ends, to keep the home front and the garden ticking over you will drive about 18,000 miles a year in all sorts of conditions. But you will see England and Wales as no one else sees England and Wales, with long enough at each Crown Court centre you visit to be able to appreciate the country and the people. You realise, when moving from Lincoln to Nottingham, that you are passing from Danelaw into Mercia. The place names, and the look of the juries, is different. You readily understand, at Newcastle, that you are nearer in spirit to Bergen than to Edinburgh, and that to the Northumbrian, after ages of mutual rieving with the Scots, the Border is a reality.

If in doubt, go to Berwick and walk round the town on the Elizabethan artillery era fortifications. Cross the Pennines from Yorkshire to Lancashire, you're in a different world. You learn that where south of the Trent people would say, 'What's going on?' North of the Trent they say, 'What's going off?' And all this without even getting involved with the Celtic fringe, the difference between the North and South Walians, or going foreign across the Tamar bridge.

You are cherished and kept sane by High Sheriffs who are one and all delightful people doing their best to smooth your path and lay on the leisure facilities which you enjoy. Because they sit on the Bench with you as much as they can, they know very well the sort of day to which you may be exposed when trying crime.

But perhaps the most rewarding part is that you get to know the local Circuit judges, and the local Bar. You entertain them socially and they entertain you. The young barristers, who, because they are just beginning, are unlikely to appear before you doing Red Judge work, have the opportunity to see that you came up the same road that they are travelling. At the end of an evening in the Bar mess both hosts and guests can be expected to have their hair well down, and if plain speaking happens to be needed it is an excellent opportunity for it to take place. You are reminded of what it was like to be a beginner, how daunting some of those old gentlemen on the Bench used to be, and of the gamesmanship which helped to get round them. They, or the shy ones if there are any, will realise that the judge, in spite of where he sits and how he looks, may be human after all. It all helps to achieve the situation that in court you will trust them, they will trust you, and both of you can get on with getting justice done without messing about.

7. London

There is a bewildering variety of work you find yourself doing in London when not away on circuit. At some time you will do a shift at the Old Bailey. You will be involved with criminal law also dealing with criminal appeals in the Court of Appeal Criminal Division. Before the war, its predecessor, the Court of Criminal Appeal, sat once a week. It was manned by three King's Bench judges, often with the Lord Chief Justice presiding.

Now the Criminal Division usually sits four days a week in three courts, each manned by a Lord Justice of Appeal presiding and normally two judges sitting with him. You will find yourself dealing with bail applications. You may find yourself sitting in the Divisional Court, which deals with judicial review of the decisions of inferior courts and other bodies, and ensures that what they have done is within their legal powers. It also deals with appeals from Magistrates' Courts on questions of law, and with habeas corpus problems. You have the ordinary civil work of the High Court, contract, personal injury, and other cases about private, as opposed to public, rights and wrongs. You have the Commercial Court, largely concerned with disputes arising from the carriage of goods by sea. Whether the overseas commercial operators whose disputes are dealt with in the Commercial Court in London come to London for that purpose because they prefer the quality of English justice, or simply because the arbitration clauses in their printed trade contracts forms so often specify that disputes are to be settled by English law, is an interesting speculation. You may find yourself operating in the Employment Appeals Tribunal, at grips with appeals from Industrial Tribunals. You are likely to find yourself spending time as a member of the Parole Board.

The Old Bailey is in a class by itself. One of its many agreeable traditions is that the judges are entertained to lunch every day by the City sheriffs. It is a very pleasant thing for the judges, who have

114

the opportunity to meet the City's other guests, and who are treated to a discreet menu so that they can work in the afternoon. On successive days, I found myself sitting next to the United States ambassador, Walter Annenberg, Vic Feather of the TUC, and the Chinese Chargé d'Affaires. With the latter I had a language difficulty.

If you are sitting in the September session, as I was in 1971, you are invited to attend the lunch, in the hall of one of the City livery companies, which accompanies the installation of the City sheriffs for the coming year. Everyone from the Old Bailey is there, and certainly in 1971 no one was expected to work in an afternoon into which excellent speeches bit fairly deep. I found myself sitting next to Bernard Waley-Cohen, ex-Lord Mayor, whom I had previously met when ski-ing at Wengen. When the soup was served I was shocked to find myself faced with a cup of consommé with royal custard shapes swimming in it. I asked Bernard what had gone wrong, why no turtle soup? 'My dear fellow,' he said, 'we've had to give up turtle soup for Conservation Year.' It is fair to add that for the next course I found myself roughing it on a grouse.

No doubt because the criminal stakes are high in London, you find keen operators in the defence teams, and for the innocent Red Judge unaccustomed to the London criminal scene there are some surprises. Readers of R. S. Surtees' *Handley Cross* will remember the unhappy affair of 'the Slender'. The Slender ran the bear-baiting establishment to which Mr Bowker, the distinguished Lincoln's Inn conveyancer's clerk, used to take his friend Mr Jorrocks and Charlie Stobbs, the distinguished conveyancer's pupil who was later to marry Mr Jorrocks' daughter Belinda. While Mr Jorrocks MFH was at Handley Cross, the Slender was taken up by the police on suspicion of doing away with an exciseman who had set out to investigate his business, and had not been heard of since. Mr Bowker kept Mr Jorrocks in the picture by correspondence.

As the trial at the Old Bailey approached, Mr Jorrocks wrote to Mr Bowker enclosing a 'five pun note' and saying, 'Tell the Slender to hire a good hard-mouthed counsel.' They are there to this day.

But the Red Judge is lucky. Because his stint at the Old Bailey is relatively short it is not he who is saddled with the long trials. As on circuit, he normally finds himself coping with homicide and rape. It

Judge for Yourself

is only the long trial of exceptional sensitivity and importance, like the secrets trials of the Cyprus airmen, which will not be dealt with by the resident Old Bailey judges. That type of case will be a special Red Judge assignment.

Criminal appeal work suffers, like all appeal work, in that the raw material is not live, but on paper. It involves heavy homework, essential to save hearing time, and in appeals against sentence the scope for effective live advocacy is limited. The hopeless appeals are eliminated by the preliminary filter which consists of consideration by a single judge. In many appeals which pass the filter and go forward, counsel will find the President of the Court asking him very early on whether he could realistically argue for a reduction in sentence of more than X. Appeals against conviction offer much more scope, and the court needs the help of counsel in analysing whether the shorthand note shows that something did go seriously wrong at the trial, so that the conviction must be regarded as unsafe.

I had to try at Newcastle in the early seventies a young man accused of robbery. A travelling fairground proprietor used to lay up his outfit for the winter in a Newcastle suburb. In the caravan in which he lived there was occasionally kept overnight a large sum of money. Some teenage boys and girls playing near the caravan in the evening of one such night saw two men obviously casing the joint, and saw where their car was parked. Later they saw them break into the van. They heard the proprietor's old lady screaming before she was silenced, and rushed to the rescue. One man went out of the window of the van and disappeared. The second ran from the van to the car, with boys and girls hanging on to him. He managed to get in. One of the girls, obviously of good Newcastle Viking ancestry, blonde hair and blue eyes, jumped on the bonnet and tried to smash the windscreen with her shoe. It had a flat heel, and she did not succeed. She had the sense to jump off as the car drove away. One of the boys wrote the registration number on the back of his hand in indelible pencil.

The police checked the number and found of course that it was false. They then set up a watch on the local social security office, using three of the girls, who had had a good look at the man during his escape, on a shift basis. One of them duly identified a man who came in to the office, and he was arrested. So sure was she of her identification that the excitement made her literally sick. The case depended entirely on identification by the children. The children were extremely convincing.

The man's defence was that he was elsewhere that evening, that he did not drive a car, and indeed had never held a driving licence. If you accepted the alibi evidence called on his behalf he would however still have had just time to drive to where the children saw the reconnaissance of the van taking place. The police check confirmed that he had never held a driving licence. Identification cases are notoriously hazardous. That he had never held a driving licence did not prove that he could not have been the getaway driver.

It did seem to me odd that if he was guilty the alibi put forward would not clear him if it was accepted. I laid all this before the jury in summing-up because apart from the children's identification there was no evidence that he was the man, but the jury convicted unanimously. Two days later prosecuting counsel came to see me. He told me that since the trial the police had discovered that the defendant's brother, who looked very like him, had recently come out of prison, and could have known that the money would be in the caravan that night. To attempt that sort of robbery would be well in character for the brother. It was quite out of character for our defendant, whose criminal activities had hitherto taken place in a more modest league. He felt uncomfortable about it. Was there anything that could be done? Our defendant wanted to appeal against conviction, but the summing-up had been so much in his favour that it looked as if it would be difficult.

I got in touch personally with the Registrar of the Court of Appeal Criminal Division because without the information about the brother an appeal would have been filtered out by the single judge. I put the new information on paper and asked him to steer the application to an experienced single judge and let him know that I was unhappy about the conviction. The Registrar got the application and all the information before Arthur James, a very fine criminal judge. Arthur refused to let it go forward, and wrote to me that in the light of the jury's verdict after such a favourable summing-up, he regarded an appeal as hopeless.

The application was renewed, after refusal, as the rules allow, to the full court. The full court with express reluctance let it go forward for hearing before a full court made up of three different judges who came to it quite fresh. Happily, they allowed the appeal. If they had not, the only course would have been to persuade the Attorney-General to refer the case back to the Court of Appeal in the light of the fresh information, and while that was being done, even if it was ultimately successful, our defendant would have remained in prison. Criminal appeals are not usually as dramatic as that.

When you sit in the Divisional Court performing the judicial review function, the variety of diet is enormous. Was the Home Secretary entitled to treat A as an illegal immigrant and order him to be deported? Was the NUM entitled to treat B as no longer in benefit as a member of the union? Could the Planning Authority proceed with an enforcement order against C to make him pull down an extension to his house?

Where someone wishes to challenge the legality of action against him under delegated legislation or the rules of any organisation to which he belongs, he can now do so by the cheap, quick procedure of application for judicial review. Sitting in the Divisional Court, what you have to do is look at the statutory instrument or the union or club rule under which the action against which the applicant complains was taken, and see whether what was done falls within it or not. Similarly, in dealing with appeals on points of law from magistrates you have to look at the facts they have found, look at the provisions of law which they had had to apply, see if they have got it right, and if not then send it back and tell them what to do with it.

Again the raw material is all on paper, not in three dimensions. It is intellectual jig-saw rather than human interest stuff, and no more my scene on the occasions when I was landed with it as a judge sitting in London, than it had been when I was Val Holmes' pupil nearly forty years before.

The Divisional Court work was in one way like the work you did in the Employment Appeals tribunal. Part of the Employment Law package passed by the Heath Government in 1971 was the creation of a statutory right in employees, subject to various conditions, not to be unfairly dismissed. The Industrial Tribunals, which already had to deal with redundancy payment problems, were to be the forum in which unfair dismissal was to be dealt with. Appeal originally lay from Industrial Tribunals to a High Court judge on law alone, by a procedure similar to the Divisional Court procedure. As part of the Heath package, appeal from the Industrial Tribunals was to be to the new National Industrial Relations Court, with two lay members, one from the employers and one from the trade union side of industry, sitting with a High Court judge.

The Labour Party and the Unions were implacably opposed to the Heath Industrial Relations Act, and when the 1974 Labour Government took office, one of its first actions was to repeal it. But that part of the Heath package which had created the right not to be unfairly dismissed was, predictably, at once re-enacted, and after a short interregnum, when appeals from the Industrial Tribunals went once again to the High Court in the person of Raymond Philips, a new court was created to hear them, called the Employment Appeals Tribunal. It was on the lines of the National Industrial Relations Court, with lay members sitting with High Court judges, administered by the Ministry of Employment and housed in great elegance in what had been Lady Astor's town house in St James's Square.

Raymond was the first president, assigned to this position for three years full-time. Ralph Kilner-Brown and I were the other two English judges attached, each half-time, with Bob McDonald as the part-time Scottish judge. The new court embraced Scotland as well as England and Wales, though not Northern Ireland or the Channel Islands or the Isle of Man. Raymond's master stroke in setting it all up was to insist on the provision of lunching facilities on the spot for its members. This he achieved in face of characteristic civil service resistance on the grounds of expense. It would of course involve recruiting someone to cook, although there were kitchen facilities already available in the house.

The compromise reached after the expenditure of much effort was Avis. Avis came from Jamaica, wore a great big smile, was easily moved to laughter, and produced lunch-time dishes with a marked West Indian flavour which some of the older members found a bit hot in the summer months, so that they settled for biscuits and cheese. Avis was on the strength officially as cleaner, but in consideration of the members bearing that proportion of her remuneration referable to her cooking, she was graciously allowed to feed us. The catering was done by the president's secretary,

Sheila, a delightful black-haired charmer from South Wales, who bought the stuff on her way in to work.

I stress the importance of the lunching facility because it is how the judges got to know and trust the lay members and how the lay members got to know and trust us. Most of them knew and trusted one another already. Those from the employers' side were personnel directors from the big corporations. From the union side we had the very experienced officers who do the work and do not make the noise. So most lay members had been negotiating familiarly with each other for years, but judges were an unfamiliar kind of animal, to be approached with reserve. Within weeks of lunching with Raymond at the head of the table, and Avis's food to warm you up, we had all from being fellow members become friends, and I think most of us found it an enriching experience.

Appeal to us from the Industrial Tribunals lay on questions of law alone. There were many people who asked themselves what sort of sense it made to have laymen as full members of a court, the function of which was to decide what the law was in relation to the appeal under consideration, not to decide matters of acceptable industrial practice. Unfair dismissal appeals, the bulk of our work at the EAT, did not on the whole involve complicated questions of law, but as matters of sex and race discrimination were added to the problems for the Industrial Tribunals, and as with industrial recession problems under the redundancy legislation became more frequent, so the statutory jigsaw, which produced our work, became more complex.

It was my experience that most of the lay members were just as capable of spelling out for themselves the message that the statutory draftsman had intended to convey as I was, and it was very seldom that the judge and his two lay members did not reach a unanimous conclusion. The advantage you had as a trained lawyer was that you were better able to steer argument by the advocates in the direction of enlightenment for the tribunal, and to keep everybody's eye on the ball.

I found EAT work harder than the judges' normal civil work. You could very often not tell beforehand whether the appeal was to be presented by Queen's Counsel, junior counsel, solicitors, trade union officials, officers from employers' organisations, the employee's friend, or even the inarticulate shop-floor worker from Luton whose first language was Serbian, with no advocate at all. At all levels of advocacy you found varying degrees of skill from 'alpha plus' to 'gamma minus'. It was necessary in consequence for the judge to do significant homework in order to get some idea whether there might be a respectable point somewhere. In each appeal you had to reach your conclusion in discussion out of court with your lay members. All this took time, and inevitably involved reserved judgements which took more time. You could see very well what my Indiana Federal judge meant in what he had said after that money-lender's case years before.

For me of course the cream of the ordinary civil work was the jury list, nearly all actions for defamation. Although the law was not straightforward at least it was familiar and was not to be agonised about. It is a field in which the Court of Appeal sometimes thinks the trial judge, making his rulings and giving his directions to the jury on the spot during the progress of the case, has got it wrong. But the fact situations which give rise to defamation actions are fascinating. There was the case of the 'Spanking Colonel', whose conduct with a girl who was hired as cook for trips on the Thames in his motor cruiser was the subject of disapprobation by the *Sunday People*. There was a campaign waged by the *Observer* against what might be called inside dealing on the Stock Exchange in which a sharp attack was mounted against a blameless Noble Lord based on wholly inaccurate facts. There was an attack by the BBC, on a distinguished Welsh landowner based on wholly inaccurate facts.

The high spot in this last case was when the tenant farmer, on information from whom the attack had largely been mounted, was being cross-examined on part of his evidence which was plainly contradicted by a document which he had signed. Counsel asked the old man if he would like to look at the document and then reconsider his evidence. He would find that it bore his signature. No, he had not got his glasses with him. Would he care to fetch them? Unfortunately, he had left them at home in Wales.

I asked him whether the problem was that he needed glasses simply for reading, though at our age his long sight was perfectly good. Yes, that's it, he said. So I told him I was in the same situation, walked along the Bench to the witness-box and invited him to borrow mine. He did, and felt bound to acknowledge that the signature was his and the evidence he had previously given was wrong.

Very few defamation actions are fought out in court, though the ones that are attract publicity. So even when the Clerk of the Lists is an old friend who knows you are familiar with and enjoy the defamation scene you will be lucky, as one among many, if you find yourself dealing with the jury list more than three or four times in fifteen years. It comprises a very small proportion of the civil. Most of the civil work consists of personal injury cases, where it is usually tragedy which is in the forefront.

There is normally no great difficulty in deciding whether A ought to pay B compensation for causing him injury. You could really reduce the law on the question to this; that you must behave reasonably vis-à-vis those who you would appreciate, if you applied your mind to it, are likely to be affected by what you do. You must not allow your hedgerow elm to grow in such a way that in a force 8 wind it is at risk of falling across the road so that the driver of the milk float runs into it next morning and is turned into a paraplegic. You must not mishandle things in the hospital resuscitation room so that the patient sustains such brain damage as to leave her a human cabbage. The real difficulty comes in deciding what is the appropriate compensation for the injury caused, remembering that you are there to do justice to both sides.

Perhaps the best way to start is to say to yourself, you are required to do the impossible. Ask a pretty girl how much money she would take to have one of her legs cut off, and she would tell you not to be so silly. Money will not put you back to square one after physical injury. But money is the only means of compensation the law can provide, and to do justice you have to fit the injury for which you are to compensate into what is inevitably an artifical compensation market. Counsel, solicitors, and trade union and insurance claims managers, who operate regularly in this field, know the market and so can in most cases compromise claims instead of fighting them, which is to everyone's advantage. If they could not, the courts would be inundated.

The cases in which you find yourself asked to decide what the amount of compensation should be are usually those in which the circumstances of the injury or the person injured are unprecedented. A recent illustration of this was that I found myself at Exeter trying a case in which five Devonport dockyard workers were claiming compensation for deafness caused by noisy conditions at work. It was not until the seventies that the legal departments of trade unions had come to the conclusion that it was a failure by employers to take reasonable care for their people's safety to expose them to a degree of noise at work, without making them wear earmuffs, which was likely to make them deaf.

The case of my five reached court with the department still saying that it had not been negligent, but that untenable stance was abandoned when it was called on, and I was left to set the appropriate figure for five different men of different ages suffering from different degrees of deafness, with hundreds of cases coming up in the pipeline for which my figures would be a precedent.

Even in personal injury cases comedy sometimes joins in. There is a rural promontory of Buckinghamshire through which you pass in driving from Watford to Windsor and back. On one hot summer Sunday, an unemployed boy from Watford drove his girl friend down to Windsor to see the sights and enjoy a picnic. Passing through the rural promontory on the return journey they decided that a little open-air love-making would be agreeable. They parked their car by the roadside and climbed the fence into field No 1. They thought this rather public for their purpose, climbed another fence into field No 2, and yet another into field No 3, which was a nice long way from the road, alongside a spinney, and covered with nice long grass to ensure privacy. They there set about fulfilling the object of the exercise.

The farmer whose fields they were in employed a farmworker of southern Italian origin whom we will call Luigi. Luigi was a very keen shot, having been brought up in Calabria to shoot anything he could see, foxes first. He had permission from the farmer to shoot rabbits for the pot when walking between his cottage and his place of work. On that very evening Luigi, who had no dog, decided to pick up a rabbit on the way home to his tea. His way lay along the edge of the spinney, a promising draw for rabbits at that time of the evening when they would be moving out into the field to graze, and would bolt back into the spinney if disturbed. Luigi put up a rabbit.

He fired at it, but missed. He observed a movement in the long grass which he quite reasonably thought to be his or another rabbit, though he could not actually see it. He fired again.

It was the lovers. The girl had a pellet or two in her bottom, the boy got a pellet in the eye. Unhappily, he lost his eye. The police, suspicious that Luigi might have been shooting at the lovers to scare them off the farmer's land, made very close enquiries on the spot, and were satisfied with Luigi's explanation that he was firing at what he thought to be a rabbit. The boy brought an action against Luigi, based on the proposition that it was *ipso facto* negligent to shoot at something you could not actually see.

This raised a point of obvious importance to farmers and landowners. The boy, understandably bitter at having lost his eye, was in no compromising mood. So what with one thing and another the case came on for trial in London before me. Here the interest lay not in what the loss of an eye rated in the way of compensation for him. That would have been easy. Query, was it the law that simply by letting off your gun at something you cannot see you are in breach of your duty to take reasonable care for the safety of someone you hit?

There were in fact one or two cases in the books bearing on the problem, but not precisely in point, and I decided it on first principle. Obviously in field No 1, on a fine summer Sunday evening you must expect movement in the long grass to be quite possibly lovers, not rabbits. In field No 2, it might be a difficult problem. But it seemed to me to be putting too high a duty on the man with the gun to say that as far from the road as field No 3, with three fences to climb between field No 3 and the road, he ought reasonably to have anticipated that movement in the long grass might be lovers, not rabbits.

Not long afterwards, Bob McDonald was visiting us at the EAT in St James's Square and told me that I now enjoyed a unique distinction. 'How come?' I said. 'Well,' said Bob, 'you are the only English judge whose very words have been quoted in the *Inverness Herald*.' Rabbits and lovers are important in Scots law as well.

As long-stop in the Commercial Court on one occasion I found myself at grips with a dispute between the contractors preparing a large industrial site on the banks of the Tyne, and the barge owners who had agreed to dump the spoil in the North Sea, and found that they were losing money because there was more spoil than they had bargained for. The difficulty arose because a figure of X cubic feet was set down in the contract. To the contractors, X cubic feet meant the space occupied by the spoil in their trucks after excavation from the ground, much greater than it had occupied when undisturbed in the ground. Any practical gardener could tell you that. The barge owners, being seamen, not gardeners, understood X cubic feet to mean the volume of the hole from which the spoil had been dug.

The dispute made a real commercial lawyers' Roman holiday, far more fun than the small print on charter parties and bills of lading. I was confident that whichever way I decided the case, it would go to the Court of Appeal. Large sums of money were involved. I plumped for the barge owners. The Court of Appeal found the other way by two to one, the one being Lord Denning. An appeal to the House of Lords was initiated, but at that stage the parties came to their senses and compromised.

Yet another London assignment, in case you might feel short on variety, was to sit as Judge in Chambers. Before Hitler's war, the judge in chambers work occupied one judge on two short days a week. It involved appeals from the Masters in Chambers over interlocutory decisions: that is, decisions on the problems which arise when cases are being knocked into triable shape. It involved dealing with applications for injunctions. It involved such esoteric matters as getting leave to bring an action against someone who you thought had done you wrong under the Mental Health Acts, or giving people who had been declared 'persistent litigants' leave to bring any action at all.

By the time I was on the Bench it was a five days a week assignment for the judge. Now it is five days a week for two judges, often plus such support as can be drummed up from any judge whose own list has collapsed. In addition to the original diet you have such things as squatters, who if they turn up at all, turn up in all shapes, sizes and colours complete with babies, nearly always unrepresented; 'Mareva' injunctions, a growth industry where people are trying to put the hooks on the other side's assets before they've won their case; and an infinite variety of other oddments.

By and large you have little or no advance warning of who or what is coming in through the door next. The last time I sat as Judge in Chambers I had to deal with the application by Mary Whitehouse for leave to bring a prosecution against *Gay News* for blasphemy, a prosecution in which her approach was finally upheld in the House of Lords.

Finally, there was the Parole Board. At any one time there are two High Court judges on the Parole Board. They sit on the panels where among other cases there are people serving life sentences to deal with. The one who has been on the board the longer becomes Vice-Chairman, and sits on the Parole Board/Home Office sub-committee which takes the first look at when lifers ought to be prepared for release. There is a story, I think apocryphal, that when it was announced that Eustace Roskill, then Chairman of Hants Quarter Sessions as well as High Court judge, was to be first Deputy Chairman, the flag on Winchester Prison was flown at half mast.

The Parole Board is a fascinating assignment. On the High Court judge panels you also have a consultant psychiatrist, a senior probation officer, often a university criminologist, and at least one member of the public. You have Home Office staff in attendance, in particular the officials whose job it is to deal with the life sentence prisoners. The homework for your fortnightly meeting I found took me six and half hours' solid reading. In my time you did not get the Parole Board assignment when you were part of your time out on circuit. Now you do. I don't see how you can add six hours' solid reading to your circuit obligations. It seemed, and seems, to me that if the Criminal Appeal homework, which is much less serious, calls for a reading day, so does the Parole Board homework. Maybe the present generation of Queen's Bench judges are such supermen that they can take it all in their stride and stay sane. My view is they should not be asked to.

Two things about the Parole Board work I found most encouraging. The prison service reports on their charges were thorough and sympathetic, and very rarely was there anyone for whom none of the reporting officers had a good word to say. Very seldom was there any difference of opinion among the members of the panel, coming from all their various disciplines and backgrounds, on what the right answer ought to be. Curiously, if someone was out on a limb it was often the criminologist.

So about the time you spent in London as a Queen's Bench judge it could be said that, taken all in all, it did not lack variety and was anything but dull.

PART FOUR

Reflections

1. Retiring

Until after World War II a High Court judge's office was a freehold. There was no age limit at which he had to retire. In the climate of the post-war years, this anachronism attracted critical attention and finally the intervention of Parliament. After all, even Bernard Shaw was beginning to lose his sharp edge at 90, and while no judge continued in operation to that age, it was not unknown for judges to reach 80 before they decided to retire or death overtook them; and very efficient some of them were. More often though judges either died or retired before that age. Most judges start as sensible people. Even if it not a question of recognising that you are beginning to lose your grip, judging is a hard-working and exacting life. If you have other interests in addition to the law, you may conclude that after the fifteen years' service required to earn you your maximum pension, enough is enough.

When Parliament decided that freeholds were wrong and there ought to be an age limit, it selected 75. Some people remain sharp at 75 or beyond. Some cease to make much sense before the 65 which is regarded as the general retiring age for men. Too many of my friends on the bench have worked themselves to death, or at any rate died, before 75. While some of the 75-year-olds resent having to retire, most people would think that age limit to be too high rather than too low. The truth is that whatever age you select will be too young for some people and too old for others. If you are fit to do your job on the eve of your seventy-fifth birthday, and don't have a stroke during the night, you are likely to be still able to do it next morning. Age limits with the best will in the world produce nonsenses. It is a criminal offence to have it off with your enthusiastic girl-friend on the eve of her sixteenth birthday, but perfectly OK next morning.

As year fifteen of my time as a Queen's Bench judge approached, and then elapsed, I became less and less enthusiastic about the

131

prospect of another six weeks' stint in my least favourite centres like Birmingham, Leeds, Sheffield, Manchester or Liverpool. However much you enjoy driving fast cars, three hundred miles per weekend in winter weather or summer traffic conditions become a burden. Yet that is what you will have to undertake if, like Candide, you are to cultivate your garden. The homework which lies behind the time you are seen to spend in open court become less acceptable unless you are a real glutton for punishment. Even five hours per day concentration in open court becomes more tiring than it used to be.

When we started on the Employment Appeals Tribunal the lay members tended to pooh-pooh the idea of a five-hour court day starting at 10.30. When we were getting into arrears with what the planners call the 'through-put' we started at 10.00 for an experimental period. After a little it was the lay members who cried for mercy. Two and a half hours' absolute concentration at a stretch is more than is demanded of you in most occupations, and is as much as most people can manage. So, I said to myself, sacrifice yourself and make way for the younger men. You may think you are still razor sharp but you may be wrong and anyway don't kid yourself that you are indispensable. When the magic fifteen years had elapsed I handed on the torch with the age limit still in the middle distance.

So now I have leisure on the grand scale for the first time since I settled down to tackle my Bar exams, way back in 1935. I have in theory leisure to do all the many things I want to do or which, like cultivating your garden, require to be done. I have leisure to cherish my wife, to read, to fish, to tie flies and to go to Normandy for reinforcements if we run out of Calvados. I have leisure above all to think. You don't get much spare thinking-outside-the-immediate-problems time at the Bar or on the Bench. Unless you ruthlessly insist on taking time out to deal with them, the pressure of work on the Bench leaves most people short of thinking time in relation to the immediate problems if they are complicated, as they sometimes are.

This seems to me the probable reason for some of the obviously bad decisions which are made, particularly by judges who regard it as a slur on their judicial virility to reserve judgement. It is not until you get to the House of Lords that you only sit four days a week and all judgements are reserved. Leisurely reflection in tranquillity on the state of the match after the revolution through which my generation has lived and worked has tempted me to express my personal opinions on assorted aspects of the administration of justice which follow.

2. Homicide

The question asked most often on circuit by the intelligent and responsible people up and down England and Wales whom you meet on the High Sheriff net is: 'Are you in favour of hanging?'

When you listen to what is said on either side you may come to the conclusion that you are in the presence of two irreconcilable moral imperatives. The abolitionist sincerely believes that deliberately to take human life is wrong. To take it in the name of the community is utterly wrong. You get into difficulty once you move from the punishment of crime into the area of defence of the community against aggression. Mahatma Gandhi showed that, at any rate if the aggressor is British, you can play things effectively the pacifist way. There is more difficulty when you think about the defence of yourself or your loved ones against an obvious killer. What are the moral considerations in the context of the kidnapper who begins to kill his hostages one by one? But 'thou shalt not kill' is number six in the Ten Commandments. The supporter of capital punishment believes with equal sincerity that some crimes, and particularly deliberate killing, are so destructive of the community that death is the only appropriate disposal for the offender, whether you look at it as a matter of punishment, or of expiation, or of the community taking reasonable care for its own safety.

I have come to the conclusion that the very real and respectable controversy arises from the history of our criminal law and the terminology in which the problem is discussed. At the root of the problem lies the law's definition of murder, and the message that the word conveys to ordinary people. Murder is, in law, any intentional killing not justified by being done in reasonable self-defence. The message the word conveys to ordinary people is that of deliberate, intentional, wicked killing, the murder you see in plays and on television and read about in detective stories.

In practice, most of the killings which result in a charge of murder are not like that, though they fall within what the law calls murder. Most commonly you are faced with the parties to a marriage which has gone terribly wrong. Husband has gone off with another woman once too often, or takes to his fists once too often, and wife takes the deadly weapon which is in every kitchen drawer and stabs him to death. Or wife nags husband once too often and he loses control and goes for the kitchen drawer equalliser and stabs her to death or strangles her with her own tights in the marital bed. These are the classic killings where people find themselves in a situation they cannot cope with. Very often when they realise what they have done they are the first to send for the ambulance and the police. There are very many other 'out of control' killing situations.

At the other end of the scale are the perfectly deliberate killings for money or for political motives or for revenge. There are killings which are in between. All, if intentional, fall within the law's definition of murder. The degree of wickedness differs enormously. Whatever the degree of wickedness, broadly speaking, until 1960 a conviction for murder meant you were sentenced to death. Since then it means you are sentenced to life imprisonment. Before 1960 whether you were hanged, and if not, how long you spent in prison, was a matter for the Home Secretary. Now, how long you spend in prison depends on the Home Secretary and the Parole Board. Their decision depends on the wickedness of the killing. The matrimonial explosion killer may be free in six or seven years. The Kray brothers and Ian Brady may never be released.

It is natural that if you have killed someone and you are charged with murder you should prefer to be convicted of manslaughter if possible. Instead of the mandatory life sentence, which means you will be released at the discretion of the executive and will remain on licence, subject to recall to prison, for life, your sentence will be at the judge's discretion.

The judge's discretion is unlimited. At the top of the scale he can pass a life sentence, at the bottom he can give you an absolute discharge. He will pass the sentence which is, in his view, appropriate to the criminality of the killing and what may be necessary for the safety of the community and to set public disquiet at rest. If the Yorkshire Ripper had been convicted of manslaughter on the grounds of diminished responsibility, as he might well have been on the medical evidence called at his trial, the judge would certainly have sentenced him to life imprisonment.

In the 'matrimonial explosion' cases, where merciful juries often return manslaughter verdicts on the grounds of provocation, the manslaughter sentence will seldom be as heavy as five years, and will sometimes be a probation order.

On one occasion even, not a 'matrimonal explosion' case, I thought it right to give an absolute discharge for manslaughter. Two ex-Parachute Regiment loners working on building sites in Bristol and lodging together were talking one evening in the pub. A says to B: 'I am due to appear in the Crown Court next week, and I am very anxious not to go. The only way out I can think of is to be ill in hospital, and the only way I can think of to manage that is to get you to stab me.' B demurred, but after another pint or two was talked into saying he would do it. The following day they met again in the pub. A said: 'Tonight's the night', and produced, still in its display packaging, a vegetable paring knife he had just bought in the supermarket. B again demurred but, pressed with the fact that he'd agreed and that A was relying on him, was again talked into it. So they went together to a nearby bombed site. They unwrapped the knife. A said, 'Stab me in the shoulder', and B did so. A said, 'That's no good, have another try', B, did so. A said, 'I think that will do, I'm going back to the pub.' B, not very comfortable about the operation, said, 'I'm going home to bed', and did just that. Halfway back to the pub, A fell down stone dead in the street. One of B's stabbing efforts had been over-successful. B was arrested, charged with murder and held in custody.

By the time he came to trial, four months later, the prosecution was satisfied that the story as I have told it was the truth, and accepted B's plea of guilty to manslaughter. The last thing he intended was that A should die. I concluded that the four months B had spent inside awaiting trial, knowing that he had killed his friend, was expiation enough. The punishment you will ultimately suffer for killing depends on the wickedness of your act and the danger you are seen to present to the community, irrespective to a large extent of whether you fall within the law's definition of murder or not.

So now, you might ask, is there real importance in the difference between 'murder' and 'manslaughter'? A killing is unlawful. As he does in cases of manslaughter now, the judge could be left to make the appropriate disposal in accordance with the circumstances and personality of the killer and the interests of the community, without the anomaly of a mandatory life sentence which everyone knows does not, except in the rarest cases, mean imprisonment for life, and without the Home Secretary being concerned with the decision of how long the killer should serve. As a matter of constitutional propriety and setting aside for the present the question of parole, should that not be a decision for the judiciary, not the executive?

Even in the old days of the mandatory death sentence, at a time in which Home Secretaries readily refrained from respiting the execution of women for murder, public opinion recognised that to pass a death sentence on a mother who, while still unbalanced as a result of giving birth, intentionally kills her unwanted baby, was wrong. The Prevention of Infanticide Act was passed to cure that injustice. Later it was recognised that to pass a death sentence on, for instance, a battered wife who finally loses control and goes berserk and kills her husband, was unjust. To cure that injustice the Common Law evolved the defence of 'provocation'. If, because of provocation, you lost control and killed, and a normal person in that situation might have done what you did, then your offence was manslaughter, not murder.

Finally it was recognised that to pass a death sentence on someone who killed because he was mentally ill, though he was not insane within the law's definition of insanity, was unjust. Now, if you kill in circumstances which meet the complicated requirements of the defence of 'diminished responsibility' set out in the Homicide Act 1957, your offence is manslaughter, not murder.

So between them, Parliament and the judges, who develop the Common Law, have started to deal with some of the anomalies which the law's definition of murder plus first the mandatory death sentence and now the mandatory life sentence produced. Would the changes made in those three instances have been necessary if you were thinking straight about the law's murder definition? The mother who kills her unwanted baby while still unbalanced has the intention to kill when she does so, but it is not a true intention formed by her normal mind. If you kill under provocation, you intend to kill, but it is not a true intention formed by your normal mind. If you kill because of mental illness, your intent to kill is not a true intent formed by your normal self.

If the judges had said that the intent required to make a killing murder must be true intent formed by someone in his right mind, a concept readily understood by ordinary people, the difficulties which arise from the requirements formulated by Parliament and the judges for the defences of diminished responsibility and provocation could have been avoided. Happily infanticide does not present such problems.

In a large proportion of murder trials, the defence put forward is diminished responsibility or provocation. Hours of jury time are consumed in the presentation of conflicting medical evidence, or in presenting the circumstances relied on as giving rise to provocation. More time is consumed by the judge summing-up the complex requirements, which have to be satisfied for those defences to succeed, in terms which can be understood by the ordinary people of whom the jury is made up. Yet more is spent by the jury wrestling with what can be a severe intellectual problem.

But for the mandatory sentence which follows the verdict 'guilty of murder', all this consumption of jury time would be unnecessary. Of course it is comfortable for the judge, after a 'guilty of murder' verdict, to be able to say to the killer in the dock: 'The law requires me to pass a sentence of life imprisonment.' In the event of a 'not guilty of murder but guilty of manslaughter' verdict he has to make up his mind what is the appropriate sentence. If the verdict is murder, he does not. Whatever sentence he passes will be thought by some to be too lenient, by others too severe, but that is an occupational hazard. Would it not be just as safe to leave to the judge what is the appropriate sentence for the killing which fits the law's definition of murder, as to leave it to him in the case of the killing which does not?

It is, after all, not difficult to recognise wickedness or danger to the community. In the fifteen years during which murder and manslaughter were part of my normal assignment, I had only one murder trial into which no element of 'situation out of the killer's control' entered at all. This was the case. An elderly couple, let us call them Mr and Mrs Smith, befriended a girl in her twenties who had three children, each by a different sire and none in wedlock. As a single parent family, she found it difficult to cope, and received kindness and help from the Smiths, whose own children were grown up and out of the nest. Mrs Smith died. Mr Smith, left with his dog for company, sought out more of the girl's company and gradually became infatuated. He asked her to marry him.

This put her in a difficulty. Her sexual needs were being satisfied by a fourth potential sire of a much more suitable age than Mr Smith, but who was married himself and not in a position to confer on her and the children the material benefits that the Smiths had conferred. So she did not say yes and she did not say no. Then she became pregnant.

At just this time her younger brother came to live with her. She consulted with him what should be done. Mr Smith was unemployed, but he had led an industrious life and had twice had large redundancy payments after long service with employers who had gone out of business. He owned his house, he owned a caravan on a site at Poole, and he had £15,000 in the bank. 'Well,' says brother, 'why don't you marry him, and we will kill him and you will get it all', and this was agreed between them.

So she said 'Yes' to Mr Smith. He made the arrangements with the Registrar. He bought a new tie. But he did not tell his own children, no doubt because he knew they would have told him not to do anything so stupid. They were married. He left his dog at home. After a party in the pub with the bride's relations, they spent the wedding night in her house. Next morning, brother and sister killed Mr Smith. They were not very good at it. The sitting room had to be redecorated, and the carpet was in such a state that they rolled his body up in it and put it behind the bedroom wardrobe, because they had not planned how to get rid of it.

The wedding had been on a Monday. By Tuesday people began to notice that Mr Smith was not around. On Thursday his daughter, who had expected him to be in touch, went to his house and found the dog, which had clearly been shut in for days. She told the police, who started to make enquiries. They asked the bride if she knew where he had gone. She said she thought he had gone visiting. It was then obvious that something must be done about the body. So brother went out and bought an old banger, and on Friday night the pair of them put it, still rolled up in the carpet, on the back seat of the banger, drove into the country, and dumped it in a ditch near Stratford-on-Avon where it was duly found.

At the trial each blamed the other for the killing. If the jury had thought that only one of them had done it but could not decide which, both must have been acquitted. The jury found both of them guilty of murder, and I passed the mandatory service of life imprisonment. If it had not been mandatory, but a matter for me to decide, I would have passed the same sentence. This was top marks for wickedness; for stupidity too. Without showing that Mr Smith was dead, she could not have got house, caravan or money.

As a contrast, consider the trial of the Kashmiris who kidnapped the Indian High Commission official in Birmingham, and later drove him into the country and shot him in cold blood. In this case, the Kashmiri who pulled the trigger, and another who was in the killing up to the neck, left England before they were caught. Another, who pleaded guilty to kidnapping, was not charged with murder because he was in the police station helping the police with their enquiries at the time of the killing. But one of the young men who was recruited to hold the diplomat prisoner in the safe house, and was included at the last moment in the execution squad, was properly convicted of murder. He knew perfectly well when he got out of the car and helped escort the diplomat up the lane in the darkness that the intention, the object of the exercise, was to shoot him, though he did not want him to be shot.

I passed a very long determinate sentence on the one who pleaded guilty to kidnapping. He was clearly a prime mover in the whole operation, and set up the safe house. In a sense, of course, this too was a top marks for stupidity case. The object was to hold the diplomat hostage in order to bring pressure on the Indian government, then headed by Indira Gandhi, to reprieve a Kashmiri separatist under sentence of death in Delhi, and due for execution in a few days. Not very promising. But the motive for the actual killing seemed to be that things had got out of hand. There was no question of the operation achieving its object, and the diplomat could not safely be left alive with the risk that he would identify his kidnappers.

So, as far as the actual killers were concerned, again top marks for wickedness, even though they had landed themselves in the mess from a political rather than a squalid mercenary motive. But the young man who was convicted played a much less wicked part either than those who mounted the operation or the man who pulled the trigger. The mandatory death sentence absolved me from having to decide how long the sentence ought to be. The decision how long he should serve will now be for the executive.

There would be an easy solution to all the difficulties which the mandatory life sentence for murder creates. It would sidestep the capital punishment controversy which bogs down on trying to draw the line between capital and non-capital murders. You could make a compete break with history and the terminology of which we are all prisoners. Abolish the crimes of murder and manslaughter entirely. Substitute the crime of 'unjustifiable homicide'. What would be left for the jury would be, was the killing in reasonable self-defence, or in any of the other few circumstances in which the law regards killing as justifiable, or by accident? But in nearly all cases there would have to be a plea of guilty to the offence charged and it would be for the judge, as now in manslaughter, to decide on the appropriate sentence.

What Parliament might consider the right sentence in the worst case might vary from time to time. Enough terrorism at home might lead Parliament to say, death is necessary. Too many bombs in pubs full of innocent people, too many hostage killings, might lead to a move in public opinion which would be irresistible. But that would be a political matter. From the point of view of the administration of justice, a single offence of 'unjustifiable homicide' in place of murder and manslaughter could, if anyone was bold enough to grasp the nettle, lead to a great saving of time, and improvement in quality, in the administration of justice.

3. Rape

Most of us have in the course of our lives been subjected to some physical abuse of our personal integrity. Some of us have been the subject of sexual assault. It can happen to people of either sex. It should therefore not be too difficult to understand the indignation with which rape, the deliberate taking of a woman against her will, is naturally and properly regarded by right-thinking people, and the call for condign punishment which it evokes. It is a crime which invades the most private and intimate sector of a woman's life, and may have far-reaching consequences on her situation if she becomes pregnant.

I have considered the problems that attend sentencing those who plead guilty or are convicted of rape in the chapter on sentencing. But while this question, guilty or not guilty, is still undecided there is another side to it. If you are convicted of rape as the result of a false accusation, it will involve consequences for you which right-thinking people might consider were even more serious than the consequences of rape for its victim. You will inevitably be sentenced to a term of imprisonment in the order of three years. The conviction will carry grave social implications for you, not only in your ordinary world outside, but also inside prison. The burglar, the conman, the bank robber may be regarded with admiration by his fellow prisoners; not the rapist, and the time he spends in prison is apt to be much nastier than theirs.

The law recognises that there is a danger of false accusations of sexual offences. The judge is required to warn the jury of that danger, and of the need for them to look for evidence from a source other than the person complaining, which tends to show the complaint is true. The law calls for this corroboration. If it is a child who makes the complaint, Parliament has enacted that without corroborative evidence there can be no conviction. If the complainant is adult, then the Common Law requires the judge to direct the jury, who must anyway not find a verdict of 'guilty' unless they are sure of guilt, that it is dangerous for them to convict without corroborative evidence, but that if they are sure that the complainant has told the truth they are at liberty to convict. What is a sensible juror to make of that? How sure is sure? Why should an adult be treated as just a little less likely to make a false sexual complaint than a child?

We may well ask, is false sexual complaint something that really happens, or is the whole corroboration thing a hangover from the male-orientated Victorian society when the Common Law rule was evolved? The reason for the rule is often explained to juries in terms that it is the easiest thing in the world for a sexual complaint to be made, and very difficult to disprove it, especially when the question is, did the woman, who now says the sexual act was against her will, willingly consent to it at the time, or act in a way which led the man to believe she was consenting? After all, the sexual act is not usually performed in front of witnesses. But then, the law also says loud and clear that it is not for the man to disprove the complaint but for the woman to prove it.

On the Bench, I have had to deal with many rape cases. In some, the accused has recognised that to fight is hopeless, has accepted advice, and has pleaded guilty. In others, although to fight is manifestly hopeless, the accused has fought tooth and nail, thinking to himself, no doubt, 'If I'm to get three years anyway, what have I got to lose?' These unfightables are the rapes which take place in circumstances where the man, or men, for they are often 'gang-bangs', could not possibly have believed that the victim was willing. In other cases, the circumstances are such that the jury has to decide whether in truth at the time the victim was willing or unwilling, or whether the man genuinely believed that she was participating willingly.

It is in such cases that you may well say to yourself, 'Thank heaven it's the jury, not I, who have to decide if the case is proved.' Sometimes they find it is. Often they find it is not. Sometimes, with hindsight, you understand why they came to their conclusion. Sometimes you do not. Sometimes they can come to no collective conclusion, and disagree.

Sometimes, however, the complaint is shown during the trial to be positively false. The most vivid and dramatic experience I had of this was the trial at Exeter Crown Court of a man on a charge of rape, where his defence was, 'Yes, we had intercourse. It was with her full consent, or if it was not, her behaviour was such that I genuinely believed she was consenting.' On the committal papers, and as opened by prosecuting counsel, the girl's story was wholly plausible, and there was evidence from sources other than herself which tended to show that she was telling the truth. She went into the witness-box. As prosecuting counsel proceeded with his examination-in-chief, her demeanour was impeccable.

Then we got to the stage at which it becomes necessary for the rape victim, in giving her evidence, to start calling a spade a spade. Some girls do so without hesitation. Others, naturally enough, feel and display extreme embarrassment. It must be very unpleasant to have to talk about such things in a court full of strangers in answer to questions by counsel topped off with the absurdity of a horsehair wig of seventeenth century design, and a judge with scarlet and, in winter, ermine, in addition to his horsehair.

The girl displayed extreme embarrassment and, for all kindly counsel's efforts, stretching the rules which govern examination-in-chief to their permissible limit, she dried up completely. Sometimes the judge, from a different angle, with a different voice, and perhaps with more experience in the art, can help in this situation. I did my best, but got, as they say in Canada, no place fast. I told her that it was essential, if justice was to be done, that the jury should hear what she had to tell them. I told her that, while this was inevitably a very unpleasant situation for her, the man in the dock was in a very unpleasant situation as well, faced with an extremely serious criminal charge. Finally I said to her that if the reason why she did not go on telling the jury what had happened was that in truth he had not raped her, now was the time to say so.

'Well,' she said, 'as a matter of fact he didn't.'

If that girl had gone on in the witness-box to tell the jury what she had told the police, they might have believed her. Her story was completely plausible. Corroborative evidence was there. She might have been unshaken by cross-examination. The man's evidence might have been disbelieved. He might have been convicted. If he had been convicted, he would have been sentenced to two years' imprisonment at the very least. He was a perfectly ordinary young man who had never been in trouble with the police. Both inside prison and in his own world outside, he would have been branded as a rapist.

Trials for rape, and no doubt rapes which never come to trial, are too often tragedy, but sometimes comedy takes over. I had to try five Pakistanis in Manchester on charges of rape and abduction. The victim was a girl whom they had met at a club which was well known to afford opportunties for Lancastrians of all ethnic origins to establish sexual relationships on a commercial basis. The most attractive of the five was charged with doing the business for them all, and, without being too specific, he negotiated a package deal by which, for an appropriate consideration, she was to accompany them to their residence and confer her favours upon them. The other four were less attractive than the negotiator. One indeed was so back-woodsy that in court we needed two interpreters to get through to his home language.

When she fully appreciated the nature of the package, the girl sought to repudiate the contract, but the other parties insisted on performance and took her off home willy nilly. The witnesses of the fact that she was protesting in transit were a charming Polish couple, past whose window they all went. Their Polish-English was not very polished, so one way and another we were in a good deal of language trouble. The following morning, the girl left the house and complained to the police that she had been raped. The defence to the rape charge was that when they all got home, she had made the best of a bad job, and it was not until next morning, when they refused to pay on the grounds that she had sought to repudiate the contract, that she decided to complain of rape. The jury found them not guilty of rape, but guilty of abduction.

Sometimes even farce intrudes. Sitting in Newcastle, I had to try a young man whom we will call Jacky Horner, borrowing from the nursery rhyme, on a charge of raping a housewife in a Northumbrian town we will call Ashington, where they actually speak the language put by Surtees into the mouth of James Pigg, in her bedroom. The housewife had had a difference with her husband which caused him, at about midnight, to sweep out of the house and off down the road into the darkness. She followed on to the doorstep to wing words after his departing back. The door blew shut, the lock locked, the children were upstairs in bed. There was a light in the neighbour's house, so she went and knocked them up. There she found a card school which included Jacky, and explained to them her predicament. Chivalry was not dead in Ashington. The players put down their hands, accompanied her to her house, and, being possessed of the appropriate skills, broke in by the kitchen window and let her in by the front door. So she got them a cup of tea before they went back to their cards, and Jacky maintained that he got the message that he would be welcome to return.

So return he did, some two hours later, and now there came what some lawyers call a conflict of evidence between the two protagonists. Jacky's version of what happened next was that she was waiting up and received him in the kitchen with open arms. Hers was that she was woken from sleep by Jacky in her bed getting on with the job, and that she objected vigorously. The jury might have treated Jacky's version with some reserve because he left the house through the bedroom window, but this was not the first point made to them by prosecuting counsel in cross-examination. The first point went like this:

Counsel: 'You say you got the message that you would be welcome to return.'

Jacky: 'Yes, sir.'

Counsel: 'And yet you agree that you did not go back to the house for two hours.'

Jacky: 'That's right, sir.'

Counsel: 'Why not?'

Jacky: 'We were playing cards.'

Counsel registers incredulity, with a meaning look at the jury, which Jacky intercepts.

Jacky, indignant: 'Yes, sir, we were playing cards, there was money in it. There was £4.10 in the kitty, and I always say, "Money before sex".'

From this body blow, the prosecution case never recovered. After a short retirement the jury returned a verdict of Not Guilty. Jacky, who had hitherto been quite at home in the dock and on obviously familiar, friendly terms with the dock officers, fell down in a dead faint, and it took some time to bring him round.

So in this field of jurisprudence things are not always what they seem. As far as I know, it is the only field in which the administration of justice has attracted critical commentary in the form of graffiti. One graffito on a bare red brick wall in the heart of Bristol demands, 'Sack rape judges'. I find this ambiguous. Query, a cry of indignation from rapists at the severity of the judges? Query, a cry from Women's Lib against their lenience? There is no ambiguity about a second graffito on the parapet of a railway bridge in Cardiff. This demands simply, 'Disarm rapists'.

4. Incest

One of the most difficult sentencing problems is created by the crime of incest. So difficult is it sometimes that it can be a comfort to remember its history. By and large, civilised man has appreciated the dangers of inbreeding, and treated incest as wrong. But by Julius Caesar's time the Ptolemaic dynasty in Egypt had practised incest as a matter of course, and the Ptolemies were a recent spin-off from Alexander the Great, conqueror of the world. There was incest among the Borgias, but not as a matter of dynastic policy as it had been with the Ptolemies, and, by the time of the Reformation, Europe at any rate was against it. In England under the Commonwealth it had become a capital offence. The Draconian approach produced a back-lash after the Restoration and incest, as such, ceased to be a criminal offence, though of course if it involved indecent assault or unlawful intercourse with children, as it well might, those offences would be punished in their own right. Incest as such became a matter for the Church, attracting such ecclesiastical remedies as public penance.

In 1908 the Prevention of Incest Act, in force today, was passed making it once more an offence, with heavy maximum penalties available for appropriate cases. Why, we may ask, in 1908? The middle of the reign of Good King Edward must have been the apogee of the permissive society among the Top People, though they did not make a song and dance about it. Were the rest any more straitlaced than they are today, or is it simply that the taboos are down now?

When I first appreciated this odd history, in the course of an incest appeal in the Criminal Division, I set about discovering why, for the first time since the Commonwealth, Parliament decided to make it a criminal offence once more. I didn't manage it. I went to *Hansard* and looked up the reports of the debates. I found that a similar Bill had been proposed two years before. I looked up the reports of the debates on that. No trace of either why it was proposed or why it was defeated. So when faced with an incest sentencing problem you have no philosophical launching pad. You have simply that the law made it in 1908 after two hundred and fifty years a serious offence once more, and the facts and the people in the case you have to deal with.

We think of incest as a rural crime, with the sex imperative taking control in an environment which prevents its proper gratification. It is mostly rural incest which is the subject of prosecution because of the scandal it creates in the small communities. The classic urban incest situation is this. After, say, fifteen years of slaving for her highly sexed husband, and producing and seeing through infancy several children, mother before she is forty is generally exhausted and sexually switched off. Father is not. If something is not done father will take his sexual gratification and his money elsewhere.

There will always be a willing Mrs X down the road. That means financial disaster for the family, so eldest daughter steps into the breach. When she has served her time and has a boy-friend of her own, then daughter number two takes over. What is the social worker, faced with this situation, to do? A prosecution will destroy the family. In the urban context there need be no scandal of the sort which would make prosecution essential in the village.

Of course incest, particularly in the common case when it is between father and immature daughter, can be in circumstances which make it extremely wicked and calls for a severe sentence. But like most situations you meet in sentencing there is usually a large misfortune + inability-to-cope factor. It is in making the right diagnosis of the balance between the two that the problem lies. Incest is essentially a private crime. The social agencies can ensure that it does not happen again. On the whole, is not the right answer to put father away for long enough for the social agencies to get it organised? In the rural context, except in the Fens and in very hilly country, the invention of the bicycle has had a beneficial effect.

5. Professional Propriety

In 1937 you learned how counsel should conduct himself in court in pupillage, and afterwards from your brothers in chambers, in the court robing rooms, and, on circuit, in the Bar mess. If you did what you ought not to, you were very soon told about it. If you argued or persisted, the word went back very smartly to the head of your chambers. He could and, if you persisted in misbehaviour, would throw you out.

One of my friends, after he had returned from World War II service in the army, being already counsel of some standing and experience, got into serious trouble from which his career at the Bar never recovered. He was defending a villain in assizes. His client had made some clear admissions, according to the police evidence, during his interrogation. His instructions to my friend were that these admissions were untrue, though he had made them, and were made because of undue and improper pressure by the police, of which he gave details. So my friend cross-examined the police, attacking them on the basis of what his client had told him about their conduct. At the close of the prosecution case he at once told the judge that he was not calling evidence, that is to say that his client was not going into the witness-box to support the accusation that had been made.

In his summing-up, the judge stigmatised the conduct of the defence in this way as serious professional misconduct. If you examine it dispassionately, that is clearly right. Counsel has a duty to do his best for his client. He has an equally cogent duty not to be a party to the perversion of justice by his client by misleading the court or the jury. My friend, by announcing immediately at the conclusion of the prosecution case that he would call no evidence, demonstrated to the judge that at the time he made the attack on the police he knew his client would not give evidence to support it. If therefore the police denied misconduct, as it was clear that they must, there would be no evidence for the jury to consider of misconduct by the police. Yet everyone knows that if mud is thrown it tends to stick, even if it is thrown without any justification.

What then was my friend to do, faced with a client who says, cross-examine the police on the basis that their interrogation was improper, and that my admissions were not made of my own free will and are not true, but I won't go into the witness-box to say so. Counsel's proper answer in this dilemma in those days was easy. I am not your mouthpiece, I am your counsel. Unless you are prepared to go into the witness-box to support what you are telling me, to attack the police as you want me to would be a breach of my duty. I must not be a party to anything calculated to pervert the course of justice. I may not throw unsupported mud at the police which you hope will stick. If you are not satisfied with the way in which I am prepared to conduct your defence, get another counsel, or defend yourself.

In those days, as now, there was no contract between counsel and lay client. In criminal cases, counsel was either instructed in the ordinary way through a solicitor, or at the instance of the court either by way of legal aid, which might or might not involve a solicitor, or a dock defence, which would not. Moreover, it was thought to be the law, on the grounds of public policy, that counsel was immune from claims for negligence on the part of a dissatisfied client. The priority was that counsel should be able to act for his client as he thought best, bearing in mind his two-fold duty, owed both to his client and to the court, without having to look over his shoulder for fear of negligence actions. The same priority is recognised by the law of libel, which gives the defence of absolute privilege to anything defamatory said or done by counsel, or indeed the judge, in the course of a trial. The interests of justice require that you should conduct your client's case, within the limits of professional propriety, without fear.

It is now no longer the law that counsel is immune from claims for negligence on the part of his client. Certainly in so far as his advisory function is concerned, if he fails to exercise reasonable care and skill he can be sued for damages for negligence like any other professional man, and must, if he wants to be protected, protect himself, like any other professional man, by insurance. No successful action has yet been brought for negligence in the conduct of a case in court. So far we still regard it as a priority in the interests of justice that counsel should be able to conduct his client's case in the often stressful trial situation without looking over his shoulder.

The scope of criminal legal aid has been enormously extended, and, except in rare circumstances, in trials in the Crown Court defendants are looked after by the full panoply of solicitors and counsel, to a greater or lesser degree at the public expense. Every effort is made to ensure that they shall have the services of counsel of their or their solicitor's choice. There has been an enormous increase in criminal work and a corresponding increase in the number of counsel who do it. For their guidance there is now a code of professional conduct, issued by the Bar Council, which is the elected supervisory body for the Bar. This code purports to spell out counsel's professional conduct obligations to his client and to the court.

Para 156 of the code is in the following terms:

(a) Every accused person has the right to decide whether to give evidence in his own defence. A barrister may properly advise his client upon this but it is the accused himself who must make the decision.

(b) If an accused person instructs his counsel that he is not guilty of the offences with which he is charged but decides not to give evidence himself, it is the duty of his counsel to put his defence before the court and, if necessary, to make positive suggestions to witnesses.

In a prosecution of thirteen defendants the principal evidence against them all and the only evidence against the majority of them consisted in admissions made to the police during interrogation. There were numerous defence teams, all but one with Queen's Counsel. With the exception of counsel for Defendant No 12, each defence counsel cross-examined the police officers who had conducted the thirteen interrogations to the effect that they had applied undue and improper pressure during the interrogation of his client. So the four police officers concerned were subjected for days on end to questions suggesting highly improper behaviour, put in very considerable detail.

It fell to me as the judge to fill page after page of my notebook with the suggestions put and the answers given by the police officers. When the defendants had in their turn given evidence about the behaviour of the police and of the fact that this had caused them to make admissions which though they did not deny making them, were in fact untrue, I would be able to remind the jury in summing-up of the evidence on both sides.

At the close of the prosecution case I had a session with counsel in the absence of the jury in order to try to get some idea of how long we were going to take in dealing with the thirteen defence cases. The prosecution case had taken a month. I was then told that Defendants Nos 2, 3, 4, 5, 6, 7, 8, 9, 10 and 11, on each of whose behalf attacks on the conduct of the police interrogations had been launched, were not going to give evidence.

In view of the detailed nature of the attacks on the police, details which I had to assume were included in the instructions to his counsel by each of these ten accused, this caused me some surprise. When they gave evidence, defendants No 1 and No 13, both sympathetic characters, one of whom was ultimately acquitted of everything, to some extent supported the attack made on the police by their counsel in respect of the interrogation of themselves. Nos 2 to 12 inclusive sat tight, as they were of course fully entitled to do, and did not venture into the witness-box and expose themselves to fire.

When the case of Defendant No 13, who gave evidence, was closed and before counsel addressed the jury, I initiated a further dialogue in the absence of the jury. Were we not now in this position; that as far as the attacks made on behalf of defendants Nos 2 to 11 on the police were concerned there was no evidence for the jury to consider to support the suggestions of impropriety that had been made?

'That's right,' said counsel.

'Well,' I said, 'what are you going to do about it? Are you going to tell them so in your closing speech, or do you prefer that I should tell them in summing-up? And you are not going to question the propriety of the police interrogation, are you?'

'Well,' they said, 'there is the evidence of Defendants Nos 1 and 13 about their interrogation to consider, and the jury are entitled to consider the way in which the police answered our questions, but we can't of course say to the jury that there's any evidence to support the specific suggestions we made.'

'Well,' I said, 'if your clients were not going to give evidence, those suggestions ought never to have been put, ought they?'

'Ah,' they said, 'look at Para 156(a) and (b) of the Code of Conduct. It's for the defendant himself to decide if he will give evidence or not, and if he decides not to, it's our duty to put his defence before the court and if necessary to make positive suggestions to witnesses.'

'Very well,' I said, 'I will explain the score to the jury when it comes to my summing-up.'

I told the jury that they had heard the police officers subjected for days to detailed suggestions of impropriety which nine of the defendants, on whose behalf they were made, had not had the guts to go into the witness-box to support; and that in respect of those nine there was no evidence whatever of impropriety on the part of the police, and that they might put two and two together and conclude that there was no foundation for the suggestions.

If the draftsman of Para 156 intended it to mean that counsel, knowing that his client would not give evidence, ought, because his client instructed him to, to cross-examine police officers to suggest, with details, improper conduct during interrogation, his idea of professional propriety differs from mine. Any conduct better calculated to pervert justice than to throw mud which is not going to be supported by evidence because your client hopes that some of it will stick would be difficult to imagine, and I cannot think that the draftsman had any such intention.

Para 156(a) is a truism. Of course it is the client, not counsel, who decides whether, when it comes to the crunch, his legs are going to carry him from the dock to the witness-box. As for Para 156(b), can the draftsman really have intended to reduce counsel to the status simply of mouthpiece? Has he shut his eyes to counsel's duty to the interests of justice?

On the Western Circuit you often come across what is known as 'the Portsmouth defence'. Where homosexuals have been attacked and robbed in the 'gay' public conveniences of the Western Circuit seaports, the robber very often says: 'He made disgraceful sexual advances to me and I had to hit him to defend myself. The £5 the police found in my pocket has no connection with the £5 he says he's lost, the dirty liar.' I hope we may not have to add to the Portsmouth defence the experience of a defence equally conventional. 'I admit I made a full confession. It was not true. The wicked police pressurised me into making it. But no way will I go into the witness-box and say so.'

It is axiomatic in our law that anything you say to the police once you are a suspect must be said of your own free will. That is why you must be cautioned and told that you are not obliged to say anything, but that anything you do say may be written down and given in evidence. At your trial anything said under interrogation, whether true or not, unless it is said of your own free will, is excluded from being given in evidence to the jury. Once the question is to be raised, was something said of your free will or not, the jury leaves court and the judge, after hearing whatever evidence anyone wishes to call about it, makes up his mind whether the evidence should be admitted or not.

Here is the best ever gambit played before me in an attempt to exclude an embarrassing admission in the course of interrogation. A serving soldier is arrested by the civil police on suspicion of committing an offence against the criminal law. He is cautioned. Very properly and sensibly he asked to see 'my officer'. 'My officer', as in duty bound, comes to the police station to see him. 'The police are accusing me of such and such a criminal offence. What am I to do?' 'Tell them the truth.' Full stop. 'My officer' departs. The police interrogating officers return. Once again the soldier is cautioned, in the same terms as before. He then proceeds to make the admission which by hindsight is very unfortunate. He would have done better to keep his mouth shut, as the caution each time said he was entitled to.

At the trial, defence counsel says he has a matter to raise in the absence of the jury. Out they go. Defence counsel submits that the evidence of what was said after his officer's visit ought to be excluded. The soldier goes into the witness-box. Yes, he was cautioned, both before and after his officer's visit. Yes, he understood the caution. But when his officer said, 'Tell them the truth' he took that to be a military order which he had no choice but to obey, so that, subsequent caution or not, nothing he said after that was of his own free will! There was of course no scintilla of impropriety on anyone's part in this. But what a lovely way out of the difficulty if the judge took the view that what the soldier said might be true, and so excluded the evidence.

I ask myself, will anyone besides me think that before attacking the police on their client's instructions counsel ought to ensure, so far as they can, that the attack will be supported by their client going into the witness-box? Will anyone beside me think that if the client says yes he will, and thereafter changes his mind, the very least that counsel should do in order to perform his duty to the court in the interests of justice is to say to the jury himself, loud and clear in his closing speech, 'You will please disregard the attack I have made on the police. My client has not gone into the witness-box to support it, and so there is no evidence which I can ask you to accept and conclude that the attack was justified'?

I hope the answer to these questions is 'Yes'. If it is not, then ideas of professional propriety have greatly changed, in a way which will be the worse for justice.

6. Juries in Fraud Cases

We do not all function at our best all the time. Sometimes when trying a civil case as judge alone you may say to yourself, I'd like a bit of help on this one. Sometimes when trying crime you say to yourself, thank God the jury has to decide guilty or not guilty, not I.

With three up in the Court of Appeal you greatly reduce the risk of things going wrong because a judge is having an off-day. The other two are there, and it's bad luck if two are having an off-day together, and No 3 cannot take them by the scruff and sort it out. When the problem gets to the House of Lords it is passed upon by five of them. Why? They are the voices of ultimate infallibility, so that it is of cardinal importance that they should get it right. Five is nearly half a jury. You are reducing the off-day risk all the time.

In the old days very many civil actions were tried by jury, not very few as now. Some people think it is wrong that it is the jury that assesses the compensation for injury to your reputation by libel. Others think that it is wrong that compensation for personal injury should be assessed by a judge alone, fitting it in to an artificial judge-made market. In the United States it is still the province of the jury, which ought to be a random sample of your 'peers', who, it is said, know the real-life score in the way the judge, in his Ivory Tower, does not.

I've never been able to understand where people get the Ivory Tower idea from. You don't need to be a villain to understand all about villainy. You only need to be a Deputy Chairman of Quarter Session, a Circuit judge in the Crown Court, or a Red Judge on circuit, to know all about the real world. And don't forget, you've been at the Bar before that. When I was a pupil in chambers I was astonished not so much by what people did. After all, I had three years at Cambridge. What astonished me was what they evidently thought they could get away with.

It is easy to understand so much disquiet about the trial by jury of large-scale fraud. It may be right that City swindles are so complex that you would not expect the ordinary Old Bailey jury to understand them. The police officers on the Fraud Squad managed it. The Director of Public Prosecutions staff managed it. On their instructions prosecuting counsel managed it, or the case would never have been launched. Was it that the jury was too thick, or that counsel has not simplified it enough to get it across? After all, the ultimate question is always, when X did so and so, was it honest or dishonest? But never mind. If the fault is in the jury, what then?

Before all jurors were made equal in 1945 there had been common juries, special juries, and City of London special juries; the two last only for civil actions. The war swept all away except juries to try crime. Special juries, which you had been able to ask for to try your spectacular libel action, and City of London special juries which you could ask for to try cases involving expertise in what went on in the City, were elitist anachronisms which were never restored.

In face of the fraud problem, can we not get back to square one? Who are Mr Fraudster X's peers? The people who work with and understand the City system. So when you have that sort of case, try X by a jury of his peers, a random sample of these people. There's no need to resort to judge alone plus skilled lay assessors. Of course two lay assessors are better than being by yourself. The strength and limitations of that system we know all about in the Employment Appeals Tribunal. So make sure you impanel a jury that knows the score and can cope, but stick to twelve to reduce the off-day factor, and leave the judge his proper function in trying crime, to see fair play as the trial goes alone, and put it fairly on the jury's plate in summing-up. Trial by your peers is the key.

7. Language

During your legal education you are required to devote time and attention to the drafting of what are called 'pleadings'. These are the documents in which are formulated and set out the statement of claim, and defence, and if necessary further matters which form the skeleton on which civil cases are prepared for trial. The formal indictment performs an equivalent function in a criminal prosecution. The Rules of Court tell you in simple language what you have to do. You are to state the facts on which your client relies as giving rise to his cause of action. At the receiving end you are to say whether he denies or admits the facts stated against him, to state any facts on which your client intends to rely which cast a different light on what is in issue, and to say, if you think it is open to you to do so, that even if he has got his facts right, as a matter of law they do not give him a cause of action.

Until 1856 that would have been too easy. The drafting of pleadings was a then complicated and formalised fandango, the slightest mistake in the course of which might cost your client his case. So you followed precedents with infinite care. A most important part of your pupillage was to copy out your pupil-master's pleadings, so that you could adapt them for your own use. A finer arrangement for the perpetuation of archaic language could hardly be worked out, unless it is the preservation of criminal statutes passed in the middle of the nineteenth century, and the use of their terminology in the drafting of indictments, and in telling juries what has to be proved before someone can be convicted of the offences those statutes enshrine.

English lawyers tend to be conservative in their professional outlook. It would be surprising if they were not when you remember that the Common Law has evolved through respect for previous decisions of the courts. So in spite of the changes in the Rules, starting in 1856 and culminating in the present Rules of Court, and designed to take the mumbo jumbo out of pleadings, you will still

157

find in pleadings today terminology which outside pleadings has been extinct for a hundred years, if indeed it ever existed outside pleadings at all.

When you draft a defence it is wise to include a final paragraph which denies everything you have not expressly admitted. Too often it takes the form: 'Save as herein before admitted each and every allegation contained in the Statement of Claim is denied as if it had been specifically set out and traversed seriatim.' The pleader has seen that memorable but ridiculous phrase in someone else's precedent. So had the someone else in someone else's. It is much less hard work to follow and adapt precedent than to think through and then express your claim in plain language.

Perhaps in the context of pleadings it does not matter very much. Maybe there my complaint is about style, because the lawyers know what one another are on about even if to the layman it looks ridiculous or incomprehensible, or both. The evil is that there is a tendency for young counsel who has been conscientiously drafting pleadings for his pupil-master to find himself the prisoner of archaic language when he finds himself on his feet in court. Again perhaps in the context of trial by judge alone it does not matter very much. The judge is familiar with archaic language and understands what young counsel is on about even if to him it sounds ridiculous. The presence of a wig upon your head changes your perspectives about the ridiculous anyway. It is when young counsel has a jury in play that you are in trouble. Young counsel, trapped in archaic terminology, asks the witness a question in terms which to that witness, who has not had the benefit of an expensive education, are incomprehensible; for example, 'What were you doing at the relevant time?' Look of total incomprehension on witness's face. So the judge intervenes. 'He means, what were you doing at a quarter past three?' Sigh of relief from the jury, though the sharper members knew what counsel meant.

Or counsel addresses the jury: 'Members of the jury, it is beyond a peradventure that this defendant could have been at the material place at the material time.' The judge must not interrupt counsel's address to the jury, so there is no cure for the look of incomprehension that that is calculated to produce. The material place and the material time can be a bit difficult. But what are you to make of 'beyond a peradventure'? It is an expression you will hear over and over again in court. Whoever heard it or read it anywhere else? All it means is 'certainly'. Why not say so?

Long words, even if they are not archaic, can be an occupational hazard for judges and have led to misunderstanding even between two people as highly educated as Circuit judge and young lady counsel, in the days when young lady counsel were rare birds, and leaders in a real breakthrough into male chauvinist territory. The scene: a provincial County Court. Young lady counsel's client in the witness-box, being examined by her in chief. His appearance, collar-length hair, Lon Chaney moustache, ear-rings, jeans, trainers, the lot, indicate that his way of life is far removed from the Circuit judge's way of life: three-piece suit, black shoes, watch chain, query bowler hat.

Client in witness-box is chewing gum. This is a common problem and a real one because it makes the evidence difficult to hear. One common way to resolve it is for judge to invite the witness to park his gum so that what he has to say can be the more readily appreciated. The witness will then park it on the underside of the witness-box counter, where it may take later witnesses by surprise.

Our judge did not use that method. He fixed young lady counsel with a look of marked disapprobation, and said, 'Miss So-and-So, your client appears to be masticating in the witness-box.' Miss So-and-So, without a moment's hesitation: 'Take your hands out of your pockets immediately, young man.'

Another great danger, more for administrators than for counsel, is to use the pro forma letter in circumstances to which it is inappropriate. An illustration of this arose from a very sad case on the Northern Circuit. A male nurse of irreproachable character was married and had a boy and a girl, aged respectively about thirteen and eleven. He was a pillar of his local church, doing the odd jobs and looking after the electrical wiring and so on. He lived in Cemetery Cottage. The accommodation was limited and he and his wife decided that it was wrong for the children at that age to continue to share the same bedroom. The only answer they could find was to board the boy with his maternal grandfather, who lived next to the pub.

The difference between father's and grandfather's way of life

mirrored the difference between living in Cemetery Cottage and next
to the pub. To the boy's parents' distress, it amused grandfather to
get him on the beer. They remonstrated, to no effect. The day came
when grandfather got the boy on so much beer that the results were
later unmistakable. Father went round to have it out with grandfather,
and was met with laughter. He lost his self-control and there was a
fight which finished up with grandfather dead.

Father was arrested and charged with murder. When the case came
on for trial the prosecution very rightly accepted his plea of not guilty
of murder but guilty of manslaughter on the grounds of provocation.
His sentence was in the order of three years' imprisonment. The judge
clearly took the view that the provocation was extreme and that it
was a strictly one-off disaster. Not long after his reception in prison
to serve his sentence, father received a letter from the nursing
organisation of which he was a member, in these terms:

> I am writing to inform you that your case was placed before the
> Committee at its recent meeting. It was agreed that the matter does
> constitute professional misconduct, but after careful consideration of all
> the circumstances it was decided not to take any further action.
> However, the Committee strongly deprecate such behaviour on the part
> of a qualified nurse. They would appreciate a written assurance from
> you that a similar incident will not occur again, since such things tend
> to impair the trust the public place in our profession.

Not to say what you mean in plain language which is normally used
by those with whom you are in communication is stupid. Of course
what is plain language to the Law Lords includes much that is not
plain language to a 21-year-old juror whose skills lie in the
diagnosis and cure of the troubles from which dishwashers suffer
rather than in the analysis of legal concepts. In Bristol there is a
famous thoroughfare called the Hotwells Road, which runs beside
the Avon where the statue of Mr Plimsoll, inventor of the Line,
broods over the entry to the Floating Harbour. The glory of the
Georgian and Regency houses in the Hotwells Road has long since
departed. Lodging-houses is what many of them have come to.

On a hot summer Sunday a tough but lonely man made friends
in one of the waterside pubs with a couple who were living in a room
on the second floor of one of the Hotwells Road lodging-houses.

After an agreeable lunch-time session on the beer the three, at closing time, armed themselves with an additional crate and adjourned to the room. There they settled down to a happy afternoon out of the sun. In due course hydraulic pressure made itself felt, and the loner relieved it out of the open window, because the mod con when installed had been sited inconveniently for the second-floor front room.

As ill luck would have it, the owner of the house was in conference on the pavement below with the manager, later to describe himself in the witness-box as Hell's Angel retired. An explanation was demanded. The explanation given by the loner, whom I was able later to describe to the jury as obviously Skin Head retired, was unsatisfactory. The consequent fight raged round the adjacent streets, to finish with a prosecution of the manager for 'causing grievous bodily harm with intent, contrary to section 18 of the Offences against the Person Act', eighteen-fifty something.

Prosecuting counsel opened the case in language of great dignity, entirely appropriate for the House of Lords. The loner then gave evidence. He was not bright and was incapable of telling the jury what had happened without nudging from counsel. Finally after he had stuck at the critical moment, counsel asked, 'Did you then urinate out of the window?' Blank incomprehension, so that I was driven to intervene and say, 'Counsel means piss, Mr So-and-So.' After that the ice was broken, we were all on net, and the rest of the trial went off splendidly.

8. Dress

The judges of the superior courts in the Western World, and in the countries of the Third World whose legal systems stem from their past as colonies of the Western countries, nearly all wear in court distinguishing robes of a greater or less degree of elaboration. The English judge's outfit is highly elaborate and crowned by the horsehair wig. At the other extreme is the United States judge who wears a very plain black gown, plainer than the gown the usher wears in an English court. In addition to their working outfits, the judges in most Western countries, and in England in particular, have a more elaborate and picturesque outfit to be worn on ceremonial, as opposed to working, occasions.

In England the High Court judge's robes, both working and ceremonial, have remained in effect unchanged since the Restoration in 1660. There they all are in the portraits, quite clearly the same to this day. Before 1660 the judges, like everyone else, wore their own hair, if they still had any. On their heads they wore something called the coif, which was not unlike a skullcap worn indoors by Jews who are really Kosher.

The ermine which adorned their winter robes was functional in two respects. It kept them warm in what must have been the icy winter temperature of their courts. Like the strip of ermine with a jewelled animal's head, now a rare collector's piece, but then commonly carried by courtiers and others who had to frequent places of public resort, the ermine attracted the fleas. As a courtier you handed your strip of ermine to a flunkey who shook off the fleas and handed it back. The ermine round the neck and cuffs of your judicial robe and up the front where it does up kept the court fleas at bay.

When at the time of the Restoration judges started, like everyone else who was anyone, to wear wigs, the wig also was functional. Personal hygiene in England had not yet returned to the level enjoyed in Roman times. To reduce the risk of catching typhus through having nits in your hair you shaved your head and wore a wig.

By the time Sam Pepys acquired his first wig they had become a matter of fashion as well as hygiene. Fashion was why Sam bought his. As you will see in the National Portrait Gallery, all the nobs, including the judges, wore enormous wigs on the general pattern which the judge's full-bottomed wig follows to this day, hairy spaniel's ears down both sides of your face. This is the origin of the expression 'big-wigs', now rather overtaken by the dirty word 'elitist'. These wigs were not very practical if instead of holding the floor yourself you had to listen to what other people had to say, as the judges did. So for their working dress they assumed the bob-wig, something which was to lead to a particular ladies' hairstyle introduced in the nineteen-twenties being called a bob. The bob-wig, with no spaniel's ears to obstruct your hearing, was what people other than the nobs used to wear.

As time went by and we worked slowly back towards the Roman standard of hygiene, so the nobs abandoned their wigs in favour of their own hair and shampoo. When war became a serious business with the French Revolution, wigs were abandoned by the Army and the Navy. The military haircut familiar in twentieth-century wars is again a matter of hygiene, because shampoo and the necessary water were seldom available in active service conditions, and typhus remained a killer. The Church of England abandoned wigs at about the time of Queen Victoria's accession. In the great painting of her coronation, the Archbishop of Canterbury is wearing a bob-wig, but that was the last of it. Now it is only the lawyers who although they use shampoo for their hair are so totally conservative that as part of their outfit in which to do justice in the superior courts they still wear the wig.

Wigs are very labour-intensive to make, and so now are very expensive indeed. This is not a serious matter for a judge, but because the Bar is expected to wear wigs when the judge does, having to get his wig can be a very serious matter for the young barrister, who has got through his legal education on scholarships and local authority grants. Is the wig really necessary? Is it even a good thing?

That it is not really necessary does not admit of serious argument. The Judicial Committee of the House of Lords does not wear wigs. It does not even wear robes. Except for United Kingdom judges and the judges of some of the countries that were our colonies, no judges, however elaborate their outfits and whatever they may have by way of fancy hats not worn in court, wear wigs; not even the Americans, who share so much of our law and our legal tradition.

In hot summer weather in courts without air-conditioning wigs off is a common cry even in conservative England. The Court of Appeal has found it possible to get on with the job bare-headed. Faced in the Victorian courtroom in Birmingham with a Queen's Counsel who was obviously at risk of heat stroke, I even had gowns and coats off as well as wigs. The world did not come to an end. No wigs in the Courts of Appeal in Guernsey and Jersey. At County Quarter Sessions, where much of the work now done by the Crown Court was done pre-Beeching, no robes at all, except the Bar, and you got on perfectly well. So justice has been, is, and can be done perfectly well without wigs.

Are wigs a good thing? Here we move from the realm of fact into opinion. I think not. They may be a good thing for the Bar. In this as in other respects the Bar is well capable of looking after itself. But for judges? Because I think wigs to be a bad thing I may not do justice to the arguments in their favour. These I understand be as follows:

1. The wig enhances the dignity of the court.

2. The wig promotes a sense of authority in the judicial process, so that you feel you are being tried not so much by a fallible human being as by an embodiment of the law itself.

3. The wig is traditional, and we should cherish, not tamper with our traditions. We tamper with them at our peril.

The iconoclast would retort, what's undignified about the House of Lords, or the Supreme Court of the United States, or any of the other superior courts in which wigs are not worn? Do the English courts become less dignified when it's wigs off in hot weather? Does not the dignity of the court depend on how the judge behaves, not how he is dressed? It's his behaviour that sets the tone for the behaviour of everyone in court.

Is it a good thing for the judge to be anonymous? Should you promote the idea that he is an embodiment of the law itself when everyone knows he is a human being dealing with human beings, not a computer programmed with the law so that when you press the buttons appropriate to the instant problem out comes the right answer? Your whole function as a judge, embodied in the word itself, is to do something no computer can do, that is, exercise judgement. A computer can no more exercise judgement in producing an answer to what is put into it than it can temper its answer with mercy. If the concept of anonymity means that the judge would prefer not to be recognised when he is out of the court context and in plain clothes, while you may sympathise is it really a consideration which should be given priority? When you consider how and why judges started to wear wigs, is it really right to think in terms of destroying a valuable tradition? The Archbishop of Canterbury no longer wears one. Is it not the robes, rather than the wig, which enshrine the tradition?

For six years at County Quarter Sessions, for five years in the Channel Islands, and off and on for nine years in the Employment Appeal Tribunal, I performed the judicial function bare-headed, and indeed other than in the islands, without robes. I did not find any difference in atmosphere or in the way you controlled the court from when I sat in robes and wig. It is how you are seen, where you sit, how you behave that matters, not how you are dressed. If you present as undignified or inadequate, putting you in robes and a wig will not cure it, but only make it worse.

But there is a more important consideration. Sometimes when you are the Red Judge dealing with crime you have to pass a severe sentence. This must be very unpleasant for the defendant in the dock. I think it is important that you should if possible get the message through to him that you are doing so because it is the only answer you can see to the problem which he presents to society; that you are not simply an establishment fancy sentencing automatic machine, so that when the jury says 'guilty of robbery', out comes five years.

If the defendant understands why you are doing what you are doing to him there is at least a chance that he may accept it, and go straight in the future. I accept of course that this may not happen very often. Many villains are not perceptive people. Many who have just been convicted of a serious offence will be in shock. But if you can get it across even once that you are as human as he is and are doing what you are because for the reasons which you give you think it is the right answer, it is I think well worth while. It involves establishing communication between defendant and judge, so that he knows you see him as a person, and are treating him as such. It is not generally easy to achieve. That you have a seventeenth-century pattern horsehair wig on your head makes it, I think, that much more difficult.

At assizes it was, as I have already mentioned, the convention that the judges moved between their lodgings and the court in ceremonial procession every day, only slightly less ceremoninal on Day Two and later than on Day One when the assize service was taken in en route. It was all part of the seven days' wonder of Her Majesty's judges bringing her justice to all the counties in the kingdom, however modest, and it was obviously right that they should go to and fro in robes. They represented the sovereign, and no one, except another judge in robes, was allowed to sit on the back seat of the limo with them. The High Sheriff had to manage his sword, and, if a cavalry-man, his spurs, as best he could on a jump seat. There was always a police car or motor-cycle escort. In Manchester a Special Branch officer rode shotgun with the driver with his pistol in a shoulder holster. Many years before, a disappointed Mancunian litigant had shot the County Court judge, happily without fatal results. Trumpets sounded on Day One as you arrived at church or at court or both. It might be the High Sheriff's own regiment, or at Winchester the Green Jackets, or the Royal Marines. At Nottingham I was once welcomed with a splendid fanfare by the Boy Scouts. It was all proper and romantic and impressive and, as I have said, sometimes the older members of the public doffed their caps as you drove past.

With the Crown Court all is changed. The Red Judge in all but the modest centres is a permanent presence even though he is not always the same judge. High Sheriff and Under Sheriff are no longer on parade every day. The journey to and from court is now part of the daily scene for the citizens, no longer a seven days' wonder. When the limo is held up in traffic alongside old bangers containing younger members of the public, they have no caps to doff and are often unable to contain their amusement at what they see alongside. And yet, bar the iconoclasts and, where walking to court is geographically feasible, bar those who want the exercise and walk, Her Majesty's judges on circuit still drive solemnly to and fro in limos which have to be large enough to accommodate their clerks, and marshals if they have them, on the jump seat. The modern limo is designed to knock off your wig as you get out unless you are very careful. Entry and exit in robes is difficult to achieve with dignity even if you don't lose your wig. In slippery weather there is usually a police lady on the pavement to rescue you as you fall.

Why do we do it? From the security point of view it makes you a most obvious target. You can't pretend you are a visiting VIP whom no one wants to shoot. You can perfectly well go to court, on foot or on wheels, simply as the French say *en gentleman*. If you are entertaining people from court to lunch with you they can ride to and fro without sharing the back seat. You will not disappoint Her Majesty's loyal subjects because on Day One you will travel with full assize ceremonial. If it became the convention thereafter to move unrobed it could result in significant economies. I have done my best by example. I have had no more success than I have in my efforts to establish that wigs are wrong. Over to my successors, and good luck.

9. Audience

The law courts in Rome and throughout the Roman Empire enjoyed the services of trained advocates to assist their professional judges to get the right answer to the problems which came before them. When the Roman administration of justice came to an end with the end of Roman rule in Britain, advocacy in Britain came to an end as well. When Henry II firmly re-established the rule of law in England by sending his judges to do royal justice round the shires when he could not go himself, the situation was restored in which advocates were needed if justice was to be done efficiently.

By the fourteenth century you find in the reports just the sort of dialogue in argument on points of law between the Bar and the judges that you can hear today, only terser. By the end of the fifteenth century, the Inns of Court had organised themselves into training and disciplinary bodies, and the judges, who had the right and the obligation to control the proceedings in their courts, had accorded sole rights of audience to the members of the four Inns and the members of Serjeants' Inn, now defunct. In this way the judges were able to assure themselves that cases would be conducted in court before them by advocates trained in the appropriate skills, and subject to the appropriate disciplines. Justice could then be done promptly and efficiently, something which is only possible where there is trust between Bench and Bar.

If you want advice about the law and how it bears upon a difficulty in which you find yourself, you can go and look up the book and work on a do-it-yourself basis. You can go to a lay friend. You can go to a solicitor. You can keep a tame lawyer of your own who works exclusively for you and may be either a solicitor or a barrister. You can run your own legal department staffed by several of them. You are not likely to have your own on the strength unless you are a large undertaking. When Val Homes retired from the Bar he became legal adviser to one of the great oil companies, and after he died he was succeeded by Hartley Shawcross, ex-Attorney-General.

If it's advice you are after, anyone can advise you. But if you have a problem which has to go to court, you can either conduct the case yourself, or you must go to a solicitor who will instruct counsel to conduct the case for you in court. In England and Wales that has been so ever since the sixteenth century, and it is so because the intervention of those who are amateurs in the art of advocacy is not conducive to the efficient administration of justice.

The judge who is faced with a litigant in person on one side and competent counsel on the other will find that he has to intervene in order to try to prevent the imbalance which that produces. Once you intervene in the conduct of the case you are at risk of losing your impartiality, or, which is nearly as bad, of being thought to lose it by the party represented by counsel against whom your intervention seems to be directed. It is wrong that you should have to act in part as advocate, not wholly as judge.

I had on one occasion to try with a jury a libel action brought against Mrs X, a widow, who thought that her late husband's fellow Masons had behaved badly towards him, and wrote a letter about it. One of them sued her. He was represented by counsel, instructed by solicitors. The pleading in which her defence was set out had been prepared by counsel for her and raised, as I remember, the defence of Qualified Privilege. So the issues which the jury had to decide were not simple, and much would depend on how her case was conducted in court.

She could not afford to instruct counsel at the trial. Although the action was brought against her, and she had not started it, because it was a defamation action she could not get legal aid. Why not? Because in 1948 Parliament, fearful of gold-digging plaintiffs and solicitous for the pockets of the newspaper proprietors, said so. Mrs X was entirely incapable of conducting her defence in court, let alone conducting it to the best advantage, and yet it was clear to me that her case called for serious consideration by the jury. To try to ensure that justice was done, I had to weigh in and to a large extent conduct it for her.

It was not easy. I had not been briefed, and had to pick it up as we went along. When it came to the summing-up I had to explain very carefully to the jury that I had taken that active part in the trial which might have surprised them simply because, as she was a litigant in person, in this complicated field there was no other way of getting her defence before them for their consideration. It was not that I was taking sides. Now would they please consider it.

It is the lay members of the Employment Appeals Tribunal, and the judges who have sat with them, who are probably best qualified to appreciate the value of good advocacy. Everyone has right of audience. The articulate layman can be the most trying. We had a splendid lady of Mitropan origin who complained of unfair dismissal by the Science Museum. Her case was that the reason for her dismissal was that she had refused to teach Russian or accord her sexual favours to the management. She had not succeeded in establishing this before the Industrial Tribunal. In order to make any sense of the appeal we had to let her talk uninterrupted for a whole day. Next day she was easily kept to the point.

Next most trying was a case which was conducted on both sides by two in-house solicitors. There was a respectable point on appeal. Neither had seen it. There were one or two specialist solicitors who were good. Most of the do-it-yourself solicitors were not. There were some excellent trade union officials, and some who were grossly incompetent. One brash young man applied for an order which as a matter of law he couldn't get. I told him so. 'I know,' he said, 'but my union wants it and what the unions want will be the law to-morrow.' Counsel varied in quality but the best of them, tempering what tended to be a dreary subject with humour, were a joy.

In all but the simplest cases, preparation for trial calls for the exercise of skills quite distinct from, though complementary to, the skills required for its presentation in court. While I was Queen's Counsel I was consulted by north country solicitors on behalf of an undertaking which constructed marine engines. They had come to the conclusion that they must sack their managing director whom they had engaged on a ten-year contract two years before, and who they thought was running them into the ground. How much would it cost? They realised they had made a dreadful mistake in engaging him.

I asked what had gone wrong, and I was then given a long catalogue of sins of commission and omission on his part. 'If you are in a position to prove that,' I said, 'you can sack him tomorrow and will be justified in doing so. The only trouble is that he will sue you, and such actions are difficult and expensive to fight successfully.'

'We can prove it,' they said. 'It's all there in the company documents.'

I told them that if they decided to fight him it would mean putting the company's operations for the two years he had been in charge under the microscope. They must produce a précis of everything he had done wrong in narrative form, in date order, cross-referenced to the documents and to the statements of anyone whose oral evidence would be needed to prove anything. I warned them that it would be laborious and costly. I suggested that the solicitors should put their brightest young man on to it full-time, and that he must have direct access to everybody and every document he asked for. I told them that if the decision to dismiss and fight was taken, they must move fast, because they would be required to put on paper in their pleadings chapter and verse of what they relied on to justify the dismissal.

After this initial strategic consultation I forgot all about it. In Andrew Bateson I had a highly competent junior counsel who could be relied on to look after the interlocutory tactics to the best advantage, and the solicitors were clearly fully competent.

The case was to be tried starting in October. In the early summer, having had a look at the material the solicitors had produced, Andrew and I went up to the north to have to look at the engines in order to understand what the documents were talking about. Large marine diesels are not all that easy to appreciate from drawings and photographs. You have for example a power stroke in both directions of movement of the pistons. There were some loose ends to clear up, and we thought a visit would be cheering for the clients' morale. I got back from holiday on 1st September, to find awaiting me three bundles of documents with over 1,000 pages in each, plus the pleadings, plus some witness statements. The documents were what mattered. They were the material on which the managing director had to be cross-examined and broken.

I spent the whole of September working on the case. Everybody had done a splendid preparation job. They had been quite right, it was all there. When the case was called on and opened on behalf of the managing director, the judge, as I had expected, exhibited signs of encouragment and sympathy in his direction. The plaintiff gave his evidence in chief with confidence. This was brave of him if he had read the documents, which had of course all been disclosed to his advisers. After I had cross-examined him for several days the judge asked counsel to see him in his room. He made it clear to my opponent that his case was in tatters, and would it not be wise to try to seek a compromise? My clients were perfectly happy to pay him a sum, modest in comparison with what they would have had to pay if they had lost, in order to be able to go back to making engines instead of spending their time in court, and so the matter came to an end.

Now I suppose, given time, that I could have done the preparatory work myself. But those who had done the preparatory work so well at solicitor level were simply not trained to deploy the material they produced in such a way that a case which, fought to a finish, must have taken at least two months, was cracked in three weeks. It would have been a ridiculous waste of my advocate's skills to spend the thick end of a year on digging out and collating the raw materials. Properly understood, the functions of solicitor and counsel in the field of litigation are distinct, and complementary. Properly exploited, the process is efficient and economical.

The illustration I have given was an extreme case. But even in a simple criminal case there is a real difference in function. The solicitor and his staff must get the story out of an often inarticulate client. They must do the detective work which may arise from the telling, or from examination of the prosecution statements. They must reduce what they have got to intelligible instructions. The skills required are quite different from the skills required to exploit their instructions in court. It was very salutory to a qualified barrister with even modest experience of advocacy to find himself acting during Hitler's war as defending officer at courts martial. You had to do the solicitor's and the advocate's work all yourself. It was a sharp lesson that we are not all Leonardos.

The solicitors' profession first became fully organised in the nineteenth century. You get a glimpse of how things were in *Pickwick Papers*, with nice Mr Perker, Mr Pickwick's solicitor, looking after him in the breach of promise action in which Serjeant Phunky was his counsel, though it was Serjeant Buzfuz who is the one who is best remembered. Periodically since then it has been proposed that the demarcation between the two parts of the profession should in the public interest be abolished or reduced. In the mid-nineteenth century the then Solicitor-General vigorously backed such a proposal. More recently it was one of the aspects of the provision of legal services to the community examined by the Benson Commission, chaired by a distinguished accountant and manned by a team well able to consider the questions without partisan prejudices.

One of the main cries of those who argue for fusion of the two branches of the profession in England is that there is no separate Bar in the United States. Chief Justice Warren Burger of the Supreme Court who was visiting England during the commission's operations, gave evidence before them. He said that both in the Federal and State jurisdictions probably only about half the lawyers appearing in the courts were really qualified to represent their clients properly and to move the case along adequately. He said that cases were dealt with more quickly in British courts than in American. The judge almost by definition has been one of the leading members of the Bar, and the advocates appearing before him are trained in the same way as the judge was trained. Even if you have a very experienced judge and he has two mediocre, badly turned, or untrained advocates before him, he has difficulty.

At first it sounds paradoxical that a system which requires you to use two lawyers instead of one if you have to go to court should be cheaper and more efficient. But consider. In 1960, Mr X, who lives in Hicksville, New York State, thinks he has been libelled. He goes to the firm of lawyers in Hicksville who handle his regular commercial and family legal business, Y and Co. Y and Co. are a modest firm set up to handle the normal problems their clients can be expected to meet in life and business. None of the partners has any specialised knowledge of the law of defamation or the strategic and tactical handling of defamation actions. I use defamation as an example of a field in which the law and the tactics are more complex than in ordinary personal injury or commercial litigation. Other examples are patents and copyright, industrial secrecy, and things of that nature which do not pose problems for such as Mr X in the ordinary way, and, like defamation, really call for specialist handling.

Y and Co are placed in a dilemma. Either they must handle Mr X's problem themselves, which they have not the necessary skills to do efficiently, or they must say to Mr X: 'Sorry, we can't handle this. Go to Z and Co, a big firm in New York City, who have an expert in this field, Mr A, who is also an advocate and who is well qualified to handle it for you.'

Because Z and Co have to carry the overheads of having Mr A on the strength as a specialist in the defamation field and in advocacy, their services will inevitably be very expensive. Y and Co may also feel that, having had to tell Mr X that they cannot handle his problem themselves, he might think that he might as well have gone to Z and Co in the first place, and that they are going to lose a client.

Compare Mr Smith in Hemel Hempstead who, like Mr X in 1960, thinks he has been libelled. He goes to Mr Jones, his family solicitor. Mr Jones says, 'We must go to counsel. If you have a case, you will need counsel to conduct it. The current experts are Colin Duncan, Neville Faulks, Helenus Milmo. You will get as good advice as there is for a modest fee, and we will take it from there.' Mr Jones has no temptation to undertake something he is not fit to handle. Because of the existence and intervention of Mr Jones, counsel's overheads are modest. Unlike Mr A, who on the work coming to a single firm will hardly be fully occupied in his special fields, counsel is economically occupied full-time in the exercise of his special skills as a defamation expert and an advocate.

Other things being equal, who is going to get the better service in all respects from his lawyers, Mr X or Mr Smith?

Why, you may ask, if the English system is superior, does it not exist in the United States? The answer lies in history. The Bar, with exclusive right of audience in the superior Courts of England and Wales and organised through the Inns of Court to educate and discipline its members, existed at the time of the first American settlements from England. Francis Drake and Walter Raleigh were both at one time in their careers student members of the Middle Temple. The lawyer settlers were brought up in the English tradition, and until Independence maintained close links with England. Five of the signatories of the Declaration of Independence were members of the Middle Temple. But the communities which they served were small and scattered. There was no progress of the King's judges on assize bringing the royal justice periodically round the colonial settlements, scattered not over England and Wales but originally up and down the eastern seaboard and then spreading over a continent.

The lawyer put his Blackstone's Commentaries in his saddle-bag and rode off to do his best to be a Leonardo, in face of problems which in the early days in frontier communities were relatively simple. The advocates were scattered. Each state had its capital. There was no equivalent of London where you could organise yourselves into a collegiate set-up for education and discipline. The judges in the scattered communities had to do the best they could to do justice with the help of whatever advocates were available to help them. Consequently you never got a separate Bar or the efficency in the public interest, so well recognised by Chief Justice Warren Burger and my Indiana Federal Judge, that goes with it.

Benson, after hearing evidence from everyone who wanted to talk about it, reported that subject to minor modifications the present division of function of the two parts of the profession was in the public interest. After so recent a pronouncement by an independent and authoritative body which had made such a thorough examination of the problem it was surprising to find the BBC in January 1986 painting a picture thus of the two parts of the profession which from the outside is difficult to recognise.

The Bar, an outwardly powerful body, faces the insecurity of misunderstanding by a sceptical public. Its independence is regarded by some as vital to society. Others see it as the most exclusive closed shop in the country. Wearing the wig and gown makes the Bar assume a feeling of superiority. It is fighting on the defensive against the solicitors who seek to invade its valuable monopoly of audience in the superior courts. The solicitors, shorn of their valuable monopoly of conveyancing, are trying to horn in on the Bar's monopoly to compensate for the effect upon their remuneration. The witty phrase 'Bar Wars' is coined as the title for the picture, and for good measure it is stressed that the motives of both parties are purely mercenary.

You really do ask yourself, is this the view of a sceptical public? Does the public really forget that what the Bar and the solicitors, each in their own way, are there to do is not to line their pockets but in the public's own interest to further the administration of justice?

Both the Bar and the solicitors have a problem, which did not exist before 1948. Till then there was legal aid for divorce for members of the services which was not intended to cover the outgoings of solicitors and counsel concerned. It gave them only token remuneration. There was a very modest amount of legal aid in criminal cases. The Bar and the solicitors operated in a free market situation, paid for by their clients. This meant of course that by and large the poor had to go without the services of the profession except through charity, but it also meant that both the Bar and the solicitors were fully independent of central and local government except for such of them as were in full-time government employment, not in private practice.

The Legal Aid and Advice Act of 1948, and the great increase in legal aid in criminal cases, changed all that. From then on the greater part of the work in what is now the Family Division of the High Court, and in the Criminal Courts, is funded by Central Government. To a lesser degree, civil litigation is also conducted with the help of legal aid, if you have insufficient resources yourself and your insurers or your trade union will not undertake your case for you. This means that a very significant proportion of the remuneration of run-of-the-mill counsel and solicitors comes from the public purse. As you would expect, the amount of fees from that source is not a matter of free negotiation between counsel, solicitor, and Central Government administrators. It is fixed by officers of the Court, who in deciding what the work is worth in each case, work within Central Government guidelines.

When the legal aid system as we know it was set up, it was deliberately intended to safeguard counsel's and solicitor's independence, and to ensure that although the money would come from Central Government, that fact was not to interfere with their traditional relations with their clients and with the court. There was to be no elaborate administrative structure like that which had been created to run the National Health Service. Not only was the profession to retain its independence, but by leaving it to do its own administration the whole set-up was to be cost-effective and economical. In the first few years it was the Law Society's proud, if apocryphal, boast that the cost of legal aid was no more than the cost of the corks in the medicine bottles of the NHS.

But if you are paid by the state can you ever remain independent of the state? It is only the Act of Settlement, following the Glorious Revolution, which secured the independence of the judges, who may have to tell ministers of the Crown that they have done something unconstitutional and they must stop. The current problem for the Bar and the solicitors, those of them the bulk of whose remuneration is earned under legal aid, is this. The enormous increase in serious crime, and to a less degree in family disputes which have to be resolved by the Courts, has produced an increase in the bill for professional services which Central Government has to meet. The increase is so great that Central Government has to have a hard look at things to see whether the bill cannot be reduced by reducing the fees. This is alarming for those who carry the heat and burden of the work and maintain a modest but respectable standard of living. Not for them the astronomical brief fee, or arrival at court in a Rolls Royce.

The state-funding problem is common to both branches of the profession. Because court work normally forms a smaller part of a solicitor's firm's total practice than it does for the Bar, who operate as individuals, its potential impact on solicitors is less. It remains to be seen the extent to which the loss of the conveyancing monopoly will hurt. But it seems very odd that anyone should suppose the two branches of the profession to be at war, as the 'Bar Wars' witticism was calculated to suggest. I know many ex-barristers who have become solicitors because that is the work they like. I know several ex-solicitors who have become successful barristers because advocacy is the work they like. There is now no difficulty in the way of moving from one branch of the profession to the other except the practical difficulty: for the barrister to find the firm that will take him to its heart: for the solicitor to steel himself to face leaving the relative financial security of his existing scene and plunge into the total financial insecurity which faces every beginner who wants to go to the Bar.

The grass on the other side of the hill tastes different no doubt.

To those who want to be advocates the Bar is the place to be. But for a few, you won't make a fortune on either side of the hill, though on the solicitors' side you are closer to where the money is and where business changes hands. For the top solicitors the sky is the limit. Think of Lord Goodman, back-room boy for governments and head of an Oxford College. For the top counsel, you too may become a lord. Even as a High Court judge your salary, while it may be a come down from your Bar turn-over, will maintain you in modest comfort, and if you live and work long enough you are cushioned in old age. It's the people who want the grass on both sides of the hill at once who make the noises. I doubt if there are very many of them.

PART FIVE

Air Experience

1. Beginnings

Hitler's war occupied some twelve per cent of my working career. Lord Devlin is reported to have observed that reformers must accept that judges, like any other body of elderly men who had lived on the whole unadventurous lives tended to be old-fashioned in their ideas. Is he right? Lord Devlin was almost fifteen when World War I ended, 34 and indispensable to the public service as counsel in 1939. But the previous generation of judges to his was exposed to World War I, from which several bore decorations for gallantry. The count of decorations for gallantry borne by my generation of judges from World War II is impressive, and life could be adventurous even without decoration. It must certainly have been a formative experience, and have affected the approach to the legal scene of the survivors. It certainly had a significant effect on mine.

In 1916 my mother was living with my grandparents at Chislehurst while my father was on his way back to England through Egypt after service in Gallipoli. One day at the tender age of three years, I was being wheeled by Nanny in my pram past Chislehurst Station on the South-Eastern and Chatham Railway to visit an aunt who lived in Bickley. In the field in the bottom of the valley, on the left of the road, there stood what must have been something like a Sopwith Pup, whose pilot had made a successful forced landing. My infant imagination was fired. The subsequent dialogue with Nanny I suppose may have been technically unenlightened, but in total the experience was formative.

By 1919 the family was firmly installed in London once more. As part of the Victory Celebrations there was a display of captured German aircraft in St James's Park. Six-year-old imagination was rekindled, and was kept burning by a brass model of a Sopwith Camel with the Lincoln Imp in the cockpit.

And so to boarding school, with paper models and drawings in the margins of textbooks, and in 1925, aged twelve, an afternoon at the

light aeroplane competitions of that year at Lympne, up the road
from our new seaside house, where the Avro Avian and the De
Havilland Moth first broke upon the world.

So now you are hooked. More models, more drawings, with Bert
Hinkler and Amy Johnson the heroes who consolidate the hold, and
then, under the aegis of the school Scientific Society, up round and
down in the front seat of a Moth at Heston, and you know you have
to do it yourself. With dual instruction in the clubs at £2 per hour
and solo at thirty shillings you can beg the means, you can borrow
the transport, and you are into your first pilot's logbook entry:

> 3 August 1934. DH 60g GAAFS. Gipsy 1 85 hp. Lympne local. Pilot
> K. K. Brown. Effect of controls and flying straight and level.

The Moth had a very low wing loading and was sensitive in heavy
hands. You found control in three dimensions less easy than the two-
dimensional handling of a car. You found that to get from A to B,
though it was a straight line and not by a road full or corners and
flocks of Romney Marsh sheep, was complicated by the fact that you
had left solid earth and were contained in an invisible fluid which
might add to its horizontal movement, almost always present though
greatly varied in speed and direction, disconcerting and often
unpredictable vertical movement, particularly disconcerting when
you were close to and endeavouring to land upon solid earth. But
as your skills were learned and each successive manoeuvre was
. mastered, although the initial romance surrounding the whole art
wore thin the satisfaction of challenge successfully met soon took its
place and kept you well and truly hooked.

> 21 Sept. 1934. Cadet G. ACSZ. Genet 140 hp. Hanworth local. 20
> mins. Self. First Solo.

After the summer near Lympne we were back in London.
Hanworth Air Park, country house in the L of a two strip grass
airfield in the suburban south-west sprawl and all among the
Metropolitan Water Board reservoirs, was accessible, and provided
dual instruction on the Avro Cadet. This was a much more refined,
powerful, and expensive aircraft than a Moth, delicate and sensitive
and a joy for the beginner to fly. With its aid the next milestone, see

my quoted logbook entry, was quickly passed after the respectable total of 10 hours 45 minutes in the air, embracing three different aircraft types. In prospect your first solo seems a bit daunting. In practice the moment comes when without any previous warning your instructor gets out at the end of a landing run and says, 'Off you go, do a couple of circuits and landings, then bring her in.'

So off you go and you do just that and there does not seem to be anything extraordinary or clever about it. The Cadet is a very kind aircraft, easier to land well than the Moth. You don't even feel that it is something calling for celebration when you get home. You set your sights on your next target, the 'A' licence.

In those days to qualify for your 'A' licence you had to have completed five hours' solo flying, you had to fly a fairly tight figure of eight pattern at ± 1,500 feet over your airfield, using, at Hanworth, a church steeple as one turning mark and a small reservoir as the other, you had to carry out a competent landing, and you had to pass an examination on a rather impractical syllabus dealing among other things with what is an aerostat and what is an aerodyne. A little homework on the book got you over the exam hurdle.

The faithful Cadet got me safely round the church steeple and the small reservoir at ± 1,500 feet, and safely back on to Hanworth grass. The logbook entry reads:

18 Dec. 34. Cadet G. ACSZ. Genet 140 hp. Hanworth local. 30 mins. Self. A licence test.

So there I was, after all of 16 hours 20 minutes' air time, a 'fully fledged' amateur civil pilot able lawfully to carry passengers, though not for reward, and to go anywhere!

2. RAF Reserve

Within six months of fledging two things became clear to the young bird. One. At thirty shillings per hour your scope, in your last year at Cambridge, to be followed by getting called to the Bar, was restricted. Of course it was fun to take up your family and your friends. You were pleased with their confidence. You hoped it might do you some good with the girls. But no way were you either by skills or resources in a 'You too can be a Lindbergh' situation. Two. The shadow of Hitler's war was looming. I had been in Germany during 1933 and 1934 and the signs were all displayed. In the spring of 1935 as part of its expansion the RAF advertised for direct entry reserve pilots with 'A' licences, ready at a small retaining fee to undertake twenty hours' flying training per year at civil flying training schools.

So here was the opportunity to increase your skills at the King's expense, and to make sure that if war came you would be doing something you enjoyed.

I answered the advertisement. There followed first a medical in Clement's Inn where you had to blow and hold up the mercury to test your resistance to anoxia. Then you were spun in a swivel chair and told to get up and walk to the window to see how giddy you got. Those are the parts I remember, though I'm sure they tested your urine. Next you went to Hendon for your air test as my logbook entry shows:

3 July 1935. Tiger Moth K 2576. Gipsy 111 120 hp. Hendon local. 25 mins. Class F.1 Reserve Test.

My first time in a service aircraft, even if only a Tiger Moth. My first meeting with a parachute. My first exposure to a small airfield with a railway embankment along one boundary and entirely surrounded by buildings. I satisfied my examining officer and

184

shortly after received the notification that I had been engaged as an Aircraftman Second Class and forthwith promoted to Sergeant, plus a money order for the retaining fee which I cashed at the W.1 Post Office in Welbeck Street. I was on my way.

In you Class F Reserve annual training in the civil schools you had hardly left behind your amateur status. The aircraft in my first fortnight in 1935 at Hanworth were the Blackburn B2 side by side seating trainers. In the succeeding years at Hatfield they were Tiger Moths. All were of civil registration, in civil livery. The management and the flying instructors were all ex-RAF, real reservists themselves. Most of the pilots under training were real reservists who had completed short service commissions and were there to keep hands in. A friend I made in 1925 was a Flight Lieutenant under whose command T. E. Lawrence had served. The proportion of Class F direct entry reservists was very small. Everyone was in civilian clothes, there were no distinctions of rank, and a modicum of service lore rubbed off on the amateurs, including such technical expressions as 'Do try to pull your finger out'.

But the training was professional, no longer simply how to get up, round and down from A to B without tears. You were into aerobatics, blind flying, then very difficult on the primary instruments alone, all you had on the light aircraft, and air photography which involved finding what you were told to photograph. You had to coax the aircraft, which were not enthusiastic about it, up to 10,000 feet and stay there for twenty minutes, with no oxygen or heating. You were taught forced landings after simulated power failure at 2,000 feet. You were required to fly to RAF stations some hundred miles off, being sensible about the weather conditions, and to bring back a certificate signed by the duty pilot with an appreciation of the quality of your landing. This proved you had been where you were told. You got confident.

After you had been up to 10,000 feet and stayed there for twenty minutes, and knew how long the whole operation took, and were used to the beauty of the view, the temptation to sport a little bit was very strong. The classic ploys from Hatfield in the Tiger Moth were aerobatics high above the East End of London and the docks; trying to overtake those crack trains of the LNER, the Silver Jubilee and the Coronation, on their straight runs north through the Fens from Peterborough; on the way home spending a little time over the nudist colony at Elstree. No one minded aerobatics over the East End. There was no air traffic control, and there was no air traffic. The Silver Jubilee and the Coronation did some 110 mph on those straights. The Tiger Moth had a notional top speed of 120 mph in level flight, but in a shallow dive you could keep up with them. Elstree was always a disappointment.

The Blackburn B2 flew like a brick. Because the seating was side by side it made the slow roll, a difficult manoeuvre for the beginner, particularly difficult. You were sitting not on, but to one side of the axis round which you were trying to roll your brick. It was very easy when inverted to allow the nose to go earthwards, and you would fall out of your roll in an inelegant and uncomfortable dive. Happily most aircraft if you will let them will sort themselves out of any tangle you can put them in other than a spin, always given enough space between you and the ground.

When I found myself at Hatfield in 1936 on Tiger Moths I said goodbye to the B2, and to Hanworth, without regret. At Hatfield we were mostly direct entry reservists, we had the Comet public house to lunch in, and things were altogether more fun. It must have been nearly the longest established civil school, and it was a noble, and still a rural, airfield. The factory was then relatively small, and on misty mornings when the start of flying was delayed you could walk out with a gun and try to shoot one of the many hares that lived on the grass. I never achieved success.

By the summer of 1938, the long run up to Munich and year four of my five-year reserve engagement, I was I think becoming slightly blasé about it all. I had even flown in a club aircraft from Heston to Le Zoute for an air rally. But now came the next step along the professional road. Because Blenheims and Fairey Battles were reaching the day bomber squadrons, their superannuated Hawker Harts were going not only to the service flying training schools, but to the civil schools as well. So in 1938, for the first time since my test in the Tiger Moth at Hendon in 1935, behold me face to face with a service aircraft once more. Very impressive it was, with its shining silver engine cowling with stub exhausts sticking out each side, its red white and blue roundels, and quite a climb to get into the cockpit.

Once there, no nonsense about ground crew swinging the propeller. They could not have reached up to it. You had a starter trolley which they plugged in, and when you pressed the button the engine turned and with luck would fire. Compared to the modest aircooled engines that had powered you so far, the Kestrel, liquid cooled, was a magnificent beast with a splendid growl. Here is the logbook entry:

25.8.38. Hart K6543. R.R. Kestrel. 560 hp. Hatfield local. 0.30. Pilot F/O Dunworth. Ex 6, 7, 8. Height 3,000'.

The Hart and its variants were charming aircraft to fly, but not all that easy. They had a rather narrow undercarriage, and if you opened the throttle incontinently on take-off they would swing vigorously. This was something new. So was the swing which could occur on landing if you were not straight into wind, and which was difficult to control with the not very efficient brakes on the rudder pedals. You could, though I never quite did, finish up with a wing tip on the ground and looking silly. They had a retractable radiator which if wound in produced a grateful warmth in the front cockpit. If you forgot to wind it in before trying to slow roll it fell in with a disconcerting bang when you were upside down. Handling Harts in the air was like handling a scaled-up Cadet, sweeter and no less sensitive and of course with much higher performance, though this is only conveyed to the pilot by the figures on his instruments. There is no difference in sensation. As every air traveller knows, when you are doing 500 mph in the back of your jet airliner for all the sensation there is you might be sitting still. In the Hart your height test was 15,000 feet instead of 10,000, but at least you could wind the radiator in to keep you warm.

After my fortnight in the summer of 1938, with Munich and the dismemberment of Czechoslovakia just round the corner, I was beginning to see myself as a hot number. In fact from the RAF point of view I was certainly not more than half baked. In addition to my four years, eight hours' flying training, I had enjoyed in 1936 five days' ground training at RAF Halton. Here half-a-dozen of us were dressed up as Sergeants, accommodated in a barrack room, and made free of the delights of the numerous Sergeants' Messes on the

camp, with beer at fourpence a pint and the real Sergeants happy
to play darts with new company. Someone told us whom we should
salute and how, and we were let loose on the range to fire Colt 4.55
automatics. But it seemed as if no one had thought through how we
should be usefully occupied for five days, and as indoctrination for
the direct entry reservist into the non-aeronautical aspects of the
RAF our five days, though very happy, were a farce. We did not
see an officer from start to finish.

Autumn 1938 meant Munich. To me it also meant more activity
as a beginner at the Bar, and less time to fly for fun. And indeed
after you had the experience of flying Harts, flying the aircraft
available in the clubs, especially in winter, was less fun than it used
to be. I had also begun to be hooked on sailing, and as a result,
pending my fifth and perhaps final fortnight of Reserve training
with its promise of more flying on Harts to come, I had only done
minutes more in the air when World War II blew up.

Among the papers you received on joining the Reserve were the
instructions on what to do in case of mobilisation. The RAF
Reserves were mobilised, so the BBC broadcasts informed me, on
1st September 1939. So with a toothbrush and pyjamas I said
goodbye to our house in Harley Street and embarked at Regents
Park Station on the underground, which took me conveniently
direct to Colindale. From there it was ten minutes walk down the
street to the guardroom at the main gate of RAF Hendon. No one
had heard about any direct entry reservists being supposed to arrive
there, and there was confusion anyway. So I homed on the
Sergeants' Mess, where I found Norman Shaw in a like case with
myself. We had a jolly evening, and slept on the settees in the
billiard room. Consultation with Station HQ next morning led to
the conclusion that, whatever the intention had been in 1935, in
1939 we were no longer required to mobilise ourselves at RAF
Hendon, and it was made clear, politely, that we were only in the
way.

'Go to the Air Ministry,' they said, 'and find out where you are
supposed to be.' So on to the underground once more.

London seemed unaffected by our night in the Hendon Sergeants'
Mess billiard room. The right bit of Air Ministry took a bit of
finding, but we ran it to earth at last in, of all places, Berkeley

Square. 'Ah,' they said, 'you should have reported to Uxbridge. We'll give you a railway warrant,' and they did. We thought this handsome, even if it was only the underground again. And so on the evening of 2nd September 1939 we arrived at Uxbridge, Lawrence's 'Mint', where to our great surprise we discovered next day we really were expected.

Quite how they got Norman and me to Uxbridge remains a mystery. It is a long way from any aircraft, though the barrack squares are splendid. Norman and I were the only direct entry reserve pilots, masquerading as Sergeants, in the place. It was the mobilisation centre for the genuine reserve tradesmen and those who in those days were unkindly known by the tradesmen as FIBACHES, *anglice* Fucking Ignorant Bloody Aircraft Hands, the RAF's faithful and invaluable hewers of wood and drawers of water. Day one, arrive, home on Sergeants' Mess, sleep in billiard room. Day two, identified by the Orderly Room, allocated beds in disused hangar brimming over with real airman reservists. Kitted out in stores. The whole outfit awaited us complete with knife, fork and spoon, housewife for sewing on buttons in emergency, and kit-bag to contain all.

There had been an administrative hitch. The outfit earmarked for No 700286 Sgt. Pilot Bristow thought he stood five feet. I noticed it. Standing six feet I could not help but notice it. I pointed out to my fellow Sergeant storekeeper that since I measured six feet it would not do for me. He only accepted this fairly obvious truth after discussion and with bad grace. I think he was upset that war had been declared on Germany that morning. So I continued for another couple of days to operate dressed discreetly *en gentleman*. At Uxbridge Norman and I were a pair of total anomalies. But when I finally did get my uniform it was 1939 vintage with collar and tie instead of a 1925 vintage button-up-to-the-Adam's-apple job like Norman's.

On day five triumph at last. The Orderly Room had worked out that the two anomalies were to go to No 9 Service Flying Training School at Hullavington in Wiltshire. Railway warrants again, and this time, complete with kit bags, overcoats, the lot, with toothbrush and pyjamas well submerged, we set out. Walk to Uxbridge Station. Change at West Drayton for local train to Reading. Change at Reading for main line to Swindon. Change at Swindon for local train to Hullavington. There, as a foretaste of things to come, there was a truck to take us to the camp. This was welcome. The odyssey had taken all day, and had disadvantages, though you could sit on your kit-bag in the corridor while enjoying the unexpired portion of the day's ration. That is how we got to the opening of the new chapter, in which the half-baked were fully baked, and the amateurs became professionals.

3. Training

Before 1935, the RAF pilot back-up consised of the real reservists, who had finished their short service engagements, a small number of direct entry commissioned reservists called the Reserve of Air Force Officers, who did an annual period of flying training, the University Air Squadrons, whose members undertook a reserve training obligation, and the Auxiliary Air Force squadrons, whose target was to achieve efficiency as great as the regular squadrons. In 1935 the Class F direct entry reserve, my lot, NCOs for economy, was invented to help provide back-up for the RAF as then being expanded in face of Hitler's impending war. In 1936 the Volunteer Reserve came into being, much more ambitious than Class F, with town centres to create local patriotism, flying training from scratch, good ground training, and tight organisation. Many of our lot transferred, anxious for more than the Class F twenty hours' flying a year.

On mobilisation, the RAFO reservists, our lot, the university air squadron boys, and some of those on the RAFVR who were beyond the elementary flying stage, were all fed into the RAF training set-up at the service flying training school stage. That is why Norman and I, after some vicissitudes, found ourselves at No 9 SFTS Hullavington.

No 9 SFTS Hullavington was housed in a superb 1935 expansion camp, built, hangars and all, of Bath stone. It had been the show station to which the foreign air attachés were taken, to see how well the RAF could do it. It was admirably laid out, with buildings which reflected credit on the architect, and which were supplied with all mod cons. Our course however was housed in the huts which had accommodated the direct entry Acting Pilot Officers of the previous courses while their wing of the officers' mess was being built. Mod con and heating were conspicuous by their absence. Since you could see the Bath stone buildings fifty miles away in fine weather, when Norman and I arrived everyone had been busy camouflaging them with paint or nets. Though no doubt wise, it seemed a pity. The weather was lovely, and after our frustrating week we were glad to get on with some flying.

The first half of the course, the Intermediate Training Squadron, was aimed at making you a competent pilot on either single or multi-engined aircraft. At Hullavington Harts were still in use as the advanced training aircraft for pilots destined, they hoped, for single-engined operations. To your previous exercises were added more aerobatics, more navigation, more instrument flying, low flying, and flying in the dark. Those destined, they feared, for multi-engined operations were converted first on to Airspeed Oxfords, designed as advanced trainers and very effective in that role, and later Avro Ansons, in the process of being taken out of squadron service, and much too easy to fly to be good trainers. No spinning or aerobatics for them. The mystery of flying with asymmetric power, that is, on only one of your two engines, plus flying at night, were their novelties and of course handling a much larger aircraft than even the Hart if they'd done time on that.

Half your day was devoted to the air. The other half was devoted to ground training. We had a single-engined aircraft flight, half of which was in the air while the other half was in ground school, and a twin-engined flight similarly divided. In ground school you were taught the principles of flight. You learned that the aerofoil, contrary to expectation, is sucked up, not pushed up, on account of Bernoulli's Theorem. You were introduced to the impact of Isaac Newton on the art. You were taught about engines by tradesman NCOs who while no doubt superb fitters were not superb teachers. You were taught navigation, which you had been practising for years. You were taught Morse, very efficiently, to the speed of eight words per minute.

The culmination of all this effort was the Wings exam. The regular short service entry, for whom the course had been designed, did not receive their Wings until at the end of their time in the Intermediate Training Squadron they had surmounted this obstacle. We reservists all arrived with Wings. My test at Hendon in 1935 had earned me mine. But it was made very clear to us that if we did not pass the Wings exam we would be thrown out, and turned into terrestrial creatures of an inferior sort. So we set-to in ground school as well as in the air.

I had got on well, my instructors and I thought, with the Hart at Hatfield in 1938. To begin with I did not get on well with the Hart in September 1939 at Hullavington. Looking back, I think the greater part of my trouble was those minutes only in the air since the previous September, and the fact that pleasant though he was I was not in tune with my first Hullavington instructor. But after some hours in the air and a change of instructor things went better, though the log entry appreciation by the Chief Instructor of my performance when I finished the Intermediate Training Squadron stage was disappointing:

Just reached average standard. Steep turns weak. Aerobatics weak.

The ground exam was no problem, even though after passing my Bar finals in 1936 I had never expected to be in the exam situation again, or to meet, in the navigation paper, that problem which I had been unable to resolve at school about the two taps running water into a bath with the plug out.

Because we were the first war course, assembled from reservists of various sorts, we were an entertaining mixed bag. Norman and I found ourselves in company with several more Class F reservists, of all shapes and sizes, from farmer Ken Eaton, through play-

(*From left to right*) Sergeant Turner (killed 1944), Sergeant Browning (solicitor, later often Mayor of Looe), Flying Officer Hartley (later Air Marshal), Flying Officer Foxley-Norris (later Air Chief Marshal), Sergeant Heap, and Pilot Officer 'Deadeye' Howell (killed 1940).

HULLAVINGTON, December 1939.

'Night flying has been cancelled'. (Bad weather).

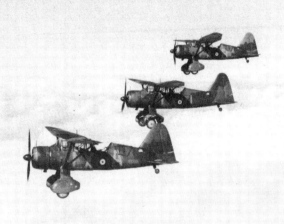

Part of 'A' Flight.
26 SQUADRON, WEST MALLING, June 1940.
'A' Flight dispersal.

boy Butler and Banner-flying-consort-to-the-leading-lady-at-the-Victoria Palace Dick Holme, to solicitor Dicky Browning. There was a splendidly moustached oil company executive in his thirties, John Longley, arrived via the Reserve of Air Force Officers. There were the leading lights of the Bristol and Nottingham RAFVR centres.

Bristol included a young man on the Bristol Aeroplane Company staff who was so important to them that he was pulled back after six weeks and lost to us. Nottingham included a dance band leader, whose recommendation for the Strand Palace Hotel, which he patronised on visits to London, was that you could guarantee to make love to the chambermaid. There were several members of the Oxford University Air Squadron. Leonard Cheshire was one. Christopher Foxley-Norris, ultimately Air Chief Marshal, another. Christopher Hartley, ex-science master at Eton, came to us via the RAF Volunteer Reserve, and became ultimately Air Marshal. We had variety, we had fun, and the school staff, air and ground, adapted to us gallantly, though we must have been a shock in contrast to their regular intake of young and innocent short service Acting Pilot Officers. I suspect those of us who were disguised as NCOs had the most fun, for we enjoyed a cross-pollination of the service sub-culture of song and story, mostly dirty, with the university equivalent. I found myself promptly co-opted to the Sergeants' Mess Entertainment Committee. Even if, like me, in the course of your university career you had majored in Sociology in the Cambridge pubs, there was much which was of long-term value to be learned in the Sergeants' Mess, which was my home, though not only at Hullavington, for eight happy months.

The next stage was the Advanced Training Squadron. Here you were treated as a qualified pilot, someone who had successfully mastered the art of flying. Now what you were to be taught was to use your aircraft as a weapon of war. Our 'weapon' was still the Hart. This may have seemed odd in the autumn of 1939 considering the Hurricanes and Spitfires and Messerschmitts and Stukas which were the actual weapons, but at least it had once been an actual weapon, and though simple and old-fashioned was no bad instrument on which to learn the job.

No more ground school. You had to do your time on the Link

Trainer, for your blind flying, and this was encouraging because you found how relatively easy it was with the full panel of artificial horizon and gyro direction indicator added to the primary instruments which were all you still had on the Hart. But otherwise you were in the air, with formation flying, camera gun work, practice dummy high dive and low-level bombing, more night flying of course, and all the excitements which made you sorry for your mates in the twin-engined flights even if they did already have artificial horizons in their Ansons. The climax ahead now was a month at Practice Camp, dropping real bombs, if only very small ones designed to produce a puff of smoke, and firing real bullets at targets on the ground or towed behind other aircraft.

Then I caught German measles. So did my ex-Class F leading-lady's-consort mate. We were out of action for three weeks, and thereafter were shunted together some thirty miles to South Cerney in Gloucestershire to finish our advanced training there. It was goodbye to Norman and many other good friends. At South Cerney we were still on Harts, but the atmosphere was very different. The course we joined had started three weeks after ours, and instead of our mixed bag was part direct entry Short Service Acting Pilot Officers, part RAF Volunteer Reserve.

South Cerney had different ideas from Hullavington on everything from discipline to the battery of sauces on the Sergeants' Mess breakfast table to help down the liver and bacon. The Flight Sergeant Discip., Chiefy Thomas, was very keen on security, and used to apostrophise you with the refrain, 'They're all spies, Sergeant.' For entertainment we had the Black Horse public house in Cirencester. The landlord had three beautiful daughters, two of whom married Sergeant Pilots on our course. But we were kept busy. It was March, so flying weather was better. We treated ourselves to take-off and landing in formation and my temporary estrangement from the Hart was forgotten.

And now practice camp was here, and off we went, early in April 1940, to RAF Porthcawl, perched in the top of Stormy Down. It would have been no fun in winter, but in April it was wonderful, with panoramic views over the Bristol Channel and the town at your feet for the accommodation of wives and sweethearts, and a very relaxed outlook on where you slept provided you were at the Flights on time.

Our air-firing ground targets were on the sand dunes where Margam Steelworks now stands. The bombing targets were moored at sea off the beach and the air-to-air firing was over the sea, pointing towards Somerset. Our aircraft had one fixed front gun, a Vickers with a belt loaded with one hundred rounds. Shallow diving at the ground targets you could see the strikes in the sand, and by how much you had missed.

There were two air-to-air exercises. In the first, a small conical target was streamed from the towing aircraft. It was designed to take station below and to one side of the tug. The tug pilot made it clear what he would do to you if you shot him up in the course of the operation in which you were meant to come up behind and hit the target if you could from as close as you could get. It sounds very unsporting, but the target was small, and aiming the aircraft was another new skill, somehow different from when all you had was a camera gun. There was a fresh target streamed for each detail, so that you could be told your results. My best result was 3/100, three better than most. It was a small target, and you tended to open fire much too far away.

But the second exercise was far more sporting, and should have been far more difficult. The tug streamed a fair-sized sleeve target directly astern. You approached on an opposite heading above and to one side, and attacked in a diving turn with strict instructions to break away downwards before you were within 15° of the line of flight of the tug, so as not to risk hitting it. This involved nice judgement of when to start your diving turn, and nice judgement of the deflection to allow, decreasing all the time, which was necessary if you were to hit the target. Imagine my surprise and delight when my first effort produced a score of 37/100, though later efforts never approached this again. They'll want Bristow on Spitfires, I said to myself.

Low-level bombing was not scientific. We did not fly low enough over the sea on the run in to the target, and you could not see where the bomb went because you were busy not flying into the sea. High dive bombing was much more sensational, but we none of us seemed to do very well. It was not an RAF speciality, and only the Navy, with its Skuas, had a dive-bombing aircraft with dive brakes. The key to accuracy, and indeed what makes it difficult to miss, is to dive at an angle of not less the 80°. 80° feels like straight down, and to aim the aircraft at a target in such a dive, though easy for the experienced pilot, is extremely daunting and therefore difficult for the relative beginner.

We never dived steeply enough, and the bombs went all over the place, with average errors in the order of 150 yards. In the US Navy, which had its dive bombers with dive brakes, you had to put ten bombs into a 50-foot circle in order to qualify for squadron service. No one seemed to worry, no doubt because no one saw the RAF in a dive-bombing role.

So we all had a wonderful time in the South Wales spring. We knew at the end of it it would be back to Cerney for a couple of days and then posting to the next destination and another goodbye to good friends. Josephine and I decided it was time to get married. Back at Cerney I learned that they did not want Bristow on Spitfires. They commissioned him as a Pilot Officer and posted him to the School of Army Co-operation at Old Sarum instead. World War II was hotting up. In the four days' break between the two incarnations, after a visit to Moss Bros for uniform, we were married.

The School of Army Co-operation at Old Sarum was the final specialised training stage. In peace, the course occupied six leisurely months. From September 1939 to April 1940 it was curtailed by half to twelve weeks. Our course in May, when the balloon went up in France and the Army Co-operation Squadrons started to take casualties, lasted four weeks.

On the ground you had a lightning indoctrination into army tactics and learned all about forward defended localities and what machine guns and artillery were supposed to do, and how you directed the guns from the air. You were told about tanks. You had your Morse Code speed pushed up to twelve words per minute, because that was how you communicated from air to ground, though at a pinch you could drop written messages in weighted streamers. You learned how to map read so that you could report where things were to within a hundred yards. The first guinea pigs for this exercise were Salisbury Plain dewponds.

In the air you converted on to the obsolete Hector, the final variant of your old faithful Hart, with an enormous air-cooled

Dagger engine of 24 cylinders and no radiator to keep you warm. Then you converted on to the Lysander, purpose-built for the Army Co-operation role. As pilot you sat in a greenhouse, ahead of the wing and well above the engine, so your view was superb. You also sat immediately above the fuel tank which in turn was immediately above the engine exhaust. If the fuel tank was hit and leaked, the act of closing the throttle on coming in to land could, and did, set fire to everything. We were glad later that year to get self-sealing tanks.

All this was mounted on a single member cantilever undercarriage structure, about the size and strength of the Sydney Harbour bridge. At each end was a wheel enclosed in a spat which also contained a Browning fixed gun and carried a stub wing on to which you could hang anything from bombs to the kitchen stove, and which was wired up to a control panel with two banks of switches, each intended to activate a different system. If it got itself wired up wrong, instead of releasing the smokescreen-producing fluid from its canister you could, and one of our pilots later did, drop the whole canister. It went through somebody's roof into somebody's bath, and the nature of the fluid it contained attracted all the cats in South Surrey. This I remember because I was sent to do the explaining.

If you had the misfortune to break your Lysander, the undercarriage usually remained intact with the rest scattered in pieces around it. Behind you, in touch through rather dubious telephonic intercom, sat your devoted air-gunner, armed initially with a single Vickers 'K' gun with which to see off the opposition.

Our four weeks were gloriously fine. We pin-pointed and reported our dewponds at the nearest we could reach to twelve words a minute while flying the aircraft with the other hand. How much more practical, we thought, voice communication by R/T would have been, and as for security, we thought the Germans as well would have mastered reading Morse at twelve words minus per minute.

We flew close tactical reconnaissance and low-level distant reconnaissance, from which the really keen were apt to return trailing telephone wires on that noble undercarriage. If you took on power cables the effect was even more unpopular, and they were likely to get the best of it. You directed actual artillery shoots on the ranges at Larkhill, though who knows if the gunners took any notice of the Morse you tansmitted to them recording what you thought to be the fall of shot. You took vertical photographs, first single pin points, then stereo pairs which through a viewer gave you a Diana-Dors-in-3D effect, and finally line overlaps which if you took several lines and got them straight and not staggered through not allowing for drift could be put together to form a mosaic.

Photography with the Lysander was easy. Not only could you see where you were going, but you had a beautiful camera sight between your feet. Of course but for your low-level tactical reconnaissance this was all 1918 stuff, pre-supposing inaccurate anti-aircraft fire and air superiority on your side. In 1940 neither of these conditions obtained, and such operations in face of the enemy were apt to be lethal.

We had a busy four weeks. It was easier for me than for some, because of my school OTC experience. The military art did not seem to have advanced greatly in ten years, and in the ground exam you could still rely on the answer to question 1 turning up as the premise to question 2, as I had discovered in 1930 when sitting for my Certificate 'A'. Boy Scout enthusiasm for maps, plus my Reserve experience in air photography, stood me in good stead in the air. But those four weeks were also my honeymoon, so that it was with some surprise that I learned I had finished top of the class.

Meanwhile the battle for France was raging, so that for us there was no hanging about, as there had been for our predecessors, in a holding unit. When we had finished the course we were posted direct, as casualty replacements, to the squadrons. I had flown as pilot on the Reserve and during my training two hundred and twenty-nine hours thirty-five minutes.

4. 26 Squadron, Lympne

My posting was to 26 Squadron. The squadron had emerged from France relatively unscathed. Like all the Lysander Squadrons in France it was a completely mobile self-contained unit. It had arrived in England with all its transport and equipment and most of its aircraft intact. I was ordered to report at Lympne. Familiar territory, and just over the airfield boundary lived one of my wife's favourite aunts, where Joey had spent part of the autumn of 1939 working in the canteen they ran for the local troops. We drove from Salisbury in our ancient Ford 10. All that map-reading training, plus familiarity with the south of England, got us safely to Lympne in spite of the removal of all road signs so that the invading Germans should not find their way as easily as they had in France and Belgium.

I duly reported on 30th May. I was allocated to 'A' Flight, one of the three flights of six aircraft of which the squadron was composed. There were accommodation problems because I had no camp kit, so everyone was delighted that I should sleep out. I found that the 'A' flight office was what had been the bar of my own flying club. Shades of K. K. Brown and Mr Warner, the barman. Flight Lieutenant Vaughan, our highly efficient regular equipment officer, later to train as a bomber pilot, issued me with my flying gear.

I was told that we were one of the squadrons which had just dropped supplies to the Calais garrison, in fact, though we did not know it, after they had been overrun. I was allocated an aircraft and Sergeant Malthouse, one of the Regulars, as air-gunner, and told to report to the Air Liaison Officer at Hawkinge at 0500 next day where I would be briefed for a sortie over Dunkirk.

It turned out to be an exquisite early summer morning. We took off from Lympne at 0450. There were a number of wrecked aircraft round the airfield at Hawkinge when we landed there, including burned-out Lysanders. That fuel tank! I reported to the ALO's office

which was all activity. I was to photograph, from 5,000 feet, the line
of the river inland from Nieuport from which guns were shelling
what was left of the Dunkirk perimeter. The camera was installed
and loaded, and off we went. In mid-Channel the scene was
reminiscent of Henley Regatta, with hundreds of assorted ships and
small craft on a dead calm sea. As we reached the Belgian coast a
summer morning fog obliterated the whole scene. Photographing
the river line was out.

We flew back to Hawkinge. Parked close to the ALO's office we
saw two beautiful light blue Spitfires which had not been there
earlier. We were told they were from PRU the brand-new Photo
Reconnaissance Unit. We were told they also were to photograph
the river line inland from Nieuport from which guns were shelling
what was left of the perimeter. Pessimism about our sortie? We were
told to fly back to Lympne. We were stood down till next day.

When we got back there was a French Air Force squadron of
Dewoitine Fighters on the airfield. In the next day or two as the
curtain came down on the Dunkirk evacuation some of our aircraft
were detached to France to operate over the German advance
towards the Somme. They did not come back. Nor did the
Dewoitines. Badger Aitken of 'B' Flight and I were given the job of
sorting out anything private which the missing Lysander crews had
left behind in their kit and sending it home to their next-of-kin.
Lympne remained intact.

On 8 June we were withdrawn to West Malling, and for 26
Squadron that was Dunkirk that was. It was later that summer that
Lympne was bombed flat.

5. 26 Squadron, West Malling

West Malling was again familiar territory for me. It had been the home of the Maidstone flying club. Our three flights were dispersed under canvas round the edges of the little grass club airfield. Squadron HQ was in club buildings, with the squash court serving as one of the offices. The officers' mess and the troops' billets were in houses well away from the airfield. At Wateringbury, a mile down the road, was the brewery which had been owned by my wife's family until taken over by Whitbreads in the nineteen-twenties. Medway water is as beneficial to brewing as the Trent at Burton. Wateringbury ale is good for morale.

The airfield was being enlarged and turned into a fighter station. On its western boundary the buildings of a permanent camp were in the process of completion but empty. The rest of the periphery, with a minor road along the north, consisted of cherry orchards just coming into fruit. Among these were dispersed our transport and our fuel and bombs and things. A tarmac perimeter track was being made, and the steam-roller part of the operation had got as far as our 'A' Flight dispersal. Those of us who had not been with the squadron in France were deeply impressed by the enthusiasm with which all ranks set-to digging slit trenches convenient for their places of work.

There was a lull, while Hitler waited for Churchill to surrender. We were given some intense low-level bombing practice on the Porton ranges. You could forget about dive bombing with a Lysander. You reached 180 mph promptly even in a shallow dive. At 200 mph, Westlands, our friendly manufacturers, expected the pilot's greenhouse to blow out, or in.

During June and early July the Army formation to which we were attached had as its front on the sea the whole coastline from Eastchurch on the Thames estuary to Thorney Island, a few miles east of Portsmouth. The RDF stations scanned high, and there was then no low-looking radar whatever. So we mounted dawn and dusk patrols to give early warning of any seaborne landing attempt, with one Lysander covering the coast from Eastchurch to Rye, and another from Rye to Thorney Island.

It was an odd sensation flying low along the familiar Sussex coast at first light, with the towns still asleep, the piers all cut off from the shore, and wire entanglements along the beaches. If you saw anything you were to report in Morse at twelve words a minute, and in case that did not work you were to drop a written message in your weighted streamer on the Army headquarters, which, in the western patrol sector where I did it, was at Washington.

Later the Canadian Lysander squadron took over the Rye to Thorney sector, when the Canadian armoured division moved into West Sussex. Until then, like the Army, we were thin on the ground. We took photographs, of majors in field boots and riding breeches in the air gunner's cockpit, so that the Army could see how cunningly what there was of it was concealed. We killed one of our best loved pilots in practice air fighting. Since France the received wisdom on how to cope with Me109s had been to get down as low as possible and hide behind trees. He got too low.

We surveyed the open spaces in Kent and East Sussex on which we thought the Ju52s might land, so that obstructions could be put in them to make the process expensive. This was a popular exercise because after marking your fields from the air you went in the CO's staff car to show the Home Guard where the obstructions should be, and the most efficient rendezvous was always the village pub. 26 Squadron's peacetime home had been Catterick, and all our drivers, including the CO's driver, Corporal Oldroyd, were Leeds busmen, whose cross-pollination with the Kent Home Guard under the unifying influence of good beer and the possibility of invasion was vigorous and interesting. You kept to yourselves the Home Guard's definition of its role as 'a body of men banded together to prevent, if necessary at the cost of their lives, the Regular British Army from retreating, according to plan, to previously prepared positions'. Anyone who remembers the radio and Press reporting of the Battle of France will recall the phrase.

We practised picking up messages, literally, from the Army. Two rifles were stuck in an open bit of ground by their bayonets, the message was attached to a line raised above the ground by the two rifle butts, and you lowered a purpose-built hook hinged below your Lysander. If you hooked the line, your air gunner wound it in and handed you the message. If not, you tried again. That was exciting for everyone, but no one was killed. We did night landing practice with a glim lamp flare path that you could not see from above 500 feet, so that the Germans would not find it. One night I couldn't find it either, and contrived to land by the light of the full moon on a stubble field, to the delight of the Plaxtol Home Guard. I did not break anything, but Mike Goodale, my Flight Commander, was not pleased.

After the lull came the Battle of Britain, fought above and all round us. One noisy morning in July my Squadron Commander sent for me. He showed me a letter from the Under Sheriff of Kent which conveyed Mr Justice Oliver's grave displeasure at the interference by aircraft noise with the proceedings of Maidstone summer assizes. What should we do about it? Resisting the temptation to write '*Inter arma silent leges*', we drafted a softish answer to turn away judicial wrath, saying that the judge ought probably to address himself to the Coastal Command Squadron stationed at Detling, since our aircraft never flew over Maidstone, but was it not Reichsmarschall Goering who was the real cause of the difficulty?

We accommodated for a day the Defiant squadron which was destroyed next day over the Straits. Bombers, including a Wellington flown by one of our South Cerney instructors, sometimes landed at night on a hastily organised flare path. As the weeks went by we were heavily bombed, both by large high-flying formations and by small groups of dive-bombing Ju88s, one of which lost two of its four aircraft to our local Bofors 40-millimetre gun.

We had aircraft destroyed on the ground, but thanks to dispersal and the slit trenches we suffered no casualties. Primarily to boost morale we mounted the Vickers 'K' guns from the 'A' Flight aircraft which had been destroyed in the 'A' flight slit trenches. This gave pleasure to one and all, including the steam-roller driver who was given his turn on a 'K' gun in exchange for giving us turns on his steam roller. Our 'K' guns did the German bombers no harm. The bombers did little harm to us because they concentrated on the new camp, which was unoccupied. Though we seemed to be making not much instant contribution to the battle, we felt it better that bombing effort should be spent on West Malling, rather than the fighter stations. Except when photographs were needed by the Army we were kept on the ground so as not to distract the fighter controllers.

Armour was added to the Lysanders here and there, and twin Brownings in the rear cockpit in place of the 'K' gun, making them fly like bricks unstable in pitch. On some, 20 millimetre cannon were attached to the spats of the noble undercarriage with a view to discouraging such German tanks as our low-level bombing might fail to destroy on the beaches. By hindsight it was as well for us that Operation Sealion was called off. In August I was in the air for no more than five hours. Finally the aircraft losses on the ground were such that on 3rd September we were withdrawn to Gatwick, where after landing it was slit-trench digging again for all hands, this time in heavy clay but with enthusiasm enhanced by the West Malling experience.

6. 26 Squadron, Gatwick

Gatwick, with the 1938 latest in circular air terminal buildings with a control tower on the top and some large sheds where the aircraft industry made things, was then a rectangular grass airfield, with a stretch of about 1,000 yards from east to west. In the prevailing wind the approach was across the London to Brighton main line, and you took off past Lowfield Heath church spire over the Brighton road. As a change from the cherry orchards, our transport, fuel and armament was all dispersed on the racecourse to the north of the field. The 'A' Flight dispersal was very snugly housed in farm outbuildings on the south perimeter. No more tents for us with autumn on the way. The troops were housed in a convenient school, the officers mess in a convenient and charming old manor house, both well away from the airfield again.

We spent the time mostly on the ground awaiting Operation Sealion, when we were to destroy them on the beaches. We were now off the main bombing road to London, and things were quiet, though we received the occasional Hurricane and Spitfire which had run out of everything on its way home. There was a corrugated iron hangar along the railway where these strays were put if they needed mending. Corporal Oldroyd found one of the Hurricanes irresistible during his lunch break. He climbed in to see what it was like, and with true Yorkshire enterprise started fiddling with the knobs and tits. Result, a 10-second eight-gun burst through the side of the hangar directly towards the railway. Luckily he did not retract the undercarriage, and since the aircraft was in its tail down at rest on the ground position all the lead vanished into the open spaces of Surrey where it did no harm.

I enjoyed a fortnight's leave in Devon, including the church bells calling out the Halstock Home Guard on the night of 15th September. In that month I flew only 1 hour 25 minutes.

It was in that month that 'B' Flight left us to go to Egypt and form a new squadron there, and that some of our pilots were posted for conversion on to fighters, and one to PRU, where he served with great distinction and in the end was killed. In France it had already become clear that the Lysander was miscast in its 1918 role in relation to the land battle, a role encapsulated in 26 Squadron's Afrikaans motto beneath the impala's head on the Coat of Arms '*N' wachter in die lug*'. As the invasion prospect faded there was for some time going to be no European land battle for us to *wacht in die lug* anyway. So what were we going to be on about?

The directing genii of the British armed forces were not always very good at strategic foresight, but once the effective novelties were disclosed in Europe in 1940 they were quick to adopt them. The capture of Fort Eban Emaël by glider-borne troops landed on top of it was enough, and the lesson was learned before it was rammed home by the invasion of Crete in 1941. Here was something for the under-employed Lysander squadrons to do with their time during the winter. We already had a Tiger Moth and a Magister for communications purposes. On 15th and 16th October we collected three brand new nice little Moth Minors from the Maintenance Unit at Aston Down.

'Master them,' they said, 'because you will be getting some soldiers who have had a little piloting experience in civilian life. You will prepare them for training as Army glider pilots, and you, Pilot Officer Bristow, in whom we, like others, have detected a propensity to teach your grandmother to suck eggs, will be in charge, and you will have an office in the hangar with bullet holes in it from which to conduct the exercise.'

Meanwhile at the beginning of October we had been assigned the job of flying by day over London above the balloon barrage on predetermined courses at predetermined heights between 12,000 and 15,000 feet, so that the new radar control on the anti-aircraft guns could be calibrated on us. Since the Lysander's operational role did not envisage flying so high we were not equipped with oxygen. Fighters, bombers, and PRU when operating at heights above 9,000 feet were required to use oxygen from the ground up. We soon found out why. The Lysander was very easy to land. Gatwick was amply large for us. The flying over London was not on the face of it exacting, though you had to be accurate with your heights, courses, and turning points. But you flew at those heights for up to three hours, and the oxygen shortage so affected you that the landing accident rate, normally minimal, rose dramatically, though the problem did not affect us all, and I was lucky. I have since examined the logbook of a DH4 day bomber pilot killed in France in 1918. They flew their photographic sorties, which lasted up to three hours, at 19,000 to 20,000 feet. All this in open cockpits, with no oxygen. Small wonder they had a high rate of landing accidents. What men!

On 4th November our soldiers arrived. My three were Lance Corporal Harrison, Lance Corporal Baker, and Driver Cooper, very helpful if your car went wrong. They were bright, they were fun, they appeared to enjoy their move from khaki into light blue surroundings, and they were obviously delighted to get back to flying after more than a year on the ground.

We had been issued with Air Publication 1732, the Instructors' Manual of Flying Training. The three of us who were to tackle the problem borrowed it from one another, studied it closely, and got on with the job. During November I spent 26 hours 45 minutes getting on with it, against 4 hours 15 minutes' worth of Lysander work.

It was only in December that I was sent to Cambridge, again familiar ground, to be taught how to do what we had been doing, at least to our own satisfaction, all through November. Between 12th and 17th December, in one of those freezing Cambridge spells where the north-east wind comes down uninterrupted from Jan Mayen and Bear Island, I spent eight and three-quarter instructive hours in a Magister and was then sent back to the Squadron qualified as a restricted 'Elementary Flying Instructor'.

For the rest of December and through January 1941 we worked away at our soldiers. Sometimes I took the air in a Lysander to take photographs. Then, at the end of January, came the news. We were to be re-armed with Tomahawks, Curtiss single-seat fighters once intended for the French, and not wanted by Fighter Command. And who was to convert the No 26 Squadron pilots, nearly all trained on biplanes with fixed undercarriages and fixed pitch propellers, and all flying Lysanders ever since? Surprise, surprise, Pilot Officer Bristow.

This time I was sent to learn how to do it before we started. Off to Upavon I went on 2nd February, in one of our Moth Minors, to the RAF Mecca, CFS. In addition to its principal work of training real flying instructors, checking the quality in all the flying training schools, and exploring the handling of all new service aircraft, the Central Flying School had a small refresher flight. This had such varied clients as senior officers returning from staff appointments to command formations equipped with aircraft which had not been heard of during their last flying assignments; ATA girls; Colonel Smith-Barry himself, creator in 1918 of the Gosport School of Special Flying from which the CFS philosophy had sprung, who was not going to be left out of World War II if he could help it; and oddments like me.

What I had to learn, and then teach, were the characteristics of the modern high performance monoplane with constant speed propeller, flaps, and retractable undercarriage. In particular, since Lysanders would not spin, you had to know the spinning behaviour and recovery, and how in a steep turn with insufficient power you would experience a high speed stall which flicked you outward directly into a spin. Not even the faithful Hart had ever managed this. The Harvard was to be our conversion instrument on the squadron. Into a Harvard I was placed by kindly and patient Flight Sergeant Jarred, who proceeded to expose me to all these mysteries in four busy hours on 2nd and 3rd February, in the afternoon of which, much enlightened, I plodded back to Gatwick in my Moth Minor. Then on 13th February I was sent, with our first three squadron pilots for conversion, to Andover, a large old-fashioned grass field. There were three beautiful new Tomahawks. There was the devoted Harvard.

For the rest of that month, first at Andover, then for a short time at Old Sarum which was dangerously small, and finally back home at Gatwick, twelve of our pilots suffered at my hands in the front seat and I suffered at theirs in the back. Fifteen mortal hours we devoted mainly to spinning and that flick stall out of a steep turn, so that in the end the sensations so induced ceased for me to be sensational. Nobody broke anything. They all got off safely on their Tomahawks. My pay off for all this selfless effort was that I had priority in flying the available Tomahawks myself.

They were of course a totally different proposition for the Army cooperation role from the Lysander, and the next thing was to see what you could do, and how you could do it. No more Morse. No more dropping message streamers or trying to pick them up. No more field-booted majors in the back, for no back seat. No more 1918 stuff. We were the first Lysander squadron to be re-armed. We were to do the pioneering. But first catch your Tomahawks, Mrs Beeton would have said, and for weeks we had none, and I was back with our soldiers and with the faithful but now rather homely Lysander, to get to which through Gatwick mud we had to wear gumboots. We flew tactical recces for the Army on exercise. We made dummy attacks on Gatwick to keep the guns awake. We took photos for the Army. On 18th April I was required to take photos of Winston's house at Chartwell. They came out well, and I hope they gave him pleasure. Two days later I collected the first of what were to be our own Tomahawks from Colerne.

Bullet Sayers and Mike Birkin (later Inspector General, Auxiliary Air Force).
EMPIRE CENTRAL FLYING SCHOOL, 1943
Squadron Leader Trevor Benson and Warrant Officer (formerly Flight Sergeant) Ryding.

Winchester, May 1985
Retirement in view

No time was wasted. On 26th April 'A' Flight was at Warmwell for air firing practice on the Lyme Bay ranges with the Tomahawks' Browning .300 wing guns. There was as yet no ammunition for the 50.cal. guns firing through the propeller in the old style. We did our target towing ourselves with the Lysanders, and as you took it in turns to tow and to shoot there was a good understanding about safe angles for approach and breakaway. I had no nil returns from quarter attacks, but never reached the dizzy heights attained at Stormy Down the year before. Back at Gatwick on 29th April I really felt I was approaching the war again.

The Germans had heavy guns on Cap Gris Nez with which they were then starting to shell convoys going through the Straits, and any shipping in Dover. To provide counter battery fire, World War I 12-inch guns on their World War I railway mountings had been extracted from their various museums and brought on rail to Kent. The first on the spot was housed in a convenient tunnel, all ready to steam out, do its stuff, and steam back again. Naturally the gunners wished to fire it, and to provide a real Roman holiday for troops who had endured a long dull cold winter it was arranged that on an 'LL' call for fire 'by one of those new Tomahawks that 26 Squadron has got' every gun within range of the trial target in Pegwell Bay was to be fired as well.

My CO sent for me. 'You will give the call for fire,' he said. 'They may take some time to get everything ready,' he said, 'but you are to be over Sandwich at 1500 hours, and you will wait till they call you on the RT to say they are all set before you give the call for fire.'

I duly flew from Gatwick to Sandwich, from over which I had a commanding view of Pegwell Bay and the target. I decided where I had better not be. You want to avoid the line of flight of a 12-inch shell. I flew up and down. I flew round and round. All by myself in that sky I felt a little exposed. An hour passed. Then another. Just when I was about to radio that I was running out of fuel they said they were sorry to have been so long, but were now ready. I gave the 'LL' call for fire. There were a number of small splashes in the target area. The large splash was impressive, but a very bad shot. By now very short of fuel, I landed at Manston. Bomb damage and slit trenches were much in evidence, and the duty crew were intrigued at having a new toy to play with. And so home.

May started with more conversion of squadron pilots; this time, for variety, on a Master which had been found for us, though we got a Harvard again later. And now we got into working out how you should do with the Tomahawk what had been Lysander work. Instead of an air gunner in the back to warn you of interference while you were concentrating on what was happening on the ground, or your camera work, or directing artillery fire, you now had another Tomahawk in loose formation looking after your tail. How were you to deal with photography with no nice camera sight for verticals? Obliques were no problem, judged by eye anyway. I was getting to know my Tomahawk. A visiting USAAF officer in plain clothes had given us the key on how to avoid the wild swing they could manage on landing.

'Never attempt the conventional three-point landing,' he said, 'we always wheel them in.'

I might have foreseen, I suppose, what happened. On 23rd May 1941 I was posted to CFS to be turned into a real flying instructor. Goodbye to 26, and much fun and good friends. I visited them again, still at Gatwick, on 27th March 1942 and was allowed to fly one of their Mustangs, with which they were the first RAF squadron to be rearmed. They were working up then for the Dieppe raid. I saw no more of them after that.

7. Flying Instructor

By May 1941 CFS had settled down to the war. Group Captain Daddy Down was the Commandant, most recent of a long line starting with Captain Paine RN in 1912, when one of the instructors was Major Trenchard. The Chief Flying Instructor was Speedy Holmes, a great RAF character who set the tone. No longer would it have been thinkable that an assistant CFI, seeing airmen with fire buckets rushing through a door in the CFI's office block to deal with a fire, should ask them whether they did not realise they were using the officers' entrance.

Dick Cox from Canada was my 'C' Flight flight commander. No one could have been more totally relaxed, and this rubbed off on us student instructors. Still wedded to single-engined aircraft, I found myself on Masters for the service flying and Avro Tutors for the elementary training. The Tutor was the military version of my Cadet from Hanworth days, and had been in use at CFS ever since as a near perfect instrument for the job. In the end even I could roll it reasonably well while talking my imaginary pupil through the manoeuvre. After a few hours with Pilot Officer Booker I found myself in the hands of Warrant Officer Williams, a man of the same stamp as Flight Sergeant Jarred. In these good hands I safely completed my course by 2nd July, putting in 68 hours' flying, eight of them at night.

Upavon was soaked in RAF tradition. It was a very bad airfield by 1941 standards, sloping off from its hilltop in two directions into the nearest Salisbury Plain valley below. No doubt it had been ideal in 1912, and the Officers' Mess was hung with photographs of the RAF greats who'd passed through ever since. The buildings were of pre-World War I vintage, with the sleeping quarters in bungalows on the Indian cantonment pattern. The weather was lovely. We flew over the northern escarpment of the Plain, over the Vale of Pewsey, and over the Marlborough Downs. The satellite where we did our

211

night flying was at New Zealand farm, miles from anywhere on the top of the Plain, a fine flat expanse, with the adjacent farm buildings screened by belts of trees all round. You were too busy really to think about the war, which seemed a long way off. I duly qualified as a real flying instructor. 'Average. S.E. Service Trainers.' Speedy Holmes's encouraging caption was, 'Should develop into a useful instructor.'

Since Joey and I were comfortably installed in Pewsey I was pleased to find myself posted to No. 1 SFTS at Netheravon, just down the road, and promoted, by the effluxion of one year from my commission, to the rank of Flying Officer. At Netheravon it was pupil pilots for the Navy who were to be trained. I cannot say the RAF had done them proud over 'S.E. Service trainers'. For the first month I found myself teaching the boys on Harts. To think yourself back on to the Hart was difficult after fifteen months' absence, and it taught you quickly what a good training aircraft the Hart was even if not furnished with the modern aids.

Then in August 'C' Flight went over to Fairey Battles, turned into trainers by putting dual control in the air gunner's cockpit. This seemed a very long way back from the pilot's cockpit in the front. With no electrical intercom, coherent speech over that distance between instructor and pupil through Gosport Tubes, unaltered since Smith Barry's day in 1918, was difficult against the noise of the Merlin engine. Was it thought that Harts would be a good introduction to the Swordfish? Was it thought that the Fairey Battle would be a good introduction to the Fulmar? You could well have thought that Netheravon airfield was good training for those destined to fly from aircraft carriers. It had what seemed like a fifty-foot wave in the middle.

The Battle was no more appropriate to the role of single-engined advanced trainer than it had proved to be to the role of day bomber in France in 1940. It was altogether too kind for the training job. You were not supposed to do aerobatics in it, or spin it. True, it had a retractable undercarriage, flaps, and a two pitch prop like the Lysander, which was something. But it was ridiculously easy to fly, and if you gave it half a chance it would land itself comfortably both by day and by night.

It provided two excitements. When after take-off you changed the prop pitch from fine to coarse the engine revs fell from 2850 to 1900 rpm in one swoop, and at night as the revs dropped sparks showered out of the stub exhausts. Often on landing the brakes, which had after all not been designed to cope with the Flying Training Command intensity of 'circuits and bumps', would fail totally, and you might roll off the airfield in a dignified manner down and away into the Salisbury Plain middle distance. In that lovely chalk country there was nothing to stop you till you reached level ground. Then a tractor would retrieve you and tow you back to the flight dispersal.

Nearly all our pupils were direct entry boys in bell-bottomed trousers and round caps, some of whom had grown beards. These, while not interfering much with talking into the Gosport Tube mouthpiece, must have been very uncomfortable crammed into an oxygen mask. They rated as ALAs, Acting Leading Naval Airmen. I also collected a Petty Officer, five Sub-Lieutenants, and two midshipmen. One of these, years after I had successfully defended him at his Court Martial for low flying, as a faithful instructor should, put a torpedo into the *Tirpitz* in Norway. They were all easy to teach, keen, competent, and broke nothing. We worked hard. Between 2 July and 5 September, I flew some 95 hours. Then I received the accolade. I was posted all the three miles back to CFS Upavon as a staff instructor. I was also promoted to Flight Lieutenant.

I now became a member of a very happy family. My guides and philosophers of the spring and early summer became very much my friends. Once again I found myself in a single-engine flight, under Dick Cox's Canadian mate Howey Marcou. We were tucked away on our own across the road from the main airfield on a short grass strip dignified by the label 'North Aerodrome'. It had the great merit of being flat, and you learnt to land in a cross-wind as a matter of course. You had to. By far the greatest proportion of the work was now done on Masters, very little on Tutors. Being supposed, at this level, to be master of all the skills, I was introduced for the first time to flying with two engines by John Burman from one of the twin-engine flights. In September I did some three hours in the Airspeed Oxford, all very dignified, and, for the first time since the Lysander, I could see the ground in front of me when taxiing, not just a large expanse of engine cowling.

You were now no longer trying to teach beginners to handle their aircraft. Your pupil instructors could do that. You had to teach them to demonstrate in the air, to co-ordinate demonstration with explanation. This is not easy in the manoeuvres which produce sensation, for example the spin and the slow roll. On the ground you showed them how to brief a pupil before flight, in the calm of the crew room, and how to unwind him after landing. Confidence and relaxation are the key to good flying, as they are to good performance in anything, and you hoped to show by your example, even when spinning or upside down, how this could be instilled.

Mark that the object of the exercise was for your pupils to train pilots who would be masters of their aircraft able and willing to fly them to the limits of their performance. Only when you have done that can you effectively start to teach pilots the use of their aircraft as a weapon of war. This was the basic CFS philosophy, stemming from Smith-Barry's 1918 Gosport School of Special Flying. This was how, the RAF believed, you would achieve a body of pilots which as a whole, not simply through talented individuals, would have a qualitative edge over the opposition. It was the RAF alone which taught its flying instructors how to teach.

So 'A' Flight beavered away all that winter on the North Aerodrome. In October I flew 40 hours; in November, 56; in December, 54; in January, 35; in February, 46. My pupil instructors were English, plus some French, and Polish. As a special treat in November I had charge for three days of my first CO in 26 Squadron, who might have gone to the Refresher flight. That was the sort of imaginative thing that endeared Speedy Holmes to his team. Another of Speedy's things concerned a distinguished radio personality who went on some gallant excursions in order to broadcast about the RAF, including flying in a Hudson over Norway. The personality was very anxious to broadcast about CFS. The personality's reputation was unfortunate. Its message was that he suffered from an aberration that Speedy did not admire. After being shown round the Station the personality asked if he might be taken up to see what the night flying instruction was like. It was a night when the Masters were on. His request was conveyed to Speedy as Chief Flying Instructor. 'Very well,' said Speedy, 'but he must not fly in the back seat.'

Night flying at New Zealand Farm that winter was sometimes rugged. There were stoves in the huts by the buildings, but for whoever was acting as aerodrome control pilot on the flare path, with the green and red Aldis lamps to tell you whether or not it was clear to take off and land, there was necessarily no shelter at all. If you started as ACP, with a flying detail later on, you could not resort to the rum ration until you'd finished. Some of the younger airmen did not care for rum. Since the aircraft came back to Upavon next morning and we were driven home in a bus this was the source of several happy journeys in the course of which you could even lose your cap. On still moonlit frosty night you could see the fog creeping up the valleys towards the New Zealand Farm plateau, and it was easy to decide when flying must stop before it reached the flarepath.

There was on the staff a wonderful hard core of ex-Halton apprentices ex-NCO pilot instructors. Shippy, who had been in the first Spitfire sqadron. Harry Stratton, very much a Wiltshire chap, who was a master aerobatic pilot. George Lillywhite, whose eyesight was more than doubtful, and who for that reason was our beam approach specialist. By comparison most of the more recent staff instructors had been, like me, on one of the pre-war reserves and remained in spirit very much amateurs. We were warmly and totally accepted by the professionals. Until now the amateurs had had a VR on the lapels of their jackets, which distinguished them in the same way as the wavy stripes distinguished RNVR from RN. But the RAF very wisely removed the outward and visible sign of difference. By 1942 you could really regard the pre-war amateurs who survived till then in the same way as the professionals who did, and who since they had borne the brunt in 1939 and 1940 were by now very much a minority.

8. Empire Central Flying School

At the beginning of 1942 the Empire Air Training Scheme was in full swing. Elementary flying training, and the training my lot had had in the Service Flying Training Schools, had all been dispersed overseas. Now the potential RAF pilot was selected in the UK after aptitude testing and some five hours testing in the air to see if he was a good prospect to be trained economically. After that he found himself in Canada, Rhodesia, South Africa, Australia, New Zealand or the United States for his EFTS and SFTS training instead of for example Hatfield or South Cerney. With the coast as the front line the home sky was considered too crowded for him and too vulnerable to intruders. So the question arose, how do you maintain the quality when your schools are all over the world? It was no longer practicable for CFS to send an examining flight round them periodically to see how they were doing.

The answer was to bring the key men from the schools to England, and by a three-month course to indoctrinate or re-indoctrinate them with the basic CFS philosophy, to familiarise them with the aircraft and the environment of the European theatre of war for which the great majority of their RAF pilots were destined, to show them operational techniques and actual operations if possible at first hand, to get the maximum cross-pollination of ideas, and generally to get them thinking about how to do the job.

So a new unit was to be created, divested of any 'teaching' function and operating at university as opposed to teacher-training level, the level at which CFS had performed its main function. The whole concept was totally new. Apart from the name, which was to be Empire Central Flying School, the new thing was to be fundamentally different, though it was still to perform what had been the CFS functions other than the training of flying instructors. This was a grave blow to CFS, which for the rest of World War II was ipso facto downgraded into one of several flying instructor schools.

How was it all to be organised, where was it to be, where were you to get the directing staff, and what were they going to do?

The prima donna's course was to be handled in university style. There were to be 'tutors', each of whom would have four students for whom he would be responsible. The tutor was to ensure that his students were familiarised by day and night with any of the elementary or service flying training aircraft which were strange to them. He was to introduce them to the wide variety of operational aircraft which were available, usually only one example of each, so that it was important that they should remain intact. He was to organise and accompany student visits, normally once a week, to operational stations. He was to ensure that his students knew about and could exploit the special facilities in the way of such things as beam approach, infra red bombing training, and synthetic night flying in which they might be interested. He was to encourage and help with what would now be called 'projects'. He was to direct the students' ground activities so as to stimulate thought and the bandying about and testing of ideas and the modification of the prejudices inevitable among instructors drawn from a world-wide background.

In addition to the Empire course there was the Handling Squadron, translated bodily from CFS and working out how all new service aircraft were to be best exploited; and the Experimental Flight, which was there to conduct any experiments in relation to pilot training the Air Ministry might require. To it were attached the Director of the Institute of Industrial Psychologists, part-time, and two of his bright young men full time, there to instil as much business efficiency as possible into pilot training.

Where was all this to be transformed from the planners' dream into three dimensions? The airfield at Upavon, for all Upavon's tradition and associations, was far too small. It turned out that the lucky station was to be Hullavington, already emptied of its service flying training school, and now sporting two concrete runways, 13,000 yards and 1,000 yards long respectively, at right angles to each other. Its permanent buildings, undamaged by enemy action, were appropriate to the requirement, and the surrounding town country scene, including such gems as Badminton and Bath, might be hoped to have a subliminal effect on students from new worlds not unlike that produced by Oxbridge or the old Scottish universities or the Inns of Court.

Who was to do it? The whole thing was the brain child of Air Vice Marshal Cochrane. As Commandant there was Air Commodore Oddie, an unorthodox RAF officer with an imaginative mind, no respecter of persons because of their situation but only because of their quality. Oddie's theme was, 'Never take what other people say about flying for granted. Try it yourself and see what happens. You'll break some aeroplanes but I will back you.'

The first Chief Flying Instructor was Anthony Selway, CFS in the early thirties and in the Middle East ever since, where he had earned the DFC by bombing the Italians in East Africa from Aden. He moved on in November 1942, ultimately to become Air Marshal, and was followed by Alfie Watts, a Vancouver lawyer by profession who had been in the Canadian equivalent of the Auxiliary Air Force before the war. The station was administered by Group Captain Lywood, with a classic RAF moustache, who efficiently kept the nuts and bolts going so that the Commandant had no distractions to prevent him giving full rein to his ideas. Wing Commander Kermode, the Prof, was chief ground instructor, with a small wind tunnel at his command.

I found myself to be one of the tutors. Some of us were from CFS, others from other Flying Instructor Schools. We were, as I remember, nearly all pre-war amateurs, and most of us University graduates. No doubt that is why we were picked for the tutor job. For example, Michael Birkin had been at Cambridge with me; Trevor Benson was an ex-Oxford schoolmaster; Hardwick Holderness was a Rhodesian Rhodes Scholar. After the first course we gathered Canadian tutors as well.

Some of the CFS old brigade came with us to run our special facilities. George Lillywhite came to deal with beam approach. On one occasion I heard him land an Oxford in fog so thick you could not see across the runway. Harry Stratton cut the aerobatics experts down to size. Joe Wheeler presided over the basic armament training scene. He was an ex-flying-boat pilot whose quality is shown by the fact that as captain of a Catalina flying the Russian Ambassador home to Murmansk in 1941 he spent the time playing chess with HE and delegated the airmanship over most of the transit to his crew.

A most notable recruit to the staff after a little while was Francis Chichester. This was before he had thought about sailing, and was in the afterglow of his astonishing achievements as an amateur airman culminating in his extraordinary New Zealand to Australia solo flight via Howe Island in a Moth on floats using a system of navigation thought out by himself. After his accident in Japan which had nearly killed him he did not reach the medical standard required by the RAF before they would let you fly. He was posted to ECFS as assistant navigation officer, rank, Flying Officer, without wings, on a scene where anything less than a Squadron Leader was a rare bird. Even I achieved that financially comforting rank in April 1943.

Francis galvanised ECFS by arriving with two hives of bees in the back of his car. His personality was such that within weeks he could twist the whole establishment round his little finger. He invented low flying navigational exercises which our students practised in light aircraft when the cloud was too low for any other flying. Alfie Watts, trying out the one which had Blenheim Palace as a turning point, came back breathless with enthusiasm saying he had been flying so low he could see the Duchess taking a bath. The indigenous staff members thought this might be British Columbian hyperbole, but it is unvarnished fact that top brass, visiting an end-of-course display, were treated to a low flying race in light aircraft piloted by students who, like Francis who had laid it on, on account of their medical category were not allowed officially to fly at all. It is a tribute to Air Commodore Oddie that under his unorthodox direction such things, so good for the general morale, were able to flourish.

We had Canadians. There were French Canadians from Quebec; bush pilots from Labrador and the north; hard core Canadians from conventional civilian backgrounds trained as flying instructors during the war; and Alfie from Vancouver, a splendid one-off leader who coped brilliantly with his unusual assignment and was loved by everyone. We had Australians, Western as well as Eastern. We had South Africans, most of whom had fought in Abyssinia and the Western Desert. We had Rhodesians, who had done much the same. We had native English, from the operational commands as well as from Flying Training Command. We had the Royal Navy. We had the US Army, the US Navy, and even a US Marine who had served with Chennault's Flying Tigers in Burma and China. We had Poles, Belgians and Czechs. My Belgian Colonel de Bock had fought the squadron of Fairey Fox biplanes he commanded in 1940 all the way south to Lyons before the French surrender, and had then gone back to Belgium and organised the transfer of the Belgian Air Force to England . 'Easy,' he said, 'when like us you are used to being occupied. The front line troops, magnificent young men, totally incorruptible, sweep through. They are followed by the reservists as occupation troops. The Town Major, who would be much happier at home with his wife, has by virtue of his office to maintain a standard of living, including a local girlfriend, that he cannot afford. So he is in your pocket almost at once. We started getting our men out in ones and twos. The last contingent went out thirty strong.'

We had a wide spectrum of aircraft for them at Hullavington. We had the old faithful elementary trainers, Tiger Moth and Magister. One of the Maggies had an experimental swivelling undercarriage so that it you were landing it out of wind you could touch down on runway without facing along it. But the problem was to swivel it to the right angle. We had Masters, and a Harvard with a flow meter to show you what happened to the fuel consumption when you rang the changes on the engine controls for boost and revs. We had the Oxfords, for the basic multi-engine work. We had a Blenheim. We had a Wellington. For a time we even had a Whitley. We had two Beaufighters. We had two Hurricanes, one fitted with a beam approach system which was used for a daily meteorological ascent to more than 20,000 feet. We had a Spitfire. We had a Mosquito. We had a Kittyhawk, to give me nostalgia for the Tomahawk. We had a Havoc and a Mitchell, to demonstrate what tricycle undercarriages were all about. The Mitchell had been fitted experimentally with a 40 mm cannon as a tank buster for North Africa. The Havoc was not improved when one of our more enthusiastic pilots insisted on slow rolling it. We had a Lancaster. We had a Hotspur glider.

As a tutor you flew them all so that you could show your students how if they wanted to. You might start the day in the Hotspur, towed up on the end of a string with no engine, and finish on the Lanc with four. You soon learned that the art was the same, though with a difference in scale and sensitivity, and your students afterwards were in a position to dispel the illusions about the difficulty and danger of flying new types of aircraft, illusions which had a tendency to flourish on the training scene.

We enjoyed various experiments, both spontaneous and official. Hardwick was determined to see if it was true that Oxfords would not come out of a spin. He went up with an enthusiastic student to suck it and see. The recovery from a spin to the right was classic, so he climbed up again and put his Oxford into a spin to the left. From this it refused to recover, but simply span flatter and flatter. He told the student to bale out, but once out of his seat the student found that centrifugal force shot him past the door to the extreme back of the cabin. Hardwick switched everything off and tried to restore the situation. The same happened to him. Happily they met mother earth in the form of a narrow Wiltshire lane with a strong quickset hedge on either side, and walked out of the wreck with more useful first-hand knowledge about Oxford spinning characteristics to pass on, and with congratulation, not criticism, from our Commandant.

You would find yourself landed with odd assignments. Michael Birkin and I were sent to Old Sarum for a day to try out the landing characteristics of the Auster, used by the Army to do the Air OP work for the gunners which the Lysanders were supposed to do in 1940. The Army pilots were breaking more Austers than was desirable landing them in small fields. I got the one to test where you sat on a piece of armour plate instead of a piece of canvas designed to accommodate itself to the shape of your bottom. It put my head against the cabin top, and after two hours was very hard on my tail.

The finest experiment of all arose because in 1943 the Blenheim, with dual control installed, was being used to convert pilots from Oxfords onto Beaufighters. The Blenheim was going out of production. You could not instal dual control in the Beaufighter. Could you get the boys off on Beaufighters without an intermediate step in a dual control aircraft? So, a proper question for ECFS to resolve. All seemed to go well. Our guinea-pig Oxford pilots were put through their Beaufighter paces with staff instructors, mercifully not me, standing behind them looking over their shoulders telling them what to do. They all went solo safely, and the operational top brass was invited to come and observe this happy outcome with its own eyes.

Our Beaufighters were atypical, having Merlin engines instead of Hercules radials. If you opened the throttles too fast with the Merlins on take-off you could produce a savage swing to port. The guinea-pigs had been warned, and had safely avoided it. On the great day, with the operational brass plus Alfie deployed outside the control tower for the demonstration, the star guinea pig, attacked by over-confidence, opened his throttles too fast. With all the stops out he swung through 45° to port and made straight for the control tower. The reactions of the audience were prompt and creditable, and so he missed them all including the tower, but the throttles stayed open, and the Beau charged between the line of parked aircraft and the adjacent hangar causing alarm and despondency to the occupiers of both until fortunately it struck the NAAFI tea wagon which scuttled it and brought it to rest.

Now and then you got assignments which at CFS would have been refresher flight jobs. Once I found myself required to check out Air Vice Marshal Hollinghurst, just returned from the position of Senior Air Staff Officer India to command a fighter group armed with Spitfires. His last flying job had been on biplanes. He was large and stout, and we had a little difficulty in getting him into the front cockpit of the Master. I feared the worst, especially as he was, I thought, a bit dour during the pre-flight briefing on the things like retractable undercarriages, flaps, and constant speed props. to which he was unaccustomed. Once off, he flew the Master beautifully, and after fifty minutes was clearly in complete command of the modern scene. He got out of the front cockpit easily, and was clearly pleased with himself as well he might be.

Another such assignment was Wing Commander Winfield, head of the Physiology Laboratory at Farnborough. Like all prewar RAF regular doctors, he had been trained as a pilot on light aircraft to the sort of standard I had achieved on the Reserve. He was deeply interested in the medical implications of high flying and wished to try it out for himself, not simply as passenger or in the decompression chamber. I had already met him on a visit with students to the RAeE. To fly as high as he wanted to he had to be able to fly a Spitfire or a Hurricane. The Farnborough staff pilots took him up in a Master, and said he would break his neck if he went off in a modern high performance aircraft by himself. So he was sent to us, and landed on my plate.

It was a fascinating experience. It was immediately clear that he was terrified, and flying by sheer determination in a state of complete tension. So all you had to do was to get him relaxed. I had him up for seventy minutes showing him that the aircraft would not bite him, was perfectly easy in spin recovery, and far easier to take off and land than the Tiger Moth of his youth. As a doctor he readily understood that it was tension which was his problem. In those seventy minutes I got him fully relaxed, and as a result fully confident. The he took the Master up and did it all over again by himself, and we sent him off back to Farnborough cleared to fly any modern single-seater he wanted, and pleased as punch.

Then there was the Great Badminton Wings for Victory Week 1943. We were the nearest RAF station to Great Badminton, where Queen Mary was living during the war years. She used to visit us informally from time to time. So it was decided to lay on a flying display for the village Wings for Victory week, designed to promote the beating of saucepans into Spitfires. Among other delights there was to be a dive bombing demonstration, with a detail of two aircraft, leader Squadron Leader Bristow, No 2 Squadron Leader Jacklin from Rhodesia. Our US Navy dive bomber pilots had told us all about this art, lost in the European theatre since the Navy's Skuas in 1940. What the Germans did was regarded by the US Navy as steep glide bombing, not dive bombing at all. In dive bombing you dive at 80°, and then the proposition is you cannot miss. To qualify in the US Navy you had to put ten bombs into a 50 foot circle.

The Master, our vehicle, was not ideal for the job. It had no dive brakes, and very quickly reached speeds in an 80° dive at which you might pull the wings off. But it was the best we had, and diving from 4,000 feet to 1,500 feet the wings stayed on on pull out. Ted Jacklin and I did a dry run on the morning of the great day. All went well. After lunch we were on cue, with Corporal Sutcliffe, our flight sweeper-upper who had begged a ride, in the back of my aircraft.

We were slightly surprised to find that the optimists had put the target for our four practice bombs a mere 150 yards in front of the stand. But if the US Navy could be that accurate, so, we decided, could we. And so, over the target, nose up, 90 knots, and half roll into whats feels and looks like a vertical dive down onto it. Practice bomb released, pull out, and withdraw low over the stables with plenty of engine noise. Bomb very close to target, and we climb up, repeat the exercise, and so home feeling pleased with ourselves, and all well but for Corporal Sutcliffe's stomach which, unused to such manoeuvres, had let him down.

Her Gracious Majesty, asked by the Group Captain what she thought of it, said simply, 'Are those young men really allowed to do that?'

We had visitors of all sorts. Some, like the Russians and Chinese, came to see what we were on about. Others, like the US Navy dive bomber pilots after Midway and the RAF low level daylight bombing pilots, to tell or show us how they did their operations so that we could pass it on.

Brian Hallows, an old mate from 9 STFS days in 1939 and 1940, gave us the Lancaster low flying demonstration. The arrival was dramatic. The first we saw of it was his Lancaster climbing over the hangars before going up into the circuit and round to land. I felt I might take a ride, and took station with my head in the astrodome, from which I thought I would get the best view. We took off. Undercarriage and flaps retracted, and then instead of going up we went down. At the far side of the first large Wiltshire field Brian picked up the starboard wing to clear some trees.

In this fashion we crossed the Cotswold edge and the Severn alluvial plain into the Monmouthshire valleys. I vividly remember looking up as we went up one which accommodated a GWR branch line and seeing the stationmaster of a rural halt digging his garden. The Lancaster is quiet till it gets to you. When we got to him, and he looked up from his spade to see this mighty aircraft flying below him up his valley, his face was a study. The low flying in a Battle for which my Netheravon midshipman had been courtmartialled was kid stuff in comparison with this.

We took our students to operational stations. Two of them finished their course as prisoners of war after going for a night bombing trip. I spent a fascinating seven and a half hours over the Bay of Biscay in a Leigh Light Wellington hunting U-boats without success, but illuminating several Breton fishing boats whose crews were clearly upset by the performance. This trip confirmed my belief that navigation is an art, not a science. Our navigator was bent over his desk for most of the seven hours, and the tail gunner spent much time throwing flame floats out of the back in aid of calculating the wind. As we went homewards in the August dawn the captain said, 'We'll shortly see the Scillies about five miles to port.' We shortly saw them about five miles to starboard.

Of course all these delights were too good to last. In December 1943 Joey and I were planning our cottage garden for 1944. Then I found myself posted to the Directorate of Flying Training, Air Ministry.

ECFS Clerihews

Air Commodore Oddie
Bears a close resemblance to God. He
Makes those in a groove
Move.

If only Group Captain Lywood
Was constructed simply of Plywood
He would not fret
I bet.

Said N.S. Trevor Ben-
Son 'I sometimes wonder when
'We will ever get through
'Rewriting A.P. 1732'.

Wing Commander Kermode
Follows a mysterious road
Discussing principles of flight
Day and night.

Where can Flight Sergeant Ryding
Be hiding?

You have to send for Flight
To put things right.

9. Conclusion

I spent the rest of World War II in the Pilot Training Branch, TFI, of the Department of the Air Member for Training. This was a fascinating and useful exposure, because it taught me how the Departments of State actually work. I learned that civil servants who could not understand a problem with which it was their job to cope were not always above hiding the file in a desk drawer rather than return it to the Registry, to the general confusion. In addition to RAF pilot training we were responsible for the initial training not only of Naval pilots, but also Army pilots for gliders and Air OPs, so I learned much about the Admiralty and the War Office.

I experienced at first hand what happens when a file in a special cover comes round calling for the answer to an impending Parliamentary Question, in our case usually to do with complaints about low flying. On one occasion my old acquaintance who had walked back to Stormy Down from Swansea had announced his impending return on leave to the girl he had married by flying so low over their nest that, it being October, he blew much of the apple crop off the trees in the adjacent orchard with his slipstream.

But while of use and interest none of this really added to the air experience, which is what I am concerned to recall. I did much visiting of training stations using the Proctors of the Communication Squadron at Hendon. This showed me that because of the English weather if as an occasional, not a full time, pilot you want to get from A to B on your own wings with a better success rate than once in three times in winter or twice in three times in summer, you had better forget it. It also taught me that meteorologists can fail to take the useful precaution of looking out of the window. I was once told in the Hendon met office that it would not be clear enough for take-off for another half hour when the sun was already shining outside. In the Air Ministry you lost touch with old friends, though of course you made new ones, an inescapable part of the process of being weaned from field work into management. The most delightful and potentially most useful of these new friends was the civil servant in charge of officer pilot postings, Mike Hunt. He it was who christened our nearest pub in Houghton Street, now sadly engulfed by LSE, the Loose Minute. Many vital conferences took place there, but not on matters of personal importance to me.

On 1st September I had one final fling. TFI, being staffed with pilots, borrowed an Anson after VE day to show the non-flying Air Ministry staff who had sweated it out in Kingsway through the V weapon time the effect of their work. The Anson lived at Gatwick, and we took turns to fly them across to the Ruhr. My turn came on a beautiful summer morning. We foregathered on what was familiar territory with TFIs naval liaison Lieutenant Commander, the red-hot civilian time-and-motion head of the Training Planning branch, and two wingless RAF officers. We embarked in the homely Anson, took off, and flew in a dignified manner to Dover and across to Dunkirk. From there we followed the Belgian beaches at some fifty feet as far as Ostend, where we turned inland to refuel at Eindhoven. Leaving Eindhoven towards the Ruhr, flying low, you saw a horizon of chimneys and factory buildings, damaged and undamaged, standing out clear and sharp without so much as a wisp of smoke to obscure their outlines. As you passed over the railway siding complexes the grass had grown so high on them that you could hardly see the tracks. The urban devastation was as thorough as the Coventry city centre, which I had flown over, and on an enormous scale. From the Ruhr we flew back to the Rhine and then south up the river to Cologne, through where the bridges would have been if they had not been lying in the water. Cologne

Cathedral looked untouched, and I have a photograph taken through the Anson window looking up at the spires. Nothing else in Cologne appeared intact. Back at Eindhoven we refuelled and acquired various goodies like cheese and nylons from the NAAFI which did not exist in London. We flew home over inundated Walcheren and across the Goodwin Sands at low water, and landed at Gatwick in the evening after six and a half fascinating hours sight-seeing from the air.

As a result of the air experience, what other than memory has stayed with me, which might not otherwise be here? These things occur to me, not in any order of relative importance.

I think I question critically what I am told about what is strange to me. If I can, I try it and see what happens. I know much more about machinery, and the language and thought processes of those who live with and use it, than I could ever otherwise have done. If I have something new to play with I read the small print carefully before I start playing. I am fascinated by the weather. I am quicker than I would otherwise have been in making decisions. Knowing how very easily I might not have been still alive and kicking I am deeply grateful to find that I am.

I flew on the Reserve and in the Service during ten years. I was in the air for altogether 1,415 hours 45 minutes, in a very wide variety of aircraft of the pre-jet age. I finished as Squadron Leader, flying instructor Category A.1. It was all of absorbing interest, never dull, and nearly always good fun. It was a good experience.

Envoi

I know very well that I have been privileged and lucky. I know I am lucky to have survived Hitler's war, which killed so many of my friends. I know I am lucky to have enjoyed so many years at the Bar and on the Bench, when so many of my friends have not survived. It is a profession which for all the hazards and the hard work has brought me a sufficient reward and enormous job satisfaction. Its hallmark is friendship. There is always a step ahead to aim at, and you are not likely to be in any one incarnation for long enough for it to become dull, though when the next step comes you will be ready for it.

I remember very well a good sailing friend. From Cambridge, where he took an engineering degree, he went to Hitler's war, and afterwards spent some years on the strength of the Foreign Office finding out about the engineering advances made in Germany during the war years. To him the Foreign Service rewards for engineers were inadequate. He joined a very large American engineering company, and became one of their principal representatives in Europe, living in a nice house outside Geneva.

I saw him there some ten years after we had last sailed together, and we talked about what had happened to us in between. I was by then a reasonably successful QC. He was within two years of his company retiring age and his American scale pension. He told me he had hated every minute of the last few years. He said you got tired of selling people elaborate machinery. He said you felt every minute that there were a dozen people after your good job who would gladly stick a knife in your back given half a chance, and that to your employers in the States you were simply a name, and your achievement was a matter of statistics. He said he couldn't wait to retire. I found it very sad.

When you live through a revolution, as my generation of lawyers has done, you don't notice it all that much as you go along. If you

229

die in harness I doubt if you would notice it at all. It is only when you can sit back in tranquillity, knowing you are not off to Chester on Monday, and think what it was like when you started and compare it to what it was like when you stopped, that it hits you. On our sundial, semi-mass produced, not custom built, is inscribed '*l'heure passe, l'amitié reste*'. True of life at the Bar and on the Bench. With all the changes, have we lost the essentials?

The object of the exercise is to do justice. If you are seeking justice, in the civil context, or if justice is seeking you, in the criminal context, you must not have to wait too long. If someone has to wait five years to get his compensation for personal injury, that's unjust. If someone has lived for two years with the shadow of prosecution for a middle-weight crime over his head it's unjust to him to pass the sentence he would have got and deserved if he'd been tried after six months. Maybe it's unjust to the community not to. So you must get on with the work and not allow time to be wasted. But the litigant or the man in the dock should leave court feeling that his case has been fully and fairly heard and he's had a proper crack of the whip. If he is left with any justification for feeling that he has not, that's injustice. So you must not rush things.

How is the middle course to be steered? It can only be done if there is trust between Bench and Bar. My experience is that while there are and always have been deplorable exceptions, trust between Bench and Bar is as it was when I first listened to those far off giants in the High Court, and the essentials are not lost. It would be stupid not to hold on to them.

Index

Index